Scribe of the Kingdom

The Art of God Incarnate: Theology and Image in Christian Tradition

The Theology of Joseph Ratzinger: An Introductory Study

Yves Congar

Theology in the Russian Diaspora: Church, Fathers, Eucharist in Nikolai Afanas'ev, 1893–1966

Holy Order: the Apostolic Ministry from the New Testament to the Second Vatican Council

From Newman to Congar: The Idea of Doctrinal Development from the Victorians to the Second Vatican Council

The Shape of Catholic Theology: An Introduction to its Sources, Principles and History

A Grammar of Consent: The Existence of God in Christian Tradition

The Holy Eucharist: From the New Testament to Pope John Paul II

Rome and the Eastern Churches: A Study in Schism

The Panther and the Hind: A Theological History of Anglicanism

Byzantine Gospel: Maximus the Confessor in Modern Scholarship

Scribe of the Kingdom

Essays on Theology and Culture

Volume II

Aidan Nichols, O.P.

Sheed & Ward
London

Comiti almo viarum

Every scribe who has been trained for the kingdom of heaven is like a householder who brings out of his treasure what is new and what is old.

Mt 13:52

ISBN 0–7220–7852 8

First published in Great Britain in 1994 by
Sheed & Ward Limited
14 Coopers Row
London EC3N 2BH

Production editor Bill Ireson
Typeset by Fakenham Photosetting, Fakenham, Norfolk
Printed and bound in Great Britain by
Biddles Limited, Guildford and Kings Lynn

Contents

Acknowledgements

The author and publisher are grateful for the following permissions to reprint:

Sobernost, for an earlier version of Chapter X, 'Bulgakov and Sophiology', in Vol. 13, 2 (1991), pp. 17–31.

New Blackfriars, for an earlier version of Chapter XI, 'Balthasar and his Christology', in Vol. 66, 781–2 (1985), pp. 317–24; of Chapter XII, 'Adrienne von Speyr and the Mystery of the Atonement', in Vol. 73, 865 (1992), pp. 542–53; of Chapter XIII, 'Walter Kasper and his Theological Programme', in Vol. 67, 787 (1986), pp. 16–24; of Chapter XVII, 'The Rise and Fall of Liberation Theology? An Evaluative Chronicle', in Vol. 72, 853 (1991), pp. 408–23; of Chapter XIX, '*Rex gentium*: History, Nationalism, Christ', in Vol. 70, 833 (1989), pp. 541–52; of Chapter XXI, 'Imaginative Eschatology: Benson's *The Lord of the World*', in Vol. 72, 845 (1991), pp. 4–8; of Chapter XXII, 'On Baptising the Visual Arts: A Friar's Meditation on Art', in Vol. 74, 868 (1993), pp. 74–84; and of Chapter XXIV, 'Ekaterina Sienskaya Abrikosova, 1882–1936: A Dominican Uniate Foundress in the Old Russia', in Vol. 72, 848 (1991), pp. 164–72.

Angelicum, for an earlier version of Chapter XIV, 'Unity and Plurality in Theology. Lonergan's *Method* and the Counter-Claims of a Theory of Paradigms', in Vol. 67 (1985), pp. 30–32.

The Chesterton Review, for an earlier version of Chapter XVI, 'Chesterton and Modernism', in Vol. 15, 1–2 (1989), pp. 157–74.

Religion in Communist Lands, for an earlier version of Chapter XVIII, 'The Story of *Praxis*: Liberation Theology's Philosophical Handmaid', in Vol. 17, 1 (1989), pp. 45–58.

Quest Journal, for an earlier version of Chapter XV, 'A Theologian Responds', in Vol. 19, Supplement (June 1987), pp. 17–19.

X
Bulgakov and Sophiology

Sergei Bulgakov was born into a priestly family in central Russia in 1871.[1] As he wrote in his *Autobiographical Notes*, 'I was born into the family of a priest, and six generations of levitical blood flowed in my veins.'[2] He grew up as a devout Orthodox child, and went to school in a minor seminary. This was quite common in the period even for boys who had shown no interest in the priesthood as a vocation. But the young Bulgakov was revolted by what he considered to be the subservient attitude of the seminarians to all forms of authority – religious, social and political. Thus, when he moved to a secular school and then to Moscow University he was already receptive to the ideas of the Russian intelligentsia, anti-monarchical and anti-Church in orientation as it had become.

Russian Marxism

The Russian intelligentsia amounted to almost a distinct 'estate' in Russian society. Belonging to no particular class, its most significant common denominator was the ideal of service to the people. Though on occasion this took a right-wing form, it more generally took a left-wing one. Bulgakov himself speedily embraced Marxism, which he regarded as a scientific instrument for analysing the conditions that produced the ills of the people, and so for predicting appropriate action to remedy those ills. However, it must be borne in mind that, until the advent of Lenin, Russian Marxism was far more open and pluralistic than it later became. In 1896, at the age of only twenty-five, Bulgakov's study of the working of the market in capitalist economies gained him the chair of political economy and statistics in the law faculty of Moscow University.[3] Soon after his marriage (1898), Bulgakov published an investigation into the relation of capitalism to the agrarian economy. This was a subject of great importance in Russia where the overwhelming majority of the population were peasants.

In the years between 1900 and 1903 Bulgakov became increasingly dissatisfied with what he saw as the ethical relativism of Marxism. He therefore tried to marry Marxist social analysis to the justification of rational ethics found in the Neo-Kantian school of philosophy. In that Kantian tradition, Bulgakov sought what he called an 'absolute sanction' for the moral and social ideals of revolution. His aim was to justify radical intervention in the historical process in terms of the *a priori* and inalienable qualities of the human subject, to establish what Kantians would term a 'transcendental justification'. Bulgakov, that is, wished to preserve the socialist ideal of Marx, but to strip it of all suggestion of determinism. Man must not be seen as a passive object swept along by the forces of economic development, but as a creative agent in history, freely acting in pursuit of fundamental values.

In 1903, while lecturing at Kiev University, Bulgakov admitted that he could no longer stand the strain of combining Marxism with idealism, with a rational ethics based on the creativity of the personal subject. He therefore announced his conversion to idealism proper. This did not necessarily involve the shedding of all his earlier thought. As we shall see, his eventual theological activity as an Orthodox priest is at least partly to be explained on the basis of his Marxian inheritance.

Idealism and Sophia

What did conversion to idealism mean for Bulgakov? Russian idealism was essentially indebted to four people, two of them German, the other two indigenous. The Germans were Hegel and Schelling; the natives the lay religious philosopher Vladimir Solov'ev, and the eclectic, even syncretistic priest-theologian Pavel Florenskii. Hegel's influence on Bulgakov is important for his sophiology. For Bulgakov accepted Hegel's criticism of the usual Christian account of the God-world relationship, namely that the world, as generally presented in Christian theology, exists alongside God, or parallel to God.

But in all other respects Bulgakov's debt to Schelling was by far the greater. Schelling's philosophy underlies Bulgakov's theology at many points, even in such comparatively non-philosophical areas as ecclesiology – so much so that Bulgakov can be called a Christian Schellengian.[4] Once again, this is especially clear for his sophiology, where Bulgakov accepted Schelling's view that God, by the necessity of his love, undergoes a kenosis or self-emptying not only in the Incarnation. This kenosis is also present in the act of creation; it is present in the work of the Holy Spirit from Pentecost onwards; it is present in the very constituting of the Holy Trinity. The other two idealist influences on Bulgakov – Solov'ev and Florenskii – contributed the crucial idea of the divine Wisdom, Sophia. Without anticipating too much of what will follow, it may be noted at this point that the Old Testament uses the figure of divine Wisdom as a way of speaking about God's creative and self-communicative power at work in the world. At the same time, Old Testament writers also speak about a human wisdom, which comes from the divine Wisdom, and puts man in a state of harmony with that greater wisdom. In the Book of Wisdom itself, wisdom is presented as the very manifestation of God. Through her, God mediates the work of creation, providential guidance and revelation. She is the subtle power of the presence of God, permeating and enspiriting all things and bringing about God's immanent presence in the creation, in revelation, in redemption.

The New Testament has more than traces of a Wisdom christology, which sees such wisdom fully incarnated in Jesus Christ. It has been argued by Louis Bouyer that there are Fathers of the Church, especially Athanasius in the East and Augustine in the West, who re-created the comprehensive Wisdom theology of the Old Testament but re-aligned on the new axis of Christ. Relying on such texts as the Second Discourse of Athanasius against the Arians and Book XII of Augustine's *Confessions*, Bouyer goes so far as to ascribe to these Fathers a fully explicit sophiology of their own, a vision of created wisdom as

> the final embodiment of the glorification of human nature in Christ, in his mystical body the Church, in the blessed Virgin Mary, first of all, and, finally, in the whole of creation, as an association of the whole of created reality, around man, with the life of God as it exists eternally in himself.[5]

Solov'ev and Florenskii may be said to have such a biblico-patristic synthesis. But they also added to it a new dimension of their own. This was based, so it would seem, on their personal religious experience. For Solov'ev, the crucial experience involved a female stranger who saved him from a traffic accident. This was a sign, as he saw it, of the all-encompassing divine Wisdom. Solov'ev held that the human task consists in realising unity between this divine Wisdom and the created world. He referred to this as 'all-unity' or 'Godmanhood'. Florenskii accepted Solov'ev's account of Wisdom-Sophia and claimed to find her presence throughout Russian religious culture, notably in the icons of the holy Wisdom of the Yaroslavl' school. Both of these Russian thinkers may be called idealists insofar as they held the ultimate reality to be spirit, spirit understood as subjectivity, the power of being a subject endowed with knowledge and love.

Bulgakov never explained where he found the idea of Sophia. But we know that in the period of his break with Marxism he was reading Solov'ev. Furthermore, Florenskii's influential *Stolp i utverzhdenie istiny* ('The Pillar and Ground of Truth') was published in 1914, only three years before Bulgakov's first sophiological treatise, *Svet nevechernii* ('The Light Unfailing'). In his autobiography, Bulgakov confines himself to describing three experiences of the reality to which the concept of Sophia applies: one of a landscape, one of a work of art, and one of an encounter with a starets in a monastery.

Having re-discovered the Orthodox Church of his childhood by way of the Russian sophiologists and his own experience, Bulgakov was back in Moscow, teaching in the university and active in that short-lived parliamentary experiment, the Duma. In the Duma, conscious as he was of the anti-Christian attitudes of the extreme left-wing parties, Bulgakov's became an increasingly conservative voice. In 1917, he published his first and fundamental theological work which gave his whole output its basic orientation. This was a reflection on Sophia.

Bulgakov was elected, in the same year, to the *sobor*, or council, of the Russian Church. It was at this time that he became a close adviser of the saintly patriarch Tikhon (Belavin), the first Russian bishop to occupy the office of patriarch since the time of Peter the Great.

In 1918 Tikhon blessed the ordination of Bulgakov to the priesthod. In the turbulent times ahead, Tikhon was to be imprisoned (1923). That same year Bulgakov was to be expelled from his homeland as a reactionary and anti-Soviet element. After brief sojourns in Istanbul and Prague he came to Paris, where he would spend the rest of his life, and where he died from cancer in 1944. For most of that period he was dean of the newly-founded Institut Saint-Serge.

The works of his maturity

Bulgakov's great period as theologian was the 1920s and 1930s. It was then that he produced his two trilogies.

The first, sometimes referred to as the 'little trilogy', was written in the 1920s, and inspired by the idea of the *deesis*, or 'supplication', in Byzantine art. *Deesis* is the name given to a group of figures in the middle of the icon-screen as found in a typical Orthodox church. Turned in supplication to Christ as divine-human mediator, the icons of the *deesis* show our Lady, John the Baptist and the angels. These are, respectively, the subjects of Bulgakov's little trilogy: *Kupina neopalimaia* ('The Unburnable Bush') on our Lady; *Drug zhenikha* ('The Friend of the Bridegroom') on John the Baptist; and *Lestvitsa Iakovlia* ('Jacob's Ladder') on the angels.

The second trilogy, sometimes called, by contrast, the 'great trilogy', takes its point of departure from Solov'ev's term 'Godmanhood', and deals with the three main elements in the reunion of the divine wisdom with mankind. As Bulgakov saw it, there were the mission of the Son, the mission of the Holy Spirit, and the role of the Church. They are described in, respectively, *Agnets Bozhii* ('The Lamb of God'), which is Bulgakov's Christology; *Uteshitel'* ('The Comforter'), which is his pneumatology; and *Nevesta Agnitsa* 'The Bride of the Lamb'), his ecclesiology.

'The Comforter'

Uteshitel' may serve to give some idea of the ethos, problematic, and particular strengths or weaknesses of Bulgakov's theological approach. So far as theological method is concerned, his study of the Paraclete stresses the primacy of Scripture, berating participants in the *Filioque* controversy (whether Orthodox or Catholic) for appearing to place the Fathers on the same dizzy eminence. His appeal to the Bible incorporates some contemporary New Testament exegesis, just as his use of texts and materials from the Christian past generally involves a recognition of historical scholarship and recourse to the tool kit of the philologist. Still he is very free in his use of Scripture; in regard to the patristic witnesses he is not only free, but critical.

What is more specifying for Bulgakov's theological enterprise, however, is what we may term his theological and philosophical principles of order – the themes by whose instrumentality the contents of Scripture and Tradition at large are to be held up to intellectual light, there to be both analytically explored and synthetically displayed. So far as a theological principle of order is concerned, Bulgakov draws an all-pervasive analogy between nature and the structure of the inner-trinitarian relationships. Thus for instance (in a way reminiscent of Augustine's comparison of the human mind to the Holy Trinity, yet also thoroughly different from his), Bulgakov compares the structure of the 'two-some' (*dvoitsa*) of Son and Spirit as revealers of the hypostasis of the Father to the structure of the mind of man as knower of truth. If the Word is the 'deep wisdom' (*premudrost'*) of Sophia, the divine all-unity, the Spirit is her 'glory' (*slava*).

But man knows truth as both 'ideal' (in the form of the coherent intelligibleness of conceptual contents) and 'real' (as referred to the actual splendour of reality). Accordingly, the Word comes to him through Sophia as the content of revelation, while the Spirit he encounters, thanks to Sophia, as revelation's beauty or glory. Thus Bulgakov looked to the sophianic energies of the Holy Trinity to provide the transcendental conditions of possibility for human creativity: man is the image of the sophianic creativity of God. The danger here lay in forgetting the sheer contingency of the creature, of natural reality.

Where a dominant *philosophical* problematic may be said to shape Bulgakov's selection and treatment of his materials, this must certainly be that of the God-world relationship. Just as the young Hegel had asked after a possible reconciliation of finite and infinite, taking as his inspiration the happy harmony of Greek religiosity (as seen by German students of his period), so Bulgakov manifests the self-same hostility to a distant God, likening Calvinism, in this respect, to Islam. For Bulgakov, there must be something mediate between the Uncreated and the created, the divine and the human, else neither creation nor incarnation can be thought or realised. Sophia, not an hypostasis, but rather *hypostasia*, or 'hypostaseity', makes possible, as an inter-mediate reality, immanent in both divine and human being, not only the incarnation but also the action of the Holy Spirit in the world. It has been pointed out that Bulgakov threatens here the divine personalism of the New Testament, since he diverts attention to an impersonal cosmic Wisdom. Yet in other ways Bulgakov's thought is almost wildly personalistic, for instance in its rejection of the concept of causality as applied to the origin of the trinitarian persons. For Bulgakov, the persons are not caused. Rather is each self-determined, self-qualified and 'self-produced'. This led him, in the course of *Uteshitel'*, to cry a plague on the houses of filioquists and monopatrists alike.

Father, Son and Spirit

What, then, of the substantive doctrine of Bulgakov's *The Paraclete*? To grasp it – and especially its implications for the Sophia theme – we must cast an eye over the conclusions Bulgakov had already reached in his christology, *The Lamb of God*.[6] The *Father*, as the absolute Subject, chooses from all eternity to be self-knowing and self-revealed in the Son, who stands to the Father, accordingly, as the Father's 'not-I' – and in this sense as his nature. In this act, the Father is engaged in a self-sacrifice: he gives himself away, he 'annihilates' himself so that the Son may be begotten. This self-gift, though made in eternity, cannot, for Bulgakov, be sundered from the Son's mission to redeem the created universe. Thus, in the light of the cross as the high-point of the Son's redemptive work, the Father's begetting of the Son can be called by Bulgakov his 'self-negation'.

On the side of the *Son*, too, there is, from the beginning, sacrifice, and even – for Bulgakov – suffering, endured in the total surrender of his will to that of the Father, whether in the everlasting triune life, or in his earthly life as the incarnate. In the Holy Trinity, the Son allows himself to be begotten, that is, to be made the image of the begetter, the Father. To be the Father's image is a sacrificial condition, since it is to know and realise oneself only in him after whose image one is made. This 'self-exhaustion' of the Son in the Father is his eternal kenosis.[7]

Where, then, does the *Spirit* enter the play of the persons? The Holy Spirit, for Bulgakov, gives 'reality' to the union of the Father and the Son. He also 'consoles' them by contributing joy and bliss to the sacrificial suffering of their love. How does this come about? First, the Spirit renders the hypostases of Father and Son fully transparent to the divine *ousia*. Second, the Spirit overcomes the 'tragedy' in the love of Father and Son: in the moment of 'sending' the Spirit, the Father receives his love; and the Spirit, thus sent by the Father, 'reposes' at the same time on the Son. Yet the Spirit too, like Father and Son, suffers sacrificially: in his case, because his hypostasis is not itself revealed. The Spirit is destined for ever to be a means to the mutual transparence of others, and hence, like a window, to be imperceptible in his function as intermediary. Yet this self-abnegation is also the Spirit's joy. As a major study of Bulgakov's pneumatology sums up:

In forsaking the possibility of revealing himself like the Father and Son, he becomes the comfort of the Father and Son, becomes the real love between them, and thus is filled with joy.[8]

Thanks to the Holy Spirit, nature in the Godhead – the not-I of the Father as absolute Subject – becomes at last fully hypostatised, fully personal. Yet the divine nature does not lose its own significance in thus being appropriated in the relations of the persons. There are 'depths of life' in God which are not simply subsumed under the relations of the trinitarian persons. In the Godhead, 'nature' exists not only for the mutual revelation of the persons but for itself as the highest of all powers, that of the *ens realissimum*, the divine Essence. And it is this divine life and power which Bulgakov calls Sophia. It is this which he regards as creation's own foundation, its principle of being.

The sophiology crisis

In the midst of writing the 'great trilogy', Bulgakov's daily round of study and teaching was rudely interrupted. In September 1935, Metropolitan Sergii (Stragorodskii) of Moscow announced that he had condemned Bulgakov's sophiological teaching as alien to the Orthodox faith.[9] In October of the same year, apparently quite independently, the bishops of the Russian Church in Exile, themselves not in communion with the Moscow patriarchate, wrote to Bulgakov's ecclesiastical superior in Paris, Metropolitan Evlogii (Georgievskii), in yet stronger terms, characterising his theology as heretical.

These attacks were not wholly unheralded. As early as 1924, the former Archbishop of Kiev, Metropolitan Antonii Khrapovitskii, presiding bishop of the Church in Exile, had accused both Florenskii and Bulgakov of adding a fourth hypostasis (person) to the Holy Trinity. And some phrases in *Svet nevechernii* could indeed give the impression that Bulgakov believed in a quadernity of Father, Son, Spirit and Sophia.[10] To this earlier attack, Bulgakov had written a reply

('Hypostasis and hypostaseity') in which he explained that the Wisdom of God is not a person and yet may be called quasi-personal for two reasons.[11] First, it is the recipient of the love of God. Second, being itself the medium whereby the world is made, it is capable of manifesting itself in innumerable persons – namely, in human beings. This answer was, no doubt, as little satisfactory to zealous Orthodox bishops as it was intelligible to ordinary readers.

The charges brought by the Orthodox hierarchy against Bulgakov in 1935 were various and weighty. The Moscow patriarchate in its *ukaz* declared that Bulgakov's teaching was not ecclesial in its intention, since it ignored the Church's own teaching and tradition, preferring at certain points openly to embrace the views of heretics condemned by the councils. Nor was it ecclesial in content, since it introduced so many new elements into the understanding of fundamental dogmas as to be, rather, reminiscent of Gnosticism.[12] Nor, finally, was it ecclesial in its practical consequences, since by presenting salvation as a cosmic process, it undermined the sense of personal sin, personal repentance, and the personal ascetic effort of the individual. Study of the Moscow patriarchate document suggests that its authors enjoyed a rather general notion of Bulgakov's system, though not an altogether inaccurate one.

In the condemnation issued by the Church in Exile, Bulgakov is accused of pride as a converted Russian intellectual who had never ceased to look down on the ordinary clergy and faithful of the Russian Church. He is a rationalist, who ignores the essentially apophatic character of Orthodox theology. And by attempting to describe positively (cataphatically) what was in the divine nature that made possible the incarnation and Pentecost, he had pried into questions which Scripture and the Fathers would never have dared to ask. At the same time, he is also a subjectivist who allows his own imagination to run riot, and suffers from 'verbal incontinence'. His sophiology is nothing more than a revival of Gnosticism which consists essentially in speculation about intermediaries between the Creator and the creature. Sophiology has no basis in the Bible, and, so far as tradition is concerned, it is a new doctrine. Unlike the Moscow text, the synodal document is both detailed and circumstantial in its accusations.

A critical memorandum, on behalf of the neo-patristically inclined members of the 'Confrèrie de saint Photius', by that other giant of Russian diaspora theology, Vladimir Lossky, played its part in the formulation of these episcopal asperities. Though not himself a lecturer at the Institut Saint-Serge, Lossky's intervention would lead in time to a rupture in that body, whereby those scholars unsympathetic to Bulgakov's speculative flights, and notably Georges Florovskii, would depart for North America.

Bulgakov's defence

How did Bulgakov respond to these charges? An answer to this question involves a positive consideration of Bulgakov's theology of wisdom. This in turn will lead to a critical evaluation of our own.

In part, Bulgakov's response was a formal one, which did not consider the material doctrinal or theological issues involved, but confined itself to the issues of authority raised by the condemnations. We can deal simply with this formal aspect of his reply. Bulgakov defended himself by saying that, sophiology does not concern the content of the revealed dogmas, but only their theological interpretation. In other words, he had denied no dogma, but was, rather, setting the dogmas in a special framework of philosophical theology. He also pointed out that hitherto sophiology had been a theological interpretation of dogma permitted in the Orthodox Church, as the careers of Solov'ev and Florenskii demonstrated. Furthermore, he considered that the condemnations, made as they were by a single hierarch or else a small group of hierarchs, contravened the Orthodox ethos of decision-making, which is essentially conciliar, and, no less importantly, followed up by regard for reception or rejection on the part of the faithful. Bulgakov held that the condemnations showed a characteristically Catholic tendency to ascribe to the hierarchy an intrinsic, *ex sese*, infallibility in all questions of truth. According to Bulgakov, this violated the freedom of theological opinion and so threatened the life of the Orthodox Church by attacking the vital interests of all theologians, no matter what their tendency.

Turning to the actual issues, Bulgakov took the opportunity to offer a succinct exposé of his doctrine, both in Russian (*O Sofii, Premudrosti Bozhiei*) and in English (*The Wisdom of God*). He maintained that, whereas many of the Fathers identify the divine Wisdom with God the Son, others ascribe it, like Bulgakov himself, to the whole Godhead. Bulgakov justified his further development of the theme of Sophia by reference to Russian church dedications, to liturgical texts and to iconography, where the Old Testament wisdom texts are linked not only to the Trinity but also to Christ, our Lady, John the Baptist, the apostles and the Angels. Such liturgies and images, he pointed out, are recognised *loci theologici* in dogmatic writing. Bulgakov interprets them to mean that there is in God from all eternity a spiritual humanity, the Wisdom of God, which is itself the object of the common love of the trinitarian persons. This pre-existent Wisdom reveals itself in the creation. Above all, it reveals itself in man, and more particularly still in Mary of Nazareth and John the Baptist, in whom the Old Testament economy comes to its climax. Then, definitively, it reveals itself in Jesus Christ. Lastly, in dependence on Christ, it finds its revelation in the apostolic Church. The same pre-existent Wisdom is also reflected in the heavenly humanity of the Angels. Thus the ensemble of church dedications, liturgical texts and icons, to which Bulgakov appealed, may be said to represent the divine Wisdom in its two modes. For it represents the

Uncreated and the created, the eternal humanity of God and the created humanity. Moreover, it represents these two in their interconnecting unity.

> All this wealth of symbolism has been preserved in the archives of ecclesiastical antiquities, but, covered by the dust of ages, it has been of no use to anyone. The time has come, however, for us to sweep away the dust of ages and to decipher the sacred script, to reinstate the tradition of the Church, in this instance all but broken, as a living tradition. It is Holy Tradition which lays such tasks upon us.[13]

For good measure, Bulgakov went on to attack the bishops for their deprecation of his own reliance on the imaginative interpretation of Christian symbols. Their criticism of him on this point showed, he said, that they themselves were little better than nominalist rationalists. Unlike his critics, he has drawn on the living tradition of the Fathers and the liturgy, and interpreted them with the controlled intuition of an Orthodox mind and heart – a procedure more genuinely Eastern than dependence on a debased, propositionalist and scholastic theology.

Furthermore, Bulgakov argues that the cataphatic uses to which he has put these traditional materials are fully justified. Basically, he has had two main purposes. First, to show what, positively speaking, relates God with the world; and second, on the basis of this first enquiry, to show (positively, once again) what made possible the union of the divine and human natures in the person of Christ. To work out some understanding of these matters is for the theologian a religious duty, whereas the bishops and their advisers are like the lazy servant in the Gospels who buried his talent in the ground. The idea of Sophia is invaluable, since it enables us to say that, in creating the world, God does not produce a reality which stands over against him. If he did so, he would cease to be the Absolute. For the Absolute, of its very nature, must constitute the reality of everything else that is.

In acting as creator, God allows his own wisdom to enter into nothingness. His wisdom begins to exist in the mode of limitation, as process or becoming. It begins to develop, taking the differentiated form of the varieties of creatures found in, and as, the world. It provides those creatures with their fundamental energy. It acts as what Aristotle had called their *entelecheia*, and so provides them with their own immanent finality or goal. It is this natural, ontological union of the world with God which is taken up in the revealed economies of the Son and the Spirit. This it is which makes it possible to conceptualise the incarnation. It is this which makes possible the transfiguration of creatures by the Holy Spirit.

Sophiology evaluated

How is Bulgakov's sophiology to be evaluated? Almost all critics, whether Orthodox, Catholic or Protestant, seem agreed that Bulgakov undoubtedly ran the risk of pantheism. Though his intention was simply to avoid a radical dualism between God and the world, his position appears to lead towards an identification of the world with God. In his kenotic love for his own creation, God allows his own essence to exist apart from his trinitarian hypostases, and to become instead enhypostatised in man. In other words, the divine Sophia and the creaturely sophia are apparently the same reality under two different modes of existing. For Bulgakov, the world is the energy of the divine *ousia*, an energy which God has placed outside himself, in nothingness, and which, by fusion with that nothingness, takes the form of process or becoming.

It is interesting to note that Bulgakov called the teaching of Gregory Palamas an incomplete sophiology. Yet his own theology of divine process, like that of his Anglo-American Episcopalian contemporary, Alfred North Whitehead, could be called an incomplete pantheism. To some degree, Bulgakov seems to have allowed a certain rationalism to penetrate his theological thought, in that he refuses to allow creation *ex nihilo* its proper status as mystery. Creation from out of nothingness is a mystery in that by means of it God lets a creature be. He lets it share in his own act of existence without, for all that, transferring to nothingness the quality of being an emanation of his own divine reality.

As a theologian, Bulgakov's most distinctive concern, deriving perhaps from his Marxist period, was the due recognition of the intrinsic value of the visible world, and of the earthly life of man. He wanted to show how the revelation of the Father in the missions of the Son and the Spirit in Christ and in the Church presupposed the intrinsic value of the cosmos in general and of man in particular; and how, furthermore, they proceeded to fulfil those values by taking them to their furthest term of development. Possibly, as has been suggested by Barbara Newman, Bulgakov's closest kindred spirit in the Western Church was Pierre Teilhard de Chardin.[14]

The enduring significance of Bulgakov's thought lies, then, in the stress he laid on the divine immanence. As he wrote in *The Wisdom of God*:

> Heaven stoops towards earth; the world is not only a world in itself, it is also the world in God, and God abides not only in heaven but also on earth with man.[15]

But the question here is whether it is not precisely by virtue of his transcendence, by his absolute difference from the world, that God can be immanent within all things and intimately present to them.

This is why the most intelligent line of defence of Bulgakov is that pioneered by Constantin Andronikof. In his contribution to the colloquium on Bulgakov's thought held in Paris in 1985, Andronikof emphasised that while, for Bulgakov, the

Absolute and the relative have, certainly, something in common, this factor

> does not render them identical but maintains them in ontological distinction ... Their conjunction (*jonction*) does not affect their otherness (*altérité*).[16]

The two worlds of heaven and earth are at once 'absolutely distinct and incommensurable', yet linked by a 'configuration' or 'conformity' which allows God to come down to the level of the creature without pulverising it, and man to mount up without being burnt up.

According to Andronikof, Bulgakov's great question was, how is it possible for God to manifest himself to us, and for humanity to have, in the Church, a life filled with grace? The answer is given by the very nature of our Creator, who is love and therefore relationship: the creature reflects the Wisdom of God, but not without the 'occultations' of evil.[17] The supreme realisation of this relation is the work of the Word taking flesh by the Holy Spirit, uniting in himself the divine world and the world of man. In his attempt to vindicate the fundamental orthodoxy of this 'realist ontology', expressed as it is in a sophiology and closely linked to the theology of the incarnation, Andronikof leans for support on the massive study of Bulgakov by yet another theologian of the Russian diaspora, Leo Zander. In his *Bog i Mir*, Zander held that Bulgakov's early work, and notably *Svet nevechernii*, can indeed be convicted of the errors with which the sophiological 'system' has been charged.[18] The book offers a 'monistic' sophiology, with only one Wisdom: Janus-like, it has two faces, created and Uncreated in turn. Moreover, this same Sophia is presented as a true subject, an hypostasis. But with the writing of the 'Chapters on trinitarity', Bulgakov introduces a 'dualist' sophiology, in which the divine *ousia* and the being of creatures are clearly differentiated, and the wisdom theme is integrated with the doctrine of the Holy Trinity.

Moreover, starting with the 1925 essay on hypostasis and hypostaseity, Bulgakov insists that Sophia is not a personal principle but rather an 'ontological principle of life'. For Andronikof, Bulgakov's finest statement of an orthodox sophiology is found in his study *Ikona i ikonopochitanie*, where he wrote:

> Sophia is the very nature of God, not only as act but as divine eternal fact; not only as power but also as effect .... In Sophia, God knows and sees himself, he loves himself, not with the mutual personal love of the three super-eternal hypostases, but as loving what is his own, his divinity, his divine life .... So Sophia is the divinity of God or the divinity in God. In this sense, Sophia is the divine world before the creation.

And the passage continues:

> For the created realm, God is Sophia, since, in Sophia and by Sophia he discloses himself as the personal tri-hypostatic God and as the creator. The world is created by and in Sophia, since there neither is nor can be any other principle of being. Consequently, the world is also Sophia, but in becoming, as a creature existing in time. Created on the foundation of Sophia, the world is destined for a condition where 'God is all in all' – to become integrally sophianic.[19]

Thus Andronikof calls Bulgakov's work an attempt to point out the positive presuppositions interleaved with the negative disjunctions of the Chalcedonian definition,[20] that famous quartet of adverbs, whereby, in the God-man, the Uncreated and the created are said to be conjoined 'without confusion, without change, without division, and without separation'.

It would be inappropriate for me, a Catholic, to venture an opinion on the orthodoxy of Bulgakov's Orthodoxy! I would strongly suggest, however, that Orthodox theologians should investigate more fully the implications – whether positive or negative for Christian doctrine – of the Schellengian philosophy which underlies Bulgakov's conceptual scheme at many points.

In conclusion, I note the balance sheet of praise and blame drawn up by Barbara Newman, herself a student of the mediaeval Western sophiologist, Hildegard of Bingen. Though Bulgakov's fundamental ontology is flawed, 'heresy' is too harsh a term for the weaknesses of his speculative system. Moreover, he discovered forgotten insights of the Fathers, uncovered elements of Orthodoxy, expressed, if obscurely, in such unusual *loci theologici* as the dedications of churches and the forms of popular devotion. Hence, while lamenting Bulgakov's neglect in the English-speaking world, Newman concludes, in future years:

> We may hope that the revelation epitomized by the dome of Hagia Sophia will again receive the attention it deserves.[21]

XI
Balthasar and his Christology

Pope John Paul II's singling out, in 1984, of the Swiss theologian Hans Urs von Balthasar (1905–88) for the Paul VI award, for his contribution to Catholic theology, almost certainly marks his emergence as the preferred Catholic theologian of the pontificate.[1] Interest in his thought is bound to increase, especially with the English translation of his masterwork *Herrlichkeit*.[2] My aim here is to present what can only be an introductory picture of the man and his work, still – amazingly – so little known in the English-speaking world in spite of the fact that he died at eighty-five years of age and had been writing for some sixty years. I am not attempting to summarise everything (that would be an impossibility) but considering the central theme of his writing, his Christology.[3]

The man

Balthasar was born in Lucerne in 1905. It is probably significant that he was born in that particular Swiss city, whose name is virtually synonymous with Catholicism in Swiss history. The centre of resistance to the Reformation in the sixteenth century, in the nineteenth it led the Catholic cantons in what was virtually a civil war of religion, the War of the *Sonderbund* (which they lost). Even today it is very much a city of churches, of religious frescoes, of bells. Balthasar is a very self-consciously *Catholic* author. He was educated by both Benedictines and Jesuits, and then in 1923 began a university education divided between four universities: Munich, Vienna, Berlin – where he heard Romano Guardini, for whom a Chair of Catholic Philosophy had been created in the heartland of Prussian Protestantism[4] – and finally Zürich.

In 1929 he presented his doctoral thesis, which had as a subject the idea of the end of the world in modern German literature, from Lessing to Ernst Bloch. Judging by his citations, Balthasar continued to regard playwrights, poets and novelists as theological sources as important as the Fathers or the Schoolmen.[5] He was prodigiously well-read in the literature of half a dozen languages and has been called the most cultivated man of his age.[6] In the year he got his doctorate, he entered the Society of Jesus. His studies with the German Jesuits he described later as a time spent languishing in a desert, even though one of his teachers was the outstanding Neo-Scholastic Erich Przywara, to whom Balthasar remained devoted.[7] From the Ignatian *Exercises* he took the personal ideal of uncompromising faithfulness to Christ the Word in the midst of a secular world.[8] His real theological awakening, however, only happened when he was sent to the French Jesuit study house at Lyons, where he found awaiting him Henri de Lubac and Jean Daniélou, both later to be cardinals of the Roman church. These were the men most closely associated with the *Nouvelle Théologie*,[9] later to be excoriated by Pope Pius XII for its patristic absorption. Pius XII saw in the return to the Fathers two undesirable hidden motives. These were, firstly, the search for a lost common ground with Orthodoxy and the Reformation, and secondly, the desire for a relatively undeveloped theology which could then be presented in a myriad new masks to modern man.[10] The orientation to the Fathers, especially the Greek Fathers, which de Lubac in particular gave Balthasar did not, in fact, diminish his respect for historic Scholasticism at the level of philosophical theology.[11] His own metaphysics consist of a repristinated Scholasticism, but he combines this with an enthusiasm for the more speculative of the Fathers, admired for the depth of their theological thought as well as for their ability to re-express an inherited faith in ways their contemporaries found immediately attractive and compelling.[12]

Balthasar did not stay with the Jesuits. In 1940 they had sent him to Basle as a chaplain to the university. From across the Swiss border, Balthasar could observe the unfolding of the Third Reich, whose ideology he believed to be a distorted form of Christian apocalyptic and the fulfilment of his own youthful ideas about the role of the eschatology theme in the German imagination. While in Basle Balthasar also observed Adrienne von Speyr. She was a convert to Catholicism and a visionary who was to write an ecstatic commentary on the Fourth Gospel and some briefer commentaries on other New Testament books, as well as theological essays of a more sober kind.[13] In 1947, the *motu proprio Provida Mater Ecclesia* created the possibility of 'secular institutes' within the Roman Catholic Church, and, believing that the *Weltgemeinschaften* of laity in vows represented the Ignatian vision in the modern world, Balthasar proposed to his superiors that he and Adrienne von Speyr together might found such an institute within the Society of Jesus. When they declined, he left the Society and in 1950 became a diocesan priest under the Bishop of Chur, in eastern Switzerland. Soon Balthasar had published so much that he was able to survive on his earnings alone, and moved to Einsiedeln, not far from Lucerne, where, in the shadow of the venerable Benedictine abbey, he built up his publishing house, the *Johannes Verlag*, named after Adrienne von Speyr's preferred evangelist. She died in 1967, but he continued to regard her as *the* great inspiration of his life, humanly speaking.

The work

Balthasar's writings are formidable in number and length. Any one area of his publications would constitute a decent life's work for a lesser man. In patristics he wrote accounts of Origen, Gregory of Nyssa and Maximus the Confessor.[14] In literature, he produced a major study of Bernanos[15] as well as translations of Claudel, Péguy and Calderón. In philosophy he turned his thesis into three massive tomes under the title *Apokalypse der deutschen Seele*,[16] from Lessing through Nietzsche to the rise of Hitler. Although a major idea of his work is the notion that the figure of Christ remained a dominant motif in German Romanticism, more significant for Balthasar's later Christology is his essay *Wahrheit: Die Wahrheit der Welt*,[17] in which he argues that the great forgotten theme of metaphysics is the theme of *beauty*.

Balthasar presents the beautiful as the 'forgotten transcendental', *pulchrum*, an aspect of everything and anything as important as *verum*, 'the true', and *bonum*, 'the good'. The beautiful is the radiance which something gives off simply because it is something, because it exists. A sequel to this essay, intended to show the theological application of its leading idea, was in fact never written, but Balthasar had given clear hints as to what it would contain. What corresponds theologically to beauty is God's *glory*. The radiance that shows itself through the communicative forms of finite being is what arouses our sense of transcendence, and so ultimately founds our theology. Thus Balthasar hit upon his key theological concept, as vital to him as *ens a se* to Thomists or 'radical infinity' to Scotists. In significant form and its attractive power, the Infinite discloses itself in finite expression, and this is supremely true in the biblical revelation. Thus Balthasar set out on his great trilogy: a theological aesthetics,[18] concerned with the perception of God's self-manifestation; a theological dramatics,[19] concerned with the content of this perception, namely God's action towards man; and a theological logic[20] dealing with the method, at once divine and human, whereby this action is expressed.

Balthasar's Christological revolution

Balthasar has insisted, however, that the manner in which his theology is to be written is Christological from start to finish.[21] He defines theology as a mediation between faith and revelation in which the Infinite, when fully expressed in the finite, i.e. made accessible as man, can only be apprehended by a convergent movement from the side of the finite, i.e. adoring, obedient faith in the God-man. Only thus can theology be Ignatian and produce 'holy worldliness' in Christian practice, testimony and self-abandonment. Balthasar aims at nothing less than a Christocentric revolution in Catholic theology. It is absolutely certain that the inspiration for this derives, ironically for such an ultra-Catholic author, from the Protestantism of Karl Barth.

In the 1940s Balthasar was not the only person interested in theology in the University of Basle. Balthasar's book on Barth,[22] regarded by some Barthians as the best book on Barth ever written,[23] while expressing reserves on Barth's account of nature, predestination and the concept of the Church, puts Barth's Christocentricity at the top of the list of the things Catholic theology can learn from the *Church Dogmatics*.[24] Not repudiating the teaching of the First Vatican Council on the possibility of a natural knowledge of God, Balthasar set out nevertheless to realise in Catholicism the kind of Christocentric revolution Barth had wrought in Protestantism: to make Christ, in Pascal's words, 'the centre, towards which all things tend'.[25] Balthasar's acerbity towards the Catholic theological scene under Paul VI derives from the sense that this overdue revolution was being resisted from several quarters: from those who used philosophical or scientific concepts in a way that could not but dilute

Christocentrism, building on German Idealism (Karl Rahner), evolutionism (Teilhard de Chardin) or Marxism (liberation theology), and from those who frittered away Christian energies on aspects of Church structure or tactics of pastoral practice, the characteristic post-conciliar obsessions.[26]

Jesus Christ as the 'Gestalt Gottes'

In his person, life, death and resurrection, Jesus Christ is the 'form of God'. As presented in the New Testament writings, the words, actions and sufferings of Jesus form an aesthetic unity, held together by the 'style' of unconditional love. Love is always beautiful, because it expresses the self-diffusiveness of being, and so is touched by being's radiance, the *pulchrum*. But the unconditional, gracious, sacrificial love of Jesus Christ expresses not just the mystery of being – finite being – but the mystery of the *Source* of being, the transcendent communion of love which we call the Trinity.[27] Thus through the *Gestalt Christi*, the love which God *is* shines through to the world. This is Balthasar's basic intuition.

The word 'intuition' is, perhaps, a fair one. Balthasar was not a New Testament scholar, not even a self-taught one like Schillebeeckx. Nor did he make a very serious attempt to incorporate modern exegetical studies into his Christology. His somewhat negative attitude towards New Testament studies followed from his belief that the identification of ever more sub-structures, redactional frameworks, 'traditions', *perikopai*, tears into fragments what is an obvious unity. The New Testament is a unity because the men who wrote it had all been bowled over by the same thing, the glory of God in the face of Christ. Thus Balthasar can say, provocatively, that New Testament science is not a science at all compared with the traditional exegesis which preceded it. To be a science you must have a method adequate to your object. Only the contemplative reading of the New Testament is adequate to the glory of God in Jesus Christ.[28]

The importance of the concept of contemplation for Balthasar's approach to Christ can be seen by comparing his view of perceiving God in Christ with the notion of looking at a painting and seeing what the artist has been doing in it.[29] In Christian faith, the captivating force (the 'subjective evidence') of the artwork which is Christ takes hold of our imaginative powers; we enter into the 'painterly world' which this discloses and, entranced by what we see, come to contemplate the glory or sovereign love of God in Christ (the 'objective evidence') as manifested in the concrete events of his life, death and resurrection.[30] So entering his glory, we become absorbed by it, but this very absorption sends us out into the world in sacrificial love like that of Jesus.

This is the *foundation* of Balthasar's Christology, but its *content* is a series of meditations on the mysteries of the life of Jesus. His Christology is highly concrete and has been compared, suggestively, to the iconography of Andrei Rublev and Georges Rouault.[31] Balthasar is not especially concerned with the ontological make-up of Christ, with the hypostatic union and its implications, except insofar as these are directly involved in an account of the mysteries of the life.[32] In each major moment ('mystery') of the life, we see some aspect of the total *Gestalt Christi*, and through this the *Gestalt Gottes* itself. Although Balthasar stresses the narrative unity of these episodes, which is founded on the *obedience* that takes the divine Son from incarnation to passion, an obedience which translates his inner-Trinitarian being as the Logos, filial responsiveness to the Father,[33] his principal interest is located very firmly in an unusual place. This place is the mystery of Christ's descent into Hell, which Balthasar explicitly calls the centre of all Christology.[34] Because the descent is the final point reached by the *kenosis*, and the *kenosis* is the supreme expression of the inner-Trinitarian love, the Christ of Holy Saturday is the consummate icon of what God is like.[35] While not relegating the crucifixion to a mere prelude, Balthasar sees the One who was raised at Easter as not primarily the Crucified but rather the One who for us went down into hell.

Balthasar's picture of the descent is taken from the visionary experiences of Adrienne von Speyr and is a world away from the concept of the triumphant preaching to the just which nearly all traditional accounts of the going down to Hell come under.[36] Balthasar stresses Christ's solidarity with the dead, his passivity, his finding himself in a situation of total self-estrangement and alienation from the Father. For Balthasar the descent 'solves' the problem of theodicy, by showing us the conditions on which God accepted our foreknown abuse of freedom: namely, his own plan to take to himself our self-damnation in Hell. It also demonstrates the costliness of our redemption: the divine Son underwent the experience of Godlessness. Finally, it shows that the God revealed by the Redeemer is a Trinity. Only if the Spirit, as *vinculum amoris* between the Father and the Son, can re-relate Father and Son in their estrangement in the descent, can the unity of the Revealed and Revealer be maintained. In this final humiliation of the *forma servi*, the glorious *forma Dei* shines forth via its lowest pitch of self-giving love.

A question

Balthasar's account of the *kenosis*, and especially of the descent, leaves a great many questions unanswered that more than manual-bound Scholastics would consider needed asking. Here, if anywhere, as Giovanni Marchesi has said, Balthasar's writing is a *visione immaginifica* rather than a true systematics.[37] But Balthasar would not necessarily deny this. I find it interesting that so much of the hymnographic tradition echoes Balthasarian themes. Certain theologians, while not formally engaged in their craft, have in fact come up with a Balthasarian theology. There are two possible conclusions to be drawn from this. *Either*, Balthasar's theology is simply

a spiritual rhetoric, suitable for preaching or devotion but no
more. *Or* such men wrote better than they knew. They
expressed that deeper response to revelation which Balthasar
calls 'aesthetic'.[38] They saw the glory of the Cross, the glory
of the self-emptying of the Word Incarnate, and behind that
the indescribable beauty of the Trinity itself.

> Praise to the holiest in the height,
> and *in the depth* be praise.
> In all his words most wonderful,
> most sure in all his ways.[39]

XII
Adrienne von Speyr and the Mystery of the Atonement

Adrienne von Speyr (1902–67) is this century's most remarkable mystical theologian: a mystic, that is, become theologically articulate. Although her place in the history of Catholic theology is, thanks to her influence on Hans Urs von Balthasar, entirely assured, her life and teaching – above all, her doctrine of the Atonement – are of considerable interest in their own right.

Adrienne's life

Adrienne von Speyr was born on 20 September 1902 in Switzerland, at La Chaux de Fonds, a French-speaking part of Canton Berne. Her father, an eye surgeon, came from a Basle family distinguished for doctors, (Protestant) clerics and businessmen. Her relationship with her mother was bad, but, to compensate, she enjoyed what her biographer calls 'a totally childlike existence in God and for God'.[1] On such matters as how to be with God in prayer, and the value of sacrifice and renunciation she was instructed *by an angel*.

Though she lived all her life in an academic milieu and became herself, as we shall see, a professional person and, moreover, had as her confessor and biographer the most learned Catholic theologian of the present century, we cannot make sense of Adrienne's mysticism unless we accept that, to her awareness, angels and saints were constantly coming and going in her life, and behind these the Holy Trinity itself. She got on well with her father, who allowed her to go with him on his hospital rounds in order to visit sick children. Similarly, in the holidays, when she stayed with an uncle who was director of a psychiatric hospital near Berne, she was found to have a great gift for calming the patients, getting through to them, and cheeering the depressed.

From these experiences came her resolve to become a doctor herself, though her own health was below par. She was often ill, and had recurrent backaches caused by inflammation of the vertebrae. She always became ill before Easter: 'because of Good Friday' the angel told her. In her prayer she looked for ways to share the suffering of the sick, and offered herself to God for that purpose.

Despite her mother's opposition, she attended a secondary school (the only girl in her form) so as to obtain the necessary qualifications for beginning medical training. Balthasar tells us that her 'charming disposition, indomitable sense of humour, and incorruptible judgment in matters of ethics and religion made her the leader of her class'.[2] In November 1917 the Protestant schoolgirl had a vision of the Mother of Christ, surrounded by angels and saints, among whom she recognised Ignatius Loyola. After this experience she found she had a small wound under the left breast over the heart: she referred to this as her 'secret', a wonderful sign that she belonged physically to God.

Some very difficult years followed. Her father, who had overtaxed his health in an effort to get a medical professorship at Basle, died. Her mother became paranoid about money and insisted that Adrienne attend a business college as well as high school. The teenager developed tuberculosis in both lungs and was given less than a year to live; she felt that, in the circumstances, nursing would be a more reasonable ambition rather than that demanded from those studying to become doctors. Adrienne therefore volunteered for a deaconess hospital in Canton Vaud, but overwork soon brought her to a state of collapse. Her mother moved the family to German-speaking Basle, even though Adrienne herself could not at this time communicate adequately in German. She appears to have been tempted to suicide soon after this period though, once overcome, her resolve to study medicine quickened. Since her family refused to support her, she financed her own training by tutoring less advanced students. Her own teachers noted the facility with which she grasped all subjects concerned with living persons, as distinct from anatomy, as also her complete satisfaction when finally allowed to work with the sick.

In 1927, when Adrienne was twenty-five, she inherited some money; holidaying at San Bernardino she met a history professor from Basle, Emil Dürr, who promptly fell in love with her. Unsure whether she should enter marriage, owing to her 'secret', she hesitated, but the couple were duly wed. Emil died suddenly in 1934 and a distraught Adrienne seemed, again, but a few steps from suicide. However, in 1936, she married Emil Dürr's assistant, Werner Kaegi, an expert on the Renaissance historian Jakob Burckhardt. Kaegi outlived her, dying in 1979.

Adrienne met Hans Urs von Balthasar in the autumn of 1940. He was then a Jesuit, thirty-five years old, and had recently been appointed student chaplain in Basle. She told him that she would like to become a Catholic. The experience of instructing her was, for Balthasar, an extraordinary one. To begin with, though she had no theological education, he had only to give her the merest outline, hardly more than a suggestion, of a subject and she would come at once to a profound understanding of it. But secondly, in his own words:

Immediately after her conversion, a veritable cataract of mystical graces poured over Adrienne in a seemingly chaotic storm that whirled her in all directions at once. Graces in prayer above all: she was transported beyond all vocal prayer of self-directed

meditation upon God in order to be set down somewhere after
an indefinite time with new understanding, new love and new
resolutions.[3]

She had numerous visionary experiences of Mary and the
saints, either individually or in groups, and was taught by
them either verbally or by means of brief symbolic scenes.

Several of the saints particularly prominent in the Latin
Catholic piety of the period – the Curé d'Ars (Jean-Baptiste
Marie Vianney), the Little Flower (Thérèse Martin) – were
involved, but so too were the apostles and many of the
Church Fathers whom Balthasar, as a patrologist, was able to
identify. On one occasion, driving home from work,
Adrienne saw a great light in front of her car, whereupon a
nearby pedestrian jumped aside. She stopped to hear a voice
say (and Balthasar describes this as the key for all that was to
follow) 'Tu vivras au ciel et sur la terre'. ('You will live in
heaven *and* on earth?')

There were also more external charisms connected with
her medical practice: inexplicable cures that became the talk
of the town. She herself was terrified by one happening, in the
spring of 1941. An angel at her bedside told her, 'Now it will
soon begin.' In the nights that followed she was asked for a
consent to God so total that it would embrace blindly everything that God might ordain for her. And here for the first
time we touch directly on the mystery of the Atonement.
What 'began' was a series of re-livings of the Passion of
Christ, and above all, of Holy Saturday, the descent into hell.
As Balthasar explains:

These passions were not so much a vision of the historical scenes
of the suffering that had taken place in Jerusalem – there were
only occasional glimpses of these, as if for clarification – rather,
they were an experience of the interior sufferings of Jesus in all
their fullness and diversity. Whole maps of suffering were filled

in precisely where no more than a blank space or a vague idea seemed to exist.[4]

These initiations into the spiritual meaning of the events of Good Friday and Holy Saturday, registered in her diaries and later published by Balthasar under the title *Kreuz und Hölle* ('Cross and Hell'), were accompanied by the reception of the stigmata, a common feature of Passion mysticism since Francis of Assisi.[5] The wounds were small, but Adrienne was extremely anxious that they should not be noticed. She felt, in fact, ashamed that something happening to her, a sinner, might have to do with the Lord's own Passion. In contrast to many other mystics, she avoided any language that might suggest identification, or even participation, speaking instead of, at most, proximity.

Throughout these years she was commenting on the books of Scripture: notably the Johannine writings, some of Paul's letters, the letters of Peter, James and Jude, the Apocalypse and parts of the Old Testament.[6] These commentaries were not written out by her as books but dictated, at first hesitantly, but later in word-perfect form. She was also coming to an understanding of what mysticism itself is. It is a particular mission or service to the Church which can be carried out only in a complete movement of self-forgetfulness, *efface-ment*, and of receptivity towards the Word of God. For Adrienne, personal states of soul are, as such, of no interest: for her, psychologising introspection involves a deviation from the mystic's true concern, the Word of God, and so a distortion of his or her mission.[7]

During the 1950s Adrienne became increasingly ill. Her heart weakened and she developed diabetes. Chronic arthritis set in and after 1954 she had to abandon her work as a doctor. Up until 1964, when she began to lose her sight, she devoured novels in French, especially Bernanos, Mauriac and Colette, as well as many women authors; she also read scholarly books about the ocean, where God in nature was very present to her. At night, except for two to three hours of sleep, she gave herself to prayer. Balthasar records that Adrienne's prayer was universal, directed to all the concerns of God's Kingdom, and an offering of self for its needs.

Anonymity and availability were two of her favourite concepts in this connexion: letting oneself be absorbed in the universality of spiritual humanity. This must be understood of her in a completely concrete sense. In prayer she was transported, she claimed, to innumerable places where her presence was needed: during the Second World War into the concentration camps; and afterwards into religious houses, especially contemplative ones, where fervour for the divine Office or prayer itself had grown cold; into confessionals where confession was simulated or lukewarm, or the priest was not up to the needs of his penitents; to seminaries; frequently to Rome, to the offices of the *Curia romana*; and into empty churches where no one went to pray. She felt herself to be in these places both spiritually and physically, and returned from these strange journeys dog-tired. At the same time she was also organising a community, the Institute of Saint John, a 'secular institute' whose members were people living the evangelical counsels but with professional jobs in the world. She also spent a lot of time in anonymous alms-giving, notably to poorly off contemplative monasteries and women without means. These alms she had sent off by letter from different parts of Switzerland and she found it delicious to imagine the bewildered delight of those who received them.

Between 1964 and 1967 Adrienne's condition deteriorated. Though she could get down the steps to her study, she had to be carried back. Her eyesight was so poor that she sometimes wrote and posted long letters without realising that the ink had run out from her pen, and so the pages were blank. For many years she had experienced a vicarious dying, as an aspect of her substitutionary suffering for the suffering of others, their sins or their purgatory. According to

Balthasar, her joyousness, courage and childlikeness (she loved children's books and dolls-houses, and frequently had them refurbished to give to children) continued till the end.

Adrienne von Speyr died on 17 September 1967 – in German-speaking countries the feast of St Hildegard of Bingen, a mediaeval mystic and theologian who had been, like her, a medical doctor. Adrienne was buried on her sixty-fifth birthday.

Adrienne and the Atonement

Balthasar recalls that, from 1941 onwards, Adrienne re-lived each year the suffering of Christ. These experiences took place during Holy Week, with Lent as their usual preparation. Balthasar, who was by her side throughout this time, was struck by the diversity within the suffering of Christ as Adrienne described it. At the Mount of Olives and on Calvary, Christ knew different kinds of fear, shame, humiliation, outrage. The 'abundance' of his physical pain is obvious; he also related himself in different ways to the sin of the world, experienced its Godforsakenness from various angles. Each year on Good Friday afternoon Adrienne went into a death-like trance interrupted only by the lance-thrust described in St John's Gospel. Shortly afterwards there began the most characteristic feature of her Passion mysticism: the descent into Hell, which lasted until the early hours of Easter Sunday morning.

As she understood things, the descent is the culmination of the Son's obedience to the Father. Moved by that obedience, he enters the realm where God is absent, where the light of faith, hope and love is extinguished, where God is cast out of his own creation. Moving through the formlessness which is the world's sin, the divine Son experiences its spiritual chaos. Balthasar describes what Adrienne told him as 'more horrible than the Hell depicted for us by the mediaeval imagination', a being engulfed in the 'chaotic mire of the anti-divine'.[8]

How did she *herself* describe the *Triduum*, the 'Three Days' in which the mystery of the Atonement was enacted? Barbara Albrecht, in her study of Adrienne,[9] provides a helpful anthology of texts on this theme drawn not only from *Kreuz und Hölle* but from her Scripture commentaries too.

Adrienne stressed as the chief presupposition of the Atonement the Son's ability to experience the gravity of human sin in a variety of distinct but interrelated ways. The incarnate Son experiences sin as God from out of his absolute purity feels it, but also, since he has Adam's integrity before the Fall, as humanity would have felt it had man never sinned. But through the Father's gift he also feels and knows the difference which sin works in man: how sin is projected, and what it is like not to repent it once committed; how too I feel when I sin in such a way that my sinful action is in dissonance from my character, and also when the sin reveals my character and makes it transparent through and through.

Like other women mystics – Catherine of Siena, Julian of Norwich – Adrienne von Speyr tries to make her meaning intelligible through homely examples.[10] For there is a mystery here: as she stresses, Christ does not take over the experiences of individual sinners directly – rather does he possess them first and foremost from out of the 'space' between the Father and the Son, and the Holy Spirit who 'circles' there makes them actual in him. He sees the guilt of the world, in its bloatedness, and in its implications, *von jeher* (from the perspective of the Eternal). And perceiving the alienation of men from the Father, he nevertheless lives among them as man, dwells with the alienated, in a world which by the mere fact of his coming is in no way altered. But in his Passion he who recognises (*erkennen*) the sin of the world for what it is also confesses it (*bekennen*). Recognition and confession are linked not only by a German word-play but by Christology: for everything the Son has and knows belongs to the Father. Dying on the Cross, he makes for all our sins a perfect confession, and simultaneously, as he represents them in their unity before the Father, does penance for them all. The Cross, for Adrienne, is the Son's confession, with Easter the Father's responding absolution.[11] This, by the way, provided Adrienne with her understanding of the sacrament of reconciliation in her study *Confession: The Encounter with Christ in Penance*. As a follower of Christ, the sinner tries to bring to light his own sins, inseparable as these are from the sin of the world, in personal confession before the Church, so as to share experientially in the great absolution of Easter.[12]

In order to experience the more starkly the distance which separates sinners from God, the Son on the Cross lays down his divinity before the Father. The Spirit takes from the hands of the dying Son the offering of his Godhead so as to place it for ever in the bosom of the Father. Or, as Adrienne re-expresses this in less imagistic and more classical doctrinal language: the Spirit allows the hypostatic union of divinity and humanity in Christ to take such a form that it expresses the difference between God and man to the uttermost degree. Out of love for the Father, the Son renounces the experience of that same love, and renounces too his understanding of that privation.[13] Here we begin to see the invasion of her theological doctrine by the mystical experience of dark night which she had each year on the first two days of the *Triduum*. Going beyond what is explicitly authorised by Scripture, she insists that the Son, in giving up the Spirit, gave over to the Father him (Spirit) who bound him (Son) to him (Father). In tones of fearful negativity and harshness, she speaks of the dying Christ as only the target of an obedience he no longer knows or can reflect on, for the object of reflection has been withdrawn, and the abandonment (*Verlassenheit*) is complete. All signs of the Father's acceptance fail: the very being and content of the Father's will are veiled to him. Jesus' self-offering becomes a 'saying "Yes" which can no longer hear its own voice'. All 'translation' of heavenly truth into earthly now breaks down for this 'abandoned man on the Cross';

there is no longer any conformity, or accommodation (*Anpassung*) between above and below; no parables are of any use now.[14]

Yet, while the Son seeks in vain for the face of the absent Father, this heart-rending openness (*Offenheit*) to the Father is outstripped by the Father's own in the silence where the Father accepts the sacrifice of the Son. This night of consummate suffering, where the Son, as Word of the Father, falls dumb is in fact the fulfilment of the compact between Father and Son, the pact they have made in love, and so the revelation of the innermost being of the Godhead. This is Adrienne's comment on Jn 25:16, 'the hour is coming when I shall no longer speak to you in figures but tell you of the Father': this suffering is 'the ultimate that man can surmise of the greatness of God'.[15] On the Cross *the Father himself becomes visible*, in the sense that the Chosen One is so identified with the Father's will that all talk of the Son's own willing or disposing becomes out of place.

But this is no mere binitarian exchange. Adrienne does not forget, even in the depths of this commerce between Father and Son, the rôle of the Spirit. During Jesus' ministry, the Spirit was, in her favourite term, the 'rule' (*Regel*) of the Son's acting: accordingly, Jesus was, in the words of the Gospels, 'led by' him. But now, at the moment when the Son's relation as man with the Father reaches its highpoint, the rôles are reversed. The Spirit obeys the Son as the latter embarks on that sending forth of the Spirit which he will complete at Easter: a sending first to the Father and then to the Church and the world.[16]

On the Cross, the Son was, moreover, *kein Eremit* ('no hermit').[17] Though Adrienne von Speyr rejects all mitigation of the Son's subjective isolation on the Cross, she stresses that the unique suffering of the Atonement was not, objectively speaking, absolutely alone. In a mysterious way, real, yet offering no lightening of his burden, the Son had co-sufferers. For the believers of the Old Covenant, summed up, for von

Speyr, in Job, the Son also suffered, 'rounding off' their sufferings by his own; yet at the same time, he took up all the
initiatives involved in their faith, suffering, and 'readiness'
(*Bereitschaft*, a key word in her vocabulary) and sent streams
of grace flowing over them from the Cross. On the Cross the
Son, implicitly, thanks the Father for the predecessors of his
new and everlasting covenant, and by fulfilling their attempts
at redemptive suffering makes them into saints of that new
covenant of his.

And with these spiritual presences, there stood at the foot
of the Cross, Mary his mother. Adrienne's entire spirituality
is so Marian that it would be unlikely for her to overlook the
Lady of Sorrows in her visions of Calvary. Her first book,
Handmaid of the Lord, was devoted to Mary, and is dominated by the motif of Marian consent:[18] for Balthasar the
fundamental attitude which pervades all von Speyr's mission.[19] In virtue of her unique election, Mary alone among
human persons can exclude from her 'Yes' to God every
limitation, whether conscious or unconscious. In her, love,
associated by Adrienne with St John, and obedience, linked
with St Ignatius, coincide, because her love expresses itself in
the *fiat*, the will to obey. As a result she becomes pure receptivity to the Incarnation of the Word. Such a perfect readiness
can be moulded into many figures, as in the great Marian
titles, but most importantly, the Church, as Bride of the
Lamb, can be formed from her. While time lasts, the Church
never fully attains to Mary's perfect consent, but she carries it
within her as her determining form, striving towards it as best
she can. In the duality of love and authority in the Church,
redeemed sinners share in the pre-redeemed consent of Mary,
which in the general Resurrection will become the consent of
the entire people of God. Mary's consent is the archetype of
Christian fruitfulnes, and in its light the contemplative life,
the attempt to remain entirely open for the Word of God, can
be seen as the necessary foundation for the active life as well.
At the Cross, Mary shares in the way proper to her as mother

in the universality of the Son's crucifixion. According to Adrienne, Mary on Calvary abdicates all right to private intimacy with her Child. She lets into the space between the Son and herself all those for whom she suffers, since he has so bound her co-suffering to his Passion that he will not work out the universal redemption without her.[20] This is, of course, von Speyr's version of the notion of Mary as *auxiliatrix*, *adiutrix* and even *mediatrix* of the Atonement, affirmed in chapter 62 of the Second Vatican Council's Dogmatic Constitution on the Church. More original is Adrienne's teaching that in the relation of Mary and John created by the Saviour from the Cross there originates the religious life of the Church. In Mary the Lord reaches back to the aboriginal consent of mankind to his coming, so as to set the new fruitfulness of the vows a-flowing from that same source. To John, the beloved disciple, he gives him, in the Cross itself, the loveliest gift he has. Here, then, love, fruitfulness and the three forms of self-surrender expressed in the traditional vows are bound together, under the shadow of the Cross, as an inseparable unity.[21]

Moving from Good Friday to Holy Saturday, this moment of the *Triduum* is for Adrienne von Speyr 'the day when the Word falls dumb', a day which she compares, daringly, to the pre-natal dwelling of the Incarnate One in Mary's womb.[22] Resting in her purity, his nearness to her took the form of reclusion and silence; now, in the womb of Sheol, what harbours him is all that is unclean, and his nearness to the mystery of Father takes the form of separation and wordlessness. In sheer obedience, the divine Son seeks the Father where he cannot be, in all that is opposed to him. If the Atonement lacked the experience of Holy Saturday, the suffering of the Redeemer would be in some way comparable to that of other men, since his death was, after all, a human dying. It is the fact that the Son must go through Hell in order to return to the Father which gives this death its uniqueness. In Hell, the Son encounters sin in its sheer objectivity, by contrast to this world where, through its embedding in human circumstance, it always has nuance, shadow, outline. But now sin loses that circumscribed character which makes it in some way bearable. At the same time, the Son also meets sin in its sheer subjectivity, the sense in which personal subjects nourish sin with their own substance, mix it with their 'I', lend it their strength. And lastly he encounters it in its aspect of sheer actuality: deep, radical potency now actualised as evil. On the Cross the Lord suffered sacrificially, by a productive love. But in Hell there is nothing in any way worthy of love: Hell is negative infinity. Behind every sin, the Son sees only one thing: the not-being-there of the Father. But this too is a saving event. As Adrienne puts it, in an important passage worth citing in full:

> The Son took sin upon him in two senses. On Good Friday, up to the moment of his death, he carried it as the personal sin of each individual human being, bearing it atoningly in his divine-human Person, by an action that was, to the highest degree that he could make it, for the sake of sinners, the action of a subject. At that moment, every sin appeared in its connexion with the sinner who had committed it, and bore his or her features. By contrast, on Holy Saturday, in his vision of the sin of the world from the standpoint of Sheol, sin loosed itself from the subject of the sinning, to the point that it became merely what is monstrous, amorphous, that which constitutes the fearfulness of Sheol, and calls forth horror in the one who sees it.[23]

Both belong equally to the Son's 'confession'.

The body of the Son's passion and death Adrienne calls his 'confession body', for he had to carry not only the personal sin of each individual human being but also original sin, and sin as such. Turning now to the climax of the *Triduum*, Easter, she affirms that Christ's risen body is his 'absolution body': as the body laid in the grave gathered to itself all confession, so the body raised from the tomb bestows itself as pure forgiveness. Hitherto the access of the Father to this earth was barred, because through sin humanity was turned away from him. The Son has turned once again to the Father the face of creation. And so the Father, who had to turn from sin, can turn again to the world. On Easter Day the Son rises visibly as man so as to arise in the invisibility of God. The Son, awakened by the Father, presents to him his work. He stands before him in his created humanity which is now in a definitive way the finished creation of the Father. The Son, who in rising receives into himself the Father's life, turns wholly to the Father, since he now lives altogether in him and from him. The risen Son is, in Adrienne's phrase, *Erde im Himmel* ('earth in heaven'). From now on, the eternal Word houses all the words of the world, and of humanity. Through the sending out of this Word we become believers; through his suffering we are re-made; through his Resurrection we too are raised up in the Word; through his journey home to the Father we too can so speak the Word of the Son to the Father as to reach the Father's heart. Through the Son's work, the Father has become 'Our Father', and since the Son's return is accomplished in the Holy Spirit, that Spirit is given to us, for now the *Kreislauf*, the 'circling course', of the love between the Father and the Son runs through the world and encloses the world in itself.[24]

An evaluation

Of the religious power of Adrienne von Speyr's understanding of the Atonement there can be no question. What some will, forgivably, find strange is her account of the descent into Hell. If it is reminiscent of Balthasar's theology of Holy Saturday in his *Mysterium Paschale* there can be little doubt that the source is Adrienne rather than the other way round.[25] It is noteworthy that, at the Roman Colloquium of September 1985 on the 'ecclesial mission of Adrienne von Speyr' – which, held as it was at the papal summer residence, Castel Gandolfo, and addressed by the pope himself, marks the Roman acceptance of her work – Balthasar went out of his way to show the consonance of her Holy Saturday mysticism with the wider tradition of Catholic theology, in the Fathers, the iconography and the already accredited mystics of the Church.[26] Even he, so committed to her as he was, finished by encouraging his hearers to leave her speculation to the theologians, but to imitate the practice which her vision of the Lord's descent sealed in her life: bearing the burdens of others and praying with fervour, notably in works of penance, that none of our brothers and sisters be finally lost.

Yet Balthasar was himself the last person to wish to sever theory, the Church's theological doctrine, from practice, her ethico-spiritual existence. In the course of the development of Catholic dogma, devotion and mysticism have played a considerable part in unfolding the glories contained in the apostolic teaching.[27] It may be that, in the Church's understanding of the Paschal mystery, Adrienne's voice will have a wider resonance in the ecclesial body of Christ.

XIII
Walter Kasper and his Theological Programme

Walter Kasper's name is by now well-known among English-speaking readers of theology: the 1984 translation of *Der Gott Jesu Christi*[1] following on the translating in 1976 of *Jesus der Christus*[2] established his reputation as a writer at once conceptually rigorous and historically well-informed. What is less understood, however, is the *total context* to which these works belong. From Kasper's background in the Tübingen school his writings can be shown to represent a total theological programme of a quite distinctive kind. This programme is not only of considerable intrinsic interest. It also has a wider church-political significance in the light of Kasper's selection as the official theologian of the Roman Synod Secretriat, encharged with the collation and theological analysis of the 'submissions' made to the Holy See by national conferences of bishops in readiness for the 1985 Synod on 'The Church after Vatican II'. His appointment offered a useful key to the debate about the intentions of the Congregation for the Doctrine of the Faith (and more generally, of the Roman Curia in its higher echelons) in the pontificate of John Paul II. In particular, it helped to determine whether these intentions are best described as 'Neo-Ultramontane', as argued (in effect) by a group of writers in *New Blackfriars* in June 1985, or rather, as I maintain, as offering a *via media* or *re-accentramento* ('re-centring') for Church and theology, amid the competing voices of left and right-wing radicalism in post-conciliar Catholicism.[3] This is a debate which has not ended with the ending of the Synod.

Kasper and the Tübingen school

Kasper was born in 1933 in Heidenheim, a town of the Swabian forest, not far from Tübingen. He began his theological studies at Tübingen in 1952, and remained there, minus a short period in Munich, until his election in 1989 as Bishop of Rottenburg-Stuttgart. That diocese has the Catholic faculty of Tübingen as the theological jewel in its crown: under the terms of the *concordat* between the Church and the *Land* of Baden–Württemberg, the bishop has ecclesial oversight of the lecturers, and so a close connexion has been maintained. Kasper is, in fact, a pure product of the Catholic Tübingen school, and since his theological programme is a restatement of the historic aims of that school, I will begin by sketching in this essential background.

The origins of the Tübingen school were somewhat fortuitous.[4] In the territorial restructuring of Germany which followed on the Revolutionary and Napoleonic wars, a large part of Catholic Swabia was handed over to the Elector of Württemberg, a Protestant. This prince, anxious to demonstrate his liberality to his newly-acquired Catholic subjects, founded a school of Catholic theology which eventually settled in 1817 at Tübingen, a pleasing university and market town on the river Neckar.[5] From its inception the Tübingen school was characterised by two features.[6] First, it was marked by devotion to the Catholic tradition in a wide sense: to the liturgy, the Fathers and the thought and literature of the Church down the centuries. Second, it was remarkably open to the stimulating, if at times slightly oddball, philosophical culture of early nineteenth-century Germany, the various strains of Romantic and Idealist thinking asociated with such names as Schiller, Schleiermacher, Schelling and Hegel.[7] Furthermore, as biblical criticism was entering into its first phase of maturity in (mainly) Protestant circles at about this time, the Catholic Tübingen school also tried to integrate this element, along with the commitment to Catholic tradition and contemporary philosophy.

The two principal concerns of the Tübingen school were fundamental theology and ecclesiology. In *fundamental theology* – and here the principal names are Johann Sebastian von Drey (1777–1853) and Franz Anton Staudenmaier (1800–56) – it confronted head-on the critique of revealed religion found in the German Enlightenment, and especially in Lessing and Kant.[8] Drey and Staudenmaier argued that reason finds its absolute foundation not in its own intellectual quality but in its acceptance of a revelation mediated in a history which is itself a transcendent fulfilment of nature. Their position may be thought of as an attempt to negotiate a channel between Idealism on the one hand, and a pure supernaturalism on the other.[9] The inherent difficulty of such an undertaking was shown up in the course of the dispute between Church authority and two contemporary German-speaking theologians, Georg Hermes and Anton Günther, which centred on the nature of the relationship between faith and rationality. The Roman Church increasingly found historic Scholasticism to be a safer, because tried-and-tested, philosophical underpinning for a revealed religion. But this tendency, which was to reach its acme with the draconian imposition of the 'doctrine of St Thomas' on Catholic faculties of philosophy and theology by Pius X and Benedict XV was never 'received' at Tübingen.[10]

In *ecclesiology*, the most characteristic idea of the Tübingen men was that of the Church as a supernatural organism: an organic society whose basis was the supernatural life given it by Christ. Since Christianity is (thus) a divine reality, it necessarily transcends any particular statement of its own content. But as time goes on, and the Church 'develops', we can glimpse different aspects of this transcendent revelation which the various historical phases of its carrier-organism show us. These notions of Johann Adam Möhler (1796–1838) have an affinity to the ideas of John Henry Newman, though the two men were working quite independently of each other.[11] Just as the more philosophical side of Tübingen theology aroused anxiety in less adventurous Catholic circles, so the ideas of Möhler (and Newman) on the Church and doctrinal development were later suspected of a too hasty surrender to the historicist spirit of the age. Be that as it may, the nineteenth-century Tübingen doctors bequeathed to their twentieth-century successors two precious possessions: first, a wholehearted commitment to the Catholic tradition in its historical fullness and integrity, and, second, a generous yet critically alert philosophical and cultural openness.[12] One has only to consider the contrasting but complementary qualities of such conciliar documents as *Lumen Gentium* and *Gaudium et Spes* to see that the Second Vatican Council was above all a Council ultimately inspired by Tübingen theology, and that it is not the Rhine but the Neckar which 'flows into the Tiber'. In Kasper's case, the two-fold Tübingen concern for tradition and philosophical originality is neatly conveyed in his first two big books. Their subjects were the concept of tradition in the surprisingly creative Roman school of the nineteenth century, and an exploration of what the non-Catholic philosopher F. W. J. von Schelling (1775–1854) has to offer a contemporary conceptualisation of God as 'the Absolute in history'.

Tradition and philosophy in Kasper

Kasper's *Die Lehre von der Tradition in der römischen Schule* was his doctoral thesis, written under the supervision of another great Tübingen man, Josef Rupert Geiselmann.[13] It is intriguing to note that the foreword extends an additional word of thanks to Leo Scheffczyk and Hans Küng: for the former is now one of the most acerbic critics of the latter, seen as an apostate from the Tübingen tradition for his practical exaltation of historical-critical method as the supreme norm of ecclesial faith.[14]

The principal contention of Kasper's study is that, by refusing to reduce the concept of the Church's *tradition* to that of her *magisterium*, Roman theologians like Giovanni Perrone, Carlo Passaglia, Clemens Schraader and Johann Baptist Franzelin can be seen as carrying out the very same task in Rome as the Tübingen school achieved in Württemberg.[15] A major work of historical scholarship, the book also carries a message for the wider Church. Though geographically Cisalpine and thoroughly homegrown, the ecclesiology of German Catholicism bears a marked family-resemblance to that of the main theological architects of the *First* Vatican Council. The implication is that the Council, and in particular its account of the Roman primacy, must have suffered distortion by being looked at through Neo-Ultramontane spectacles. Writing in 1962, just as the *Second* Vatican Council opened, Kasper expresses the classical Tübingen commitment to tradition as the chief, and perennially fruitful, principle of authority for Christian theology. While not downplaying the role of the magisterium, Kasper situates it where it belongs: in the making of partial, but abidingly valuable, determinations of the content of tradition. The *leit-motif* is already announced on the first page, in an appreciative citation from Perrone's *Il Protestantesimo e la regola di fede*: 'To transcend tradition is assuredly nothing other than to destroy Christianity itself.'[16]

In 1965 Kasper took the opportunity, in an extended essay on Schelling, *Das Absolute in der Geschichte*, to put into words the other aspect of the Tübingen inheritance: openness to philosophical culture in the search for a conceptuality for the faith expressed in tradition.[17] The essay deals with an author little studied in the United Kingdom, and scarcely more so in the English-speaking world outside the British Isles.[18] To understand Kasper's aims in this second book it may be helpful to situate it within the somewhat bewildering complexity of Schelling studies in Continental Europe. Following Père Xavier de Tilliette's monumental survey of Schelling scholarship, the German philosopher has been presented in three ways, corresponding to three historical periods.[19] From his death until the end of the nineteenth century, he pursued an honorary existence as a fill-in between Fichte and Hegel. With Edward von Hartmann's *Schellings philosophisches System*, written in 1897, he began to be studied for his own sake, but with the accent on his 'polyvalence': his ambiguities and shifts of direction. Then, in 1927, with Adolf Allwohn's *Der Mythos bei Schelling*, the idea began to be mooted that Schelling's development was coherent, that his 'last' or 'positive' philosophy was a major contribution to the philosophy of religion, and that he had something of contemporary importance to offer to an account of man-in-the-world who is also man-before-God. The idea that Schelling might enable theologians to address their non-believing contemporaries had been anticipated by Paul Tillich, who wrote a dissertation on him at Breslau in 1910.[20] Even more striking, however, is the fact that Jürgen Habermas, by the 1960s a major figure in German Neo-Marxism, had devoted *his* dissertation to Schelling under a title which must surely have provided Kasper's model: *Das Absolute und die Geschichte*.[21]

Schelling's thought had already been drawn on theologically by the nineteenth-century Tübingen school, and especially by Staudenmaier. Kasper evidently believed, as a result of the slice of intellectual history I have briefly summarised above, that he might usefully resume and take further Staudenmaier's project. In real terms, what did this mean? The key to the unity of Schelling's development, to his philosophical originality *and* his contemporary relevance, lies in his concept of *die Freiheit*, 'freedom'. Over against his own Fichtean beginnings, now seen as a 'system of necessity', Schelling affirms with increasing clarity the primacy of the unforseeably free, and of the real as knowable only *a poster-*

iori: in the last analysis, this involves a notion of God as sovereignly free and creative, a notion which has in fact emerged from the event of Christianity.[22] Schelling thus critically limits Idealism by showing that reason does not have power over itself, but is always anticipated by the God of positive philosophy who is its own incomprehensible origin.[23] As Tilliette puts it, '*L'Absolu* de la raison est l'Absolu *de la raison*'.[24] Thus Kasper found himself able to argue that he was not departing from strict philosophical rationality in posing the question, how does the Absolute come out of itself (in the free act of creating)? How do we (as *finite* spirits) come forth from the Absolute and (as *free* spirits) posit ourselves as other than and – alas – opposed to God?[25] Kasper finds the illumination he needs to answer these questions in the Church's faith in God as Trinity. And he locates the means to overcome the schism between God's infinite freedom and our finite freedom (with all its baleful consequences in the experiences of sin, guilt and meaninglessness) in the redemptive work of Jesus Christ.

Kasper's prescription for theology

The working out of these themes was to produce in time Kasper's two master-works, *Der Gott Jesu Christi* and *Jesus der Christus*. These treatises contain frequent brief statements of his Tübingen inheritance, but the fullest expression of his theological programme is found in *Die Methoden der Dogmatik. Einheit und Vielheit*, of which an English translation appeared in Ireland in 1967.[26] Here we find just what by now we should expect: a twin stress on, first, *tradition*, for the spirit 'comes into its own only by encountering tradition', and, second, *concern with philosophical intelligibility in a given historical moment*, which in our case is a moment when faith is in crisis, doubting the possibility of saying anything coherent about God.[27] As Kasper will later write:

A renewal of both tradition and speculation is needed, precisely in the present much-deplored stagnation of theology.[28]

Only two years after the Second Vatican Council had closed, Kasper lamented the fact that a justifiable criticism of the a-worldliness of theology in the past (*not*, of course, that of the Tübingen school!) now threatens to drive us to the other extreme, giving rise to a secular theology that is at variance with tradition.[29] Fifteen years later, writing in the pontificate of John Paul II, Kasper sees no reason to modify these judgments:

> In view of the many reductionist theological programmes now in existence it is unfortunately not a redundancy to say that, especially today, a theological theology is the need of the hour and the only appropriate answer to modern atheism.[30]

Kasper argues that the preservation of the transcendence of God, over against all attempts, however well-intentioned, to transform God into a means to inner-worldly ends, is *also* the preservation of the transcendence of the human person, and so of the 'freedom and inalienable rights of humanity'.[31]

> It is undoubtedly pleonastic to speak ... of theological theology as a programme; the formula 'theological theology' makes sense only as a polemical formula which serves to remind theology of its own proper theme ... [Theology's contribution] must take the form of the confession of the Trinity. Precisely because this confession takes seriously the Godness of God, his freedom in love, it is able to rescue the freedom in love and for love that has been given us by God through Jesus Christ in the Holy Spirit, and thus to rescue the humanity of man at a time when it is most threatened.[32]

Thus a return to the theocentrism of 'the church Fathers and the other great doctors of the Church' (and Kasper's dogmatic writings are deeply and minutely informed by both) is no flight from contemporary theological creativity and liberty of spirit but, on the contrary, its necessary presupposition.

Kasper's criticism of much post-conciliar theology is paradoxically animated, therefore, by a Schellengian commitment to *freedom*. This freedom is not, however, the 'negative' freedom of unlimited self-determination but, in Sir Isaiah Berlin's phrase, the 'positive' freedom which consists in the efficacious possibility of being determined by the truth – a truth which is also the good for man.[33]

A question

But how does Kasper know that his own account of the liberating truth of the God of Jesus Christ is itself satisfactory in ways that others apparently are not? In point of fact, a certain partiality enters into Kasper's theological judgment just because of his acute sensitivity to the tragedy of the West: the elimination of the mystery of man *via* the elimination of the mystery of God. Yet the intellectual and spiritual problem of atheism is not so central, we are led to believe, for the churches of the Third World as it is for those of the First and Second. The universally valid elements in his programme are, one may suggest, twofold: first, its Trinitarian and christological theocentrism, and, second, its insistence that in choosing a philosophy as *ancilla fidei* one must choose one that

> in opposition to every narrowing and obscuring of the human horizon keeps open the question about the meaning of the whole, and precisely in this way serves the humanness of humanity.[34]

The Tübingen project of combining traditionalism with openness to the times is *instantiated* in Kasper's work but it is not *exhaustively realised* there. In the universe of theological discourse, as in the Church as a whole, *positive* freedom, which in the last analysis is inseparable from the divine gift of creation and grace, must be held together with *negative* freedom, which is the human task of incarnating creation and grace in a myriad cultural forms.

The principles involved have been beautifully stated by Cardinal Joseph Ratzinger, in a conference at the Centre d'Etudes Saint-Louis de France in Rome. In an exposition of positive freedom, Ratzinger remarks:

> In the Church, the debate (about freedom) concerns liberty in its deepest sense, as openness to the divine Being in order to become a sharer in Its life. ... The fundamental right of Christians is the right to the whole faith ... All other liberties in the Church are ordered to this foundational right.[35]

And he continues in an equally striking allusion to negative freedom:

> Under this common denominator of faith we must leave a wide space for differing projects and forms of spiritual life, and, analogously, to differing forms of thought, so that each with its own richness may contribute to the faith of the Church ... What is in question is, on the one hand, the basic right of the faithful to a faith which is pure, and, on the other, the right to express this faith in the thought and language of their own time.[36]

From these measured words, which would have gladdened the hearts of the Tübingen doctors, it is hard to excogitate a nightmare of papalist *revanchisme*. The pastoral magisterium must ensure that its practice is as excellent as its theory. The rest of the Church has the right and duty to expect of the Roman see, to which so much responsibility has been entrusted, the same sobriety of tone and equity of judgment in all its actions.

XIV
Lonergan's *Method in Theology* and the Theory of Paradigms

The topic of theology's essential unity and legitimate plurality has become, rightly, fashionable – not least with the publication in 1972 of the International Theological Commission's statement 'L'unità della fede e il pluralismo teologico',[1] itself a response to the state of theology today. Although the Commission was primarily concerned with the unity of the *content* of theology *vis-à-vis* its manifold expression, and the distinguished Canadian Jesuit Bernard Lonergan (1904–84) in his *Method in Theology*,[2] which appeared that same year, is principally taken up with what is common to all theological method *vis-à-vis* the specificities of actual theologies from different periods and authors, their tasks are interrelated. An error about theological method may lead to a distortion in theological content; and conversely, the theological content of the Church's faith may itself help to indicate an appropriate theological method. Here I propose to consider Lonergan's *Method* in the perspective of unity and plurality, and to suggest that for all its many virtues it may have located necessary unity and desirable plurality at the wrong points.

The 'transcendental method'

Since *Method* is as difficult as it is brilliant, I shall relate my comments to an exposition of what I take to be its central drift. Lonergan opens his book by distinguishing three senses of 'method'. First, there is the method involved in a form of art and this, says Lonergan, consists in following the example of a master.[3] If we take 'art' here in the sense of 'fine art', this is disconcerting because, clearly, learning the ropes of a discipline such as writing poetry would include such things as becoming familiar with the poetic forms and techniques of past and present, sharpening one's awareness of one's possible subject-matter, growing in *Einfühlung* with the works of the poets of one's own literary tradition. But really by 'art' here Lonergan means 'skill'. It is a shame that he did, because literary criticism must surely be a helpful analogue for theological interpretation, given that the Christian religion is so extremely bound to its own self-expression in texts.

Second, by method we could mean what people mean by method in the sciences.[4] If theological method were artistic (or technical) method, we would pick a master (Augustine, Thomas, Lonergan himself) and try to imitate him; but if it were scientific, we would take the method of a 'successful' science as our norm and follow its procedures analogically. In other words, while making all possible allowances for the difference between studying the finite world and studying God's self-revelation, we would nevertheless try to realise the same kind of objectivity of methods and results. Ever since the early modern period, the typical 'successful' science has been physics. Because the particular procedures of this particular science are difficult to relate, formally speaking, to theological procedures, the academic community is less and less willing to give theology a place in the charmed circle of genuine sciences. Lonergan gives this as the reason why he has turned instead to his own 'transcendental method'. The concept of theology as a science (*scientia fidei, scientia divina*) is, however, too venerable to be dispatched so quickly. Not even all physicists, or all natural scientists, would agree that the privileging of physics or other natural sciences is epistemologically justified. They could accept that any authentic science is an intellectual discipline working with a combination of authoritative principles and rational enquiry. And this is, in effect, the account of a science found in Thomas who can call theology a science because it draws its own principles from God's own knowledge of himself and works with them in a way that is according to reason.[5]

However, even though one may hesitate in accepting Lonergan's reasons for abandoning the notion of theology as science (and as art!), one may in fact find that his concrete proposals for a successor are of great interest. The 'transcendental method' now expounded, and based on Lonergan's earlier work *Insight: An Essay on Human Understanding*[6] has in itself nothing to do, of course, with transcendence in the sense of God, the grace of God, or anything specifically religious. 'Transcendental' here has principally the meaning found in Kant, who uses it to refer to any fundamental aspect of the mind that contributes to the activity of knowing. Lonergan's transcendental method consists in trying to identify the most basic steps – or 'operations' as he calls them – which we can take with our minds: such things as seeing, hearing, imagining, understanding, reflecting, judging and so on.[7] These steps, he points out, never exist in their pure state. They always have some definite goal to which they are related. Thus, we never find ourselves simply imagining, but rather, for example, imagining being on the beach at Torremolinos; we are never simply understanding, but rather, for example, understanding the third axiom of Euclid. Technically, then, the operations are 'intentional': they 'intend' or reach out to their proper objects and make them present to the knowing subject. When that subject is aware of himself operating, or taking mental steps, this awareness is not itself an operation, according to Lonergan, but is consciousness itself: I become aware that I am me, knowing. It might be wondered whether Lonergan's list of verbs is altogether satisfactory, whether, for instance, seeing, imagining and reflecting would not more naturally be taken to be forms of understanding, rather than activities laid side by side with understanding. But surely Lonergan's general picture is right, even if it needs correcting here and there.

Continuing to follow the outlines of this picture: Lonergan goes on to say that there are four levels at which we can take mental steps. These are: first, the empirical – sorting out things and facts, stamps, butterflies, names and dates of theological authors and so on; second, intellectual – when we understand or have insight into these things and facts; third, rational – when we come to make judgments about them on the basis of insight; and fourth, responsible – when we find a meaning for them in terms of our own lives.

Corresponding to these four levels or types of mental step there is an appropriate form of consciousness: each makes us aware of ourselves as a knowing agent in a different way. Also corresponding to them are certain key concepts, each of which covers everything involved in each level and the special awareness that goes with it. Thus, at the level of understanding, we have the concept of the intelligible – that which is intrinsically capable of being understood. At the level of the rational, we have the concept of what is true or real; and at the level of the responsible, we have the concept of value, what is truly good. These concepts, Lonergan holds, are found in all cultures. No one can be human and at the same time be unable to use the ideas of what can be understood, what is real and what is good.

But at the empirical level there is no concept of this kind. There we find only different categories, different ways of sorting out things which vary from culture to culture. For instance, among the Eskimos there are a great number of different ideas, I understand, to do with snow, and different words for different types of snow; whereas among a people with no experience of snow (perhaps the Hottentot of the Kalahari desert), there might be no word for snow at all. So there is no transcendental or universal concept attaching to the empirical, even though it is from the empirical realm that all mental journeys set forth. Finally, to each level of mental step there corresponds a mental virtue which each of us should practice. These are: be attentive (to the facts), be intelligent (try to understand them), be reasonable (make rational judgments on them), be responsible (use them properly in your life). Lonergan says that if you do these things, you are practising the transcendental method without knowing it. Echoing the Gospel of John, Blessed are those who have not seen but yet believe!

The transcendental method resolves itself, therefore, into a series of commonplaces. This need not be an adverse criticism, for the theory of knowledge is chiefly meant to enlighten us on what we are doing all the time anyway – *chiefly* but not perhaps exclusively. Some theories of knowledge explain or re-state commonplaces but also indicate ways in which more interesting sorts of less everyday knowledge about ourselves or the world are possible. Kant's theory of the imagination, for instance, both helps us to understand why we enjoy looking at beautiful things and also suggests that this kind of mental activity may lead us to a kind of awe or reverence which has its objective correlate in the fundamental mystery of existence.[8] There are very occasionally glimpses of such a visionary aspect to Lonergan's epistemology: as when he says, in a fashion reminiscent of Blondel,[9] that the levels of consciousness may be seen as 'successive stages in the unfolding of a single thrust, the eros of the human spirit'.[10]

But if Lonergan's theory of knowledge is not terribly exciting, it is at least straightforward. He calls it the 'anthropological' element in theological method, the element that derives from us humans – when we do theology we do not cease to be human, we do not suddenly find our minds working in ways different from the ways they work outside of theology.

One wonders if this is wholly true in every respect. To take the analogy of doctrinal development in order to illuminate the individual's development in *fides quaerens intellectum*: such development in the corporate mind of the Church has not proved explicable except through the invocation of a variety of comparisons, the mind of the poet critically reconsidering his text, the mind of the child becoming adult, and so forth. The development of the Church's corporate mind is a supernatural process related to, but not identical with, any one kind of natural human growth in understanding. Various kinds of growth in understanding throw light on it, but in itself it is *sui generis* or unique, because of the unique rôle of the Holy Spirit in the Church's knowledge of her own faith.[11] When Thomas says that the supernatural light of faith is necessary for theological activity[12] he may be construed as saying that what is true for the common mind of the Church must needs be true for the individual mind of the theologian. Grace acts upon without destroying our natural equipment as mental agents. Could not even the transcendental method, elemental as it is, be open to transformation in terms of the obediential potency of the human spirit before supernatural grace? Not that Lonergan wishes to exclude grace. On the contrary, if we turn to the second or religious element in his theological method we shall see that it is about nothing but grace. Before turning to this, however, it will be well to delay a moment on the two intervening chapters in his *Method*, on ethics ('the human good') and semantics ('meaning').

The 'eros of the human spirit' is at its highest reach, in responsible judgment on understood fact, a 'drive towards value'. In one of the many lyrical passages of writing in *Method*, Lonergan says of the transcendental notion of value, or the good, that it

> so invites, presses, harries us, that we could rest only in an encounter with a goodness completely beyond its powers of criticism.[13]

Corresponding to our intentional self-transcendence towards

an unconditional truth, there is also our moral self-transcendence towards an unconditional value.

> In the measure that that summit is reached, then the supreme value is God, and other values are God's expression of his love in this world, in its aspirations and in its goals.

The same chapter on ethics also includes, surprisingly, an important section on 'beliefs', which for Lonergan are the kind of publicly, corporately mediated moral certainties which Cardinal Newman saw as the proper objects of the 'illative sense'. Human knowledge is here presented as a common fund from which one draws by believing. This same common fund may also be spoken of in terms of *meaning*. Here its vehicles include interpersonal relations, language, symbols, works of art. From the elements of meaning communicated to us in all of these there arises a world of meaning, a cosmos. The 'real world', the wider realm within which our existence is set, is only accessible as mediated by meaning, and since meaning can go astray, our possession of it is insecure. The self-transcending impulse of the human spirit can only be satisfied by going beyond all possible worlds mediated by meaning to the security of the further realm where God is known and loved.

Transcendental method and faith

This brings us to the strictly religious component in the method. For Lonergan, the question of God arises necessarily from the very nature of man as a knowing agent. Suppose we ask ourselves how it is that our mental operations produce results, for instance, the high-powered technology of lasers, computers and spacecraft. The only possible explanation is that the world itself has that kind of intelligibility which can be penetrated by minds; and the only explanation for *this* is that the world itself was brought into being by a reality analogous to the mind itself. And this is what all men would call God.

But although the question of God is implicit in all our questioning, to raise the question of God is not to be a believer. Even to answer it by saying 'Yes' does not in itself make one a religious person. Because we can ask, 'Why is the world intelligible? Why is there such a thing as rationality? Why is such reflection finally worthwhile?' We show that we have a capacity for transcending ourselves towards God. But to ask these questions is not in itself to actualise this capacity: it is not in itself to be united with God. The fulfilment of this capacity for transcending ourselves which is already present in our intentionality is not a kind of knowledge at all. It is a being in love with God, or what Lonergan calls a 'being in love in an unrestricted fashion'.[15] This being in love with God is not a product of anything we do at all, but is the result of sanctifying grace.

In the moment of conversion, grace abolishes the purely human limits within which our knowing and choosing went on. It substitutes a new 'horizon'. We are conscious that something has happened, but we do not directly gain any extra knowledge by it. Our understanding and judgment are defeated by this basic experience of grace. The heart is flooded with love: that is all we can say. This experience is directly of God himself, as the infinite mystery of love behind the world. It is not channelled or 'mediated' by the world, and so it is not contained in, nor perhaps even coloured by, the meanings we have found in the world.

Of course to express this experience of grace and to describe it to others we must use concepts and images drawn from the world. But this is simply what Lonergan calls the 'outer word' of the experience, a kind of suit of clothes we lend it so that it can step out into the street.[16] In itself the word, the *verbum Dei*, is a purely inner reality, beyond concepts and language. We simply know in a way that is strictly ineffable that the love of God (in Paul's words) 'has been shed abroad in our hearts by the Spirit which has been given us'. This knowledge Lonergan terms 'faith'. Faith is a knowledge born of religious love.

What are the implications of this account of coming to faith? First, we should note that faith here cannot be specifically Christian faith, as nothing has been said about Christ, the Bible or the Church. This means that either Lonergan regards Christian faith as just one example of real or true faith, to set beside others, or that he will later find some way of saying how Christian faith is qualitatively distinct. Second, it may be questioned whether Lonergan's notion of a conversion experience which is all inner word is really credible, or, to put it another way, whether the distinction between inner and outer here is capable of bearing the weight Lonergan gives it.

Is it possible to have an experience without also having some words and ideas to help one get hold of that experience? Without language or ideas how could we identify the experience as one of falling in love with God, or falling in love in an unrestricted fashion? Even to recognise the feeling of love requires some ability to label feelings correctly, and what Lonergan is talking about is much more than simply a feeling.

Suppose that religion as a cultural reality ceased to exist, that people lost all access to religious literature and religious language, that everything to do with the religious history of man vanished from the face of the earth, that the very word 'God' became just a meaningless sound. In such a situation, how could I begin to identify the conversion experience which is so central to Lonergan's *Method*? These are questions which philosophers in a more empirically minded tradition have put on a point which will concern us more shortly, as it is on the combination of the transcendental method and the inner word of sanctifying grace that for Lonergan the unity of theology will partly rest.

Lonergan's next step is to clarify the relation between faith (in his sense) and belief. Belief for Lonergan in the religious context is the intellectual system adopted in a given culture to express the change of horizon, or ultimate framework, which faith brings. In comparison with faith, belief is rather secondary. But surely this cannot mean that Lonergan regards Christian doctrine as dispensable in comparison with a faith which is open in principle to Muslims, Hindus and followers of no particular religion at all? No, for according to Lonergan, in the case of Christianity God himself has entered into history. Therefore in this religion, both inner and outer word come from God. In Christianity, as in other religions, the inner word, sanctifying grace, is divine. But only in Christianity is the way it is expressed also divinely guaranteed.

Here Lonergan answers in his own way the question I put a moment ago about the distinctiveness of Christian faith. But since the outer word is rather secondary for Lonergan, the distinctiveness of the Christian faith on his view is not a very interesting distinctiveness. It means in effect that Christianity has the key to what is going on in the other religions, and perhaps outside them too. It does not mean that something different is going on in Christianity. Christianity is a true belief system because its outer word comes from God, but then a belief system seems so secondary compared with Lonerganian faith.

Transcendental method and theology

Acceptance of the inner and outer word of God's grace nevertheless makes an enquiring person, someone using the transcendental method, into a theologian. And so Lonergan moves on at last to talk about theology as such; 'at last' because the book is now through a third of its course. Although the author in a gracious note apologised in advance for the lack of references to actual theologies or theologians, this silence must have worried many readers. It is entailed in Lonergan's starting-point, which is not the historical practice of theology in the Church, but the transcendental method. Nevertheless, since method in theology must mean a description of something which is implicit in the writing of actual theologies, the price to be paid is high.

Finally, then, we come to the writing of theology itself. Lonergan's account of theology turns out to be an account of what he calls 'functional specialties' in theology. Specialisation in theology, if one may follow Père Yves Congar's *A History of Theology*, is essentially a product of the seventeenth century, and it certainly came to have some very undesirable results, notably the divorce between systematic and historical theology which underlies the Modernist crisis.[17] Lonergan recognises that at the present time the sheer amount of information available in historical theology makes specialisation of some kind necessary, especially if we include biblical studies under this label. But specialisation is usually what Lonergan calls 'field' or 'subject' specialisation. One man studies the Bible, another the Fathers; or as a result of, say, the study of the biblical data, one man takes as his subject the history of Israel, another the history of the Ancient Near East. It is in the nature of specialisation of this kind, Lonergan points out, that it does not indicate how to put the pieces together again. For him, specialisation of the wrong kind is perhaps the main cause of contemporary theological malaise. In its place he proposes functional specialisation, an alternative view of specialisation. Here the various disciplines within theology are distinguished as intrinsically related, successive parts of one process.[18] These parts or phases correspond to the stages of the transcendental method with which we began. Just as taking a mature, rational, 'insightful' view of some object requires the mental steps which the transcendental method identifies, so taking a mature, rational, 'insightful' view of the theological object does as well.

Lonergan's first four specialties are research, interpretation, history and dialectics, the last having a special semantic use of Lonergan's own.

For Lonergan *research* means the establishing of data and especially textual criticism. While he leaves open the possibility that the data or texts concerned may represent Tradition as well as Scripture, for the most part he proceeds as though they were in effect co-terminous with the Bible. Since Tradition as the proper ambience for reading Scripture consists in more than texts – it includes for instance, liturgical rites, the witness of Christian art, the *sensus fidelium* – the stress on texts may be surprising. It derives from the need to find a determinate 'first level' corresponding to that of sense awareness in the transcendental method. The latter says (in general): Be attentive to the facts; and so in theology it says: Be attentive to the texts.

The meaning of *interpretation* is everything entailed in a proper 'reading' of the text, the kind of thing that goes on in biblical commentaries. 'Higher' critics, to use an archaism, try to gain insight into the texts which 'lower' or textual critics have established. For Lonergan this corresponds to the rôle of understanding in the transcendental method: Be not only attentive but be intelligent too.

Next comes *history*, that is, narrating and so judging what actually happened. On the basis of textual monuments and their interpretation, historians set to work to produce accounts of *wie es eigentlich gewesen*, despite the inescapability of individual standpoint. In the context of method in theology this will mean histories of Israel, lives of Jesus, histories of the early Church, and in dependence on this, accounts of the history of thought and action in later Christian times. So for Lonergan *history* corresponds to the rôle of judgment in the transcendental method: Be reasonable. Be not only attentive and intelligent, but make reasonable judgments also.

Last, in this group of four disciplines, is *dialectics*. This has nothing to do with dialectics in the mediaeval sense of logical studies. For Lonergan, dialectics means unravelling conflicts concerning the facts, and their meaning and value, which may have arisen so far in research, interpretation and history. Concretely, dialectics is, in a generous sense of the word, apologetics. All major differences, Lonergan thinks, in evaluating the foregoing will turn out on inspection to be differences in people's basic sense of reality. For instance, whether I think the Feeding of the Five Thousand is the report of a genuine miracle or a kind of disguised parable may well turn on what I think in general about the possibilty of miracles. Dialectics presents me with this kind of consideration and invites me to choose the world-view I think best; in effect to submit myself to that 'horizon' which seems the most ultimate intellectually, morally, religiously. So it corresponds to the fourth mental step in the transcendental method: Be responsible. Be not only attentive, intelligent and reasonable, but be responsible also. However, in the case of theology, only conversion can enable me to be responsible *vis-à-vis* God. Since we do not choose God but he us by flooding us with his grace, only a personal encounter with God can enable me to choose rightly among the options presented by dialectics and to see the data of theology as they should be seen.

In saying as much we have moved over into Lonergan's second group of specialties: foundations, doctrines, systematics and communications. It is only with these that theology requires a personal engagement. *Foundations* studies the nature of conversion as the key event which makes possible a personally-committed application of the transcendental method to theology. The reality it studies, though, as its name suggests (fundamental), is only isomorphic with the Gospel kerygma, or the essence of Christian revelation. The Gospel is formally reminiscent of this true foundation, and for Christians no doubt a uniquely valuable exemplification of it:

It is something very cognate to the Christian gospel, which cries out: Repent! The kingdom of God is at hand.[19]

From the combination of conversion and transcendental method, categories suitable for theological writing are derived: thus, Lonergan's *Method* itself is an instance of a foundational study become self-aware.

But we remember that the inner word of conversion requires an outer word which in the case of Christianity is divinely guaranteed, and also a belief system articulating further this outer word. Lonergan now turns to the *doctrines* in which these come to expression. By 'doctrines' is meant here dogmatic theology. The kerygmatic heart of Christian revelation, other particular teachings of that revelation and the authoritative interpretation of those teachings by the Church in answer to new questions in Christian history all derive, for Lonergan, from the outer word of grace and so from Christ himself. Therefore they must be taken *au sérieux* by anyone who has undergone conversion in a Christian environment. The status of the *fides quae* in his presentation seems, however, somewhat undermined by two considerations. The first is the relative inferiority of the outer word compared with the inner; the second is his suggestion that in the specialty *doctrines*, i.e. in dogmatic theology, one will expect to discriminate among the doctrines empirically available in the Church's (or churches') tradition(s) about Christian origins by reference to *foundations*, that is, to the fundamental experience of religious conversion.[20] Lonergan justifies this somewhat startling proposal by arguing that

Church doctrines and theological doctrines pertain to different contexts. Church doctrines are the content of the Church's witness to Christ; they express the set of meanings and values that inform individual and collective Christian living. Theological doctrines are part of an academic discipline, concerned to know and understand the Christian tradition and to further its development.[21]

One would have thought that the contents of Tradition, present in the Church as rule of faith (*regula fidei*) and as the concrete Christian life (*institutio christiana*) would be present in theology as a wisdom or science. If not, then theology is safeguarding its status as an academic discipline at the expense of its office as an ecclesial ministry – the one thing Catholic theology, by definition, cannot afford to do. Lonergan hopes to save the situation by speaking of the 'interacting contexts' of Church and theological doctrines but we need to know not simply that they have influenced each other historically but that they are consistent in meaning. Lonergan is clear that the theologian personally must be an orthodox believer; but how is this to be expressed vocationally, professionally?

Just as conversion expresses itself pluralistically in the endless variety of persons in an indefinite variety of cultures, so the outer world of Christian revelation is also subject to the same conditions, and so is found in many forms. The God-given meaning of dogmas may stay the same, but their formulation – shades of Pope Paul VI's *Mysterium Ecclesiae* and, behind that, Pope John XXIII's opening speech to the Second Vatican Council – will differ from age to age. How then are the various expressions of the faith to be exhibited as one? By a 'methodical theology', a theology conformable to Lonergan's *Method*, which is able to identify and explain the different shapes inner and outer word have taken in myriad forms of human consciousness. It is the Lonerganian theologian who is able to identify the orthodoxy of all of these (Jewish Christianity, Hellenistic Christianity, North African Christianity, and so forth) by showing how they are variously differentiated forms of the Word of God. In so doing he has rendered the Church a service no other could perform (it seems) and so earned his right to his autonomy in his 'academic discipline'.[22]

Lonergan now turns to *systematics*, or speculative theology. Here the aim is not simply to set forth Christian doctrine but to promote understanding of the realities it speaks of. This seems a strange distinction, since to set forth Christian doctrine well would presumably *be* to promote such understanding! Lonergan has a new specialty here because he thinks (historically, quite correctly) that in the Catholic tradition dogmatic theology may legitimately be couched in a philosophic key. We try to express God, Christ, grace and the other theological realities in terms of a general philosophy of reality. Finally, in the last specialty, *communications*, Lonergan speaks of the passing on of the Christian message and applies to it some of the ideas he has developed in the course of his *Method*.

Unity and plurality according to Lonergan's Method

What is Lonergan's own account of the unity and plurality in theology? His most explicit statement falls under *systematics*.[23] The unity of theology for him lies in: first, the transcendental method itself; second, the gift of God's love; third, the permanent element in the dogmas of the Church; and fourth, a factor not mentioned hitherto, the occurrence of theological classics (with an explicit mention of Thomas) which are enduring 'achievements of the human spirit'. These are the quaternity that 'make for continuity'. Over against this, there is the effect of the pluralism of culture and the inadequacies of the imperfectly converted upon the development of a Christian mind: a sea not of relativism but of 'perspectivism' from which only a theology instructed by *Method* can save us.

What are we to make of this formal statement? And of the informal statement which is Lonergan's book, on a topic that, as the International Theological Commission has reminded us,

has its ultimate foundation in the mystery of Christ which, while being a mystery of universal recapitulation and reconciliation, surpasses the possibilities of expression of any historical period and thus escapes exhaustive systematisation.[24]

Lonergan's *Method* is in many ways a *tour de force*, and breathes, unlike much theological writing of recent times, an admirable spirit of devotion amid its intellectual rigour. One is the more reluctant for this reason to offer a negative critique of Lonergan's own re-statement of this essential relationship of the one and the many. But on the first alleged constitutive feature of theological unity, the transcendental method, we have already noted some *lacunae* which may need to be filled, at least as that method is applied to the study of the Church's faith. In the upshot, it is not sufficiently clear that *Method* enlightens us as to how, say, Origen, Thomas, Balthasar are great theologians. The primary task of an essay on method in any discipline is, while accepting the working consensus of the appropriate studying community on the greatness of certain masters, to explain how they achieved their results. No doubt Lonergan would not deny the greatness of the names I have cited (his reverence for Thomas is palpable) but one may take leave to doubt whether the transcendental method has helped to explain it.

Second, the invisible grace of God cannot establish the unity of theology, because it can be asserted, in principle, of Muslims and Hindus, of believers of all kinds and of no obvious kind at all, and so is impotent to determine the unity of specifically Christian theology. Third, the permanence of dogmas as an expression of the God-given outer word of grace certainly establishes doctrinal constraints for theology. But its standing is called into question by Lonergan in two ways. In the first place, as a derivation from the outer word, it is doubly derivative from the inner word, the heart of the God-man relationship, and partakes of that secondary quality which attaches to all beliefs in comparison with Lonerganian faith. In the second place, the exact nature of the authority of dogma for the theologian in his professional capacity is left obscure in the text. Finally, the presence of theological classics, defined purely as achievements of the human spirit as such, no more guarantees the unity of Christian theological tradition than does the presence of any classic. There is an ambiguity here which pertains also to the concept of 'the analogical imagination' in Lonergan's disciple David Tracy.

Unity and plurality: a counter-proposal

What then does the unity of theology consist in? First of all surely, it consists in a common fascination with the mystery of Jesus Christ, as the revealer of the Father and the bearer of the Spirit. It is by being some form of response to this unique *Gestalt, figura,* as Balthasar would say, that theology deserves the accolade 'Christian'. Second, I suggest, it consists in the fact that all Christian theology worth the name includes *in some way* five components: philosophy as *preambula fidei* and, since nature contributes a necessary sub-structure to grace, a source of concepts for the disciplined exploration of revelation which is theology; Scripture and Tradition as the founts of revelation; Christian experience and the contemporary magisterium as aids to the discernment of revelation.[25] This is not an appropriate place to develop this proposal, but I think the study of actual theologies in Catholic Christian practice will bear it out.

Next, plurality in theology. For Lonergan, plurality derives from the fact that the unitary transcendental method, drawing on the unitary grace of God, expressed in the Christian case in the secondary but still identifiable permanent elements in 'common doctrine', must express itself in a variety of cultures.[26] The aim and method of theology is or should always be the same; it is the language (in the widest sense) of theology that differs. But though it is fashionable and to a degree justified to stress the difficulties of cross-cultural communication, the actual historical ways in which theologies have 'taken' or failed to 'take' in a given environment are not mainly of this kind.

Why did Bernard and Abelard disagree about theology? Not because they could not understand each other; they understood each other only too well. Rather, they adopted different kinds of theology, within the same rule of faith, because they wanted theology to do different things. Bernard wanted it to assist personal living; Abelard, to meet the demands of rational enquiry. Why did the mediaeval Russian church accept and continue the kind of theology practised by the Greek Fathers? Linguistically and culturally (developmentally, if you will) one was a Mediterranean people inside a classical culture, the other a Slav people outside it. They agreed on theology because the Russians accepted the idea of what theology should be which the Greeks offered them. Even if we can point to similarities between their situations which help explain why they accepted it, it was the acceptance itself which created the unity of theological culture.

So where then should plurality in theology lie? It seems to me that it most properly lies in the different kinds of question which people put to divine revelation.[27] In looking at the history of theology, this becomes manifest. For Justin Martyr, theology asks how divine revelation fulfils and goes beyond the insights of pagan sages; for Clement of Alexandria it asks how divine revelation can bring us human and spiritual maturity; for Anselm, theology is a search for intellectual joy when we see why divine revelation has the form it has and no other; for the early Karl Barth, theology considers how the Gospel judges this world; for Balthasar, how it brings into the world a beauty or glory, *Herrlichkeit*, beyond all description. Theology can be all of these things because, first, revelation suggests all of them to the believer, and second, human nature under grace is rich and complex enough to take up the hint.

More systematically, we can say that all theology works

with some central model or metaphor around which it organises its material. The notion that a given theology always works with a central *model* derives from contemporary philosophy of science;[28] the notion that a theology is organised around a central *metaphor* comes from people who write about the nature of literature.[29] So in origin the concept of a model and the concept of a metaphor are very different; nevertheless, what they are saying is very similar. In the contemporary philosophy of science it is no longer held that scientific theories are (straightforwardly) objective descriptions of what the universe is like. Instead, a scientific theory says something like, 'Imagine that ... e.g. light is a set of waves, or that a gas is like a set of billiard balls in constant motion: does this help us to understand how things behave?' If it does, we can say that the real world is *in some way like* the model we are using. But the model is not a photograph of reality; it is a pedagogic device, a comparison, to help us get hold of something which is otherwise very elusive. The same is true of metaphors in literature. Suppose that an author organises what he has to say about human life around the metaphor of a journey (a very common organising metaphor in literature in fact: found in Homer, Dante, Bunyan). Of course, life is not literally a journey unless we happen to have been born on the Great Trek or Younghusband's march to Lhasa. But life is in some ways *like* a journey, and so the metaphor of a journey illumines the mysterious reality of life itself.

In more traditional terms, people have spoken here of *analogy*. There is an analogy between the world and God, such that by speaking in language drawn from the world we can say something about the utterly elusive and mysterious reality behind the world which is God.

All theology, then, works with models, metaphors or analogies. For the sake of brevity, let us call these different kinds of *paradigm*, different kinds of basic referent that people choose for the purposes of illuminating comparison. When one theology succeeds another, what is happening? There is a change in the central paradigm being used.[30] In the theology of Bernard, the central paradigm is that of two people having a relationship: theology is like getting more familiar with another person on the basis of what they tell you of themselves. In the theology of Thomas, the basic paradigm is the mind being granted the possibility of a new kind of knowledge: the light of faith transforming the powers of the mind so that one day the mind can be filled with the *lumen gloriae*, anticipated here and now in the *intellectus fidei* which is theology. Bernard's theology is not bad theology, any more than Newton's physics is bad physics. Newtonian physics in its own sphere works very well, and helps us to understand many things. Apples still fall onto people's heads even after Einstein. So the theology of Thomas is not necessarily better than that of Bernard: the claim is almost meaningless. It is better for certain purposes, for the rational articulation of doctrine within the framework of a metaphysics of being. But if that is not what you want theology to do, then Thomist theology will not help you.

Historians of theology have often noted how for a particular doctrine the favoured theological image shifts from one age to another. Thus in the doctrine of the Atonement, for the early Fathers, the death of Christ is a sacrifice; for Anselm it is man's payment of the debt owed to God in justice; for Abelard it is the perfect act of forgiveness. In each case there is a comparison being drawn with some human experience or activity. That such paradigms for basic doctrines are in movement is indisputable to anyone who looks at the writings, paintings or even music left behind in history by the Church.

What has not been so often remarked is that theology itself is subject to the same kinds of shift. Theology can think of itself as a mystical exploration (Denys); as a reflection on history (Wolfhart Pannenberg); as a science (Thomas); as a spectator looking at an incomparable work of art (Balthasar). It can even think of itself as a duplicate of the transcendental method! People writing in terms of each of these models can produce good theology; it is not the model itself which makes theology good or bad but what is done with it. So long as theology remains a response to the objective form of revelation in Christ, a response which includes in some fashion philosophy (or reason), Scripture and Tradition, in the light of experience and magisterium, it has a right to a place in the sun.

Does this mean that we have no criterion for judging one type of theology to be superior to another? Granted that the conditions mentioned above are met, this would seem to be so. For all such criteria could only be stated in terms drawn from a particular type of theology – and this would beg the question. We can, of course, say which type of theology we prefer, which we find most interesting, most congenial, most useful for our purposes in the Church (whatever these may be), but we cannot say absolutely that one is better than another. The ideal of 'a normative pattern of recurrent and related operations yielding cumulative and progressive results' is a chimaera.

And does *this* mean that the Church has nothing useful to say about the plurality of theologies, so long as each meets our minimum conditions? No, there is one very useful thing that the Church can say, and which is hinted at in the citation from the International Theological Commission's document quoted above. Given the nature of revelation, the divine truth is best seen when looked at from a variety of angles in turn. Because revelation is divine it is inexhaustible, and to think that Thomas or Karl Rahner has had the last word is a kind of blasphemy. By looking at revelation through the eyes of each type of theologian we are more likely to see revelation in the round. So the cooperation, and even the competition, of various theologies is desirable for the Church's contemplation of her own faith.[31] This is why the contemporary magisterium is right to be saying, *ceteris paribus*, to the representatives of these different theological schools and tendencies: in the words of the Chinese poem, 'Let a thousand flowers bloom.'

XV
Eros, Friendship, Charity: a Comment on a Curial Letter of 1986

Development is not revolution

The letter on pastoral care for homosexual persons, published in 1986 by the Congregation for the Doctrine of the Faith, has disappointed those seeking a major revision of the Church's ethical doctrine which would justify homophile and more specifically homogenital activity. Such requests for doctrinal development are not infrequently misconceived in that they ignore two considerations. First, authentic doctrinal development is always homogeneous, not heterogeneous. In other words, a later, more 'advanced' state of doctrine manifests the same fundamental principles as an earlier, more embryonic stage. Should we ask in what, then, the difference between the two states consists – what *is* 'development' here? – we come upon the idea that, second, authentic doctrinal development is essentially an explicitation of what was implicit, tacit, acted on in a taken-for-granted way when the original apostolic revelation was constitutively established in the primitive Church. What is progressive is not revelation, but its articulation.

Those who ask the Church to embrace a radically different understanding of the human body (of the human person as embodied) – which a reversal of the traditional condemnation of homogenital activity would entail – are asking her to revolutionise the fundamental Judaeo–Christian anthropology itself. This, at any rate, is the claim of the letter to which I shall return in a moment.

The Church and the natural law

Some people would agree that, were the Church's teaching on same-sex activity to be thought of as based on revelation, a decisive change could be ruled out on the grounds I have just given: namely, that authentic doctrinal development must be homogeneous and explicitatory, not heterogeneous and innovating. But, they might object, the Church's teaching is (also, or exclusively) based on the natural law, the interpretation of which is not subject to these restrictive conditions. Allowing for the moment that the Church's teaching on homosexuality may derive formally from appeal to the natural law, it is nevertheless, I believe, a mistake to regard the Church's grasp of the natural law as something materially distinct at all points from her understanding of revelation. Although the natural law tradition, as found in the Catholic Christian context as elsewhere, does appeal to general structures of intelligibility in the world around us, and offers a reading of them to the reasonable judgment of all men and women of goodwill, nevertheless, when operating precisely in that ecclesial context, it does not wholly prescind from revelation in so doing. It considers the world about us as (*a*) created, *viz.* a world where the 'natures of things' (to adapt Lucretius) are already filled with a purposeful significance, since being creatively understood and willed to be (by God) is the manner in which things have come to exist. Natural law in the Christian context also considers the world as (*b*) more deeply understood when seen in the light of God's revelation in Scripture, part of which consists of the propounding of a natural theology, a natural wisdom, which, though it may in principle be within the range of capability of the human mind and heart as such (as Thomas Aquinas points out), in practice, owing to original sin, may also need the help of revelation and its accompanying grace to be perceived by us (as Pope Pius XII stressed in his 1950 encyclical, *Humani Generis*). It follows that whilst, in appealing to natural law, the Church hopes that non-Christian rationality will respond to the account of the world and human existence within it that she offers (since it is in fact true), she does not depend for her own perception of the truth of this account exclusively on the arguments that such rationality deploys. Thus, although the Church's understanding of the natural law may be refined and filled out by the advance of the human sciences, it is more deeply dependent – materially speaking – on revelation itself. This being so, the principles which govern doctrinal development from the original revelation – homogeneity, explicitation of the implicit – are relevant here also.

Thus, the 'theology of creation' on which the letter founds its reiteration of the traditional teaching is not an uneasy compromise between natural law argumentation and appeal to divine faith. Rather does it identify the area of overlap between the natural law and revelation: an overlap which is crucial for this difficult area of sexual morality in which the claim of 'nature', the givenness of things, the already constituted meanings which man finds in the world as he awakes to consciousness (whether as an individual or as a species), must be balanced against the claims of 'persons', the still-to-be-realised meanings that men and women usher into existence by the exercise of their own creative freedom in the human project. In what I have called this area of overlap the 1987 letter finds its central thesis, which is that human beings are called to reflect the inner unity of their Creator through the complementarity of the sexes. The human body has a 'spousal significance' although this in-built significance is, in the present world-order, clouded by sin.

Mirroring our fallen humanity

The sin of which the letter speaks is, I suggest, primarily original sin and not actual sin. Original sin is the inherited condition into which fallen humanity is born, a condition of inner dislocation in which human powers tend to their proper objects in a confused and uncertain manner, and get in each other's way as a result of a radical disharmony that neither education nor the exercise of willpower can ever wholly correct. The homosexual condition, I would tentatively propose, is one which mirrors this universal condition of humankind in a particular way. The *erōs*, or desiring, erotic love whose rationale is the complementarity of male and female becomes tangled up with the *philia*, or companionable, sharing love whose rationale is brotherhood and sisterhood. Perhaps at some level, this particular dislocation in the relation of powers and their objects is, for post-Adamic man, itself a universal feature of being human. It is when it comes to dominate permanently the sexual emotions of an individual that we come to speak of a 'homosexual orientation'. The rooting of such an orientation in original sin (rather than actual or personal sin) explains why, for the letter, it is both intrinsically disordered and yet in no way reduces the moral dignity of those whom it affects. Only the willed enactment of such an orientation in specific actions brings with it personal culpability, for here – as with other consequences of the Fall like irascibility and power-hunger – we ratify original sin in a mini-Fall of our own. To adopt, and adapt, the language of the letter, the element of evil in homosexual acts (they may often have elements of good though without being thereby morally justified) is, as with adultery, the element that insults the bride and bridegroom, and beyond them offends that other, even more primordial, expression of the 'inner unity of the Creator', the nuptial love of Christ for his Church. In human marriage, the love of *erōs* and the love of *philia* can be integrated in the third classical genre of love, the love of *agapē*, which in its patience, long-suffering and ever-readiness to forgive, imitates the Crucified. This is so because marriage is a sacrament, and carries with it the distinctive grace of all sacraments. Homosexual union cannot be a sacrament for the simple reason that the order of redemption cannot overthrow that of creation, for both are equally founded on God. The way of the Catholic whose sexual orientation is to persons of the same sex (I will not say 'Catholic homosexual' since that would be to operate that 'reduction' of persons to an aspect of themselves against which the letter rightly protests) lies along the path of a purification of *philia* from its erotic component in the discovery of the possibilities, both human and spiritual, of chaste companionship.

Part Three

Theology and Society

XVI
Chesterton and Modernism

At the beginning of *The Victorian Age in Literature*, G. K. Chesterton (1874–1936) assures his readers, ironically, that he will not 'make religion more important than it was to Keble, or politics more sacred than they were to Mill'.[1] In his juxtaposition of religion and politics, Chesterton would have been well understood by many of those involved in the Modernist crisis, though not by all. In England, exceptionally, theological Modernism and social Modernism were almost wholly distinct. The Jesuit, George Tyrrell, wrote to his lay mentor, the Baron Friedrich von Hügel:

> If it is only a question of social progress and educational reform, the world can look after itself and I see no use in lugging religion into the business.[2]

The Anglican Modernists, who knew not so much a crisis as the decorous formation of a party, would have agreed. In Continental Europe, on the other hand, and especially in Italy, Church authority experienced the two varieties of Modernism, theological and social, as two heads of the one hydra. The secularisation of the Christian mind, by the adoption of an historical–critical approach to Christian origins, and the secularisation of the Christian State, by appeal to ideas sprung ultimately from the French Revolution, seemed to many Churchmen, in the pontificate of Pius X (1903–14), related, indeed inseparable evils. They were two prongs of the same attack on Catholic civilisation.

Let us take a characteristic text of the 'integral' Catholicism of the period: a form of Catholicism never officially identified with orthodoxy, yet unofficially supported in what has been called the 'bureaucratic paranoia' of the closing years of Pius X's reign. The text reads:

> We are integral Roman Catholics. As the word indicates, the integral Roman Catholic accepts *in toto* the doctrine, the discipline and the directions of the Holy See along with all their legitimate consequences for the individual and society ... Thus, he is completely counter-revolutionary, since he is not only an adversary of the Jacobin Revolution and radical sectarianism, but also of religious and social liberalism ... We are fighting for the principle and the fate of authority, of tradition, of religious and social order in both the Catholic meaning of these words and in their logical deductions. We view the spirit and the fact of so-called liberal and democratic Catholicism, as well as intellectual and practical Modernism, whether radical or moderate, and all their consequences as wounds on the human body of the Church.[3]

This uncompromising document belongs to the confidential papers of a clandestine ecclesiastical organisation, *La Sapinière*, alias the 'sodality of Pius', *Sodalitium Pianum*. Founded by a priest-academic of the diocese of Perugia, Umberto Benigni, author of a five-volume *Social History of the Church*, begun at the height of the Modernist crisis, and completed in the year prior to his death in 1934, this society was supposed to answer the eternal question, *Quis custodiet custodes?* The papacy had already set in place a formidable armoury of instruments for the control of Modernism, ranging from the administration of an anti-Modernist oath to the establishment, in every diocese, of committees of vigilance under the presidency of the local bishop. Benigni's organisation, *plus papale que le pape*, was itself to be, eventually, delated, and finally suppressed by Pope Benedict XV in 1921. In the meantime, the 'sodality' had succeeded in generating a general atmosphere of mutual suspicion and anxiety, especially among the learned clergy, in its pursuit of Modernists of all brands, both theological and social, which, as we can now see, it did not care nicely to distinguish. The historical criticism which was the main preferred tool of Modernists in the Church was, after all, known to be among the devices of anti-clerical Radicals outside the Church who saw in modern science and scholarship an invaluable weapon in the struggle against Catholicism and its legitimating rôle in the traditional régimes of Europe and beyond.

What would an integralist Catholic of the pontificate of Pius X or of Benedict XV have made of Gilbert Keith Chesterton? Though grateful for Chesterton's opposition to Modernism at the theological level, in matters of faith, the integralist would have seen him as a most dangerous social Modernist in matters of morals. What such an integralist might not have noted, however, unless he read Chesterton's work with some considerable care, was this: Chesterton became an anti-Modernist in theology so as to defend his Modernism in social ethics. He became an orthodox Christian because he saw Christian orthodoxy as, ultimately, the only convincing way to defend Liberalism in political society. To the European Catholic mind, this could only be accounted one of those paradoxes for which Chesterton would become famous.

During the years of his gradual conversion to Christianity in its Anglo-Catholic form, Chesterton was a supporter of the Liberal Party: his political ideal was the radical Liberalism of W. E. Gladstone's last ministries. He approved of such Liberalism for what he regarded as its espousal of the cause of the common man – as expressed in the destruction of monopolies in land, in government and in religion, as well as in championing the rights of small nations. In the years of the strange death of Liberal England, from Campbell-Bannerman to Asquith and from Asquith to Lloyd George, Chesterton would become increasingly disillusioned with the actual Liberal Party, both for its subservience to a managerial élite composed of old aristocracy and new plutocracy, and for the benevolent eye which it cast on the socialist idea of the all-providing State, where the common man's loss of freedom would be veiled in a gossamer coffin of State security: bread and circuses. Yet, in his disillusion, Chesterton insisted that he had not abandoned Liberalism, but Liberalism had abandoned him. Eventually, he turned to Distributism which he believed, on perhaps imperfect grounds, to be for Englishmen the social Gospel of Leo XIII and of his contemporary successor, Pius XI. Fundamentally, Chesterton accepted the three key values of the Great Revolution of the West: liberty, equality and fraternity. He knew, of course, that the French Revolution had quickly taken an anti-clerical and indeed an anti-Christian turn; but, like Hilaire Belloc, he held this to be an accident of history, a product of the short-sightedness of churchmen and revolutionaries alike. If the Jacobins had only sat down with the doctors of the Sorbonne, or so one might piously hope, they would have seen, as Chesterton himself saw, that liberty, equality and fraternity hang in the air unless they have dogma to sustain them. They find their foundation only in the supernatural revealed doctrine of man as the divine image, and their means of preservation in its companion doctrines of the Fall of man and his Restoration by Grace, which tell us of the ceaseless watching and praying required if liberty, equality and fraternity are to flourish in such a world as ours. Thus as early as 1905, in a lay sermon preached on behalf of the Christian Social Union at St Paul's, Covent Garden, Chesterton declared that he was a Christian because he was a Liberal, and three years later expanded this combination of personal experience and wider reflection into his greatest work as an Anglican, *Orthodoxy*, in which he explains how Liberal ideas, once developed, turn out to be what Christianity had affirmed in its ancient Creeds. All social sanities are to be found as the implicates and residues of Catholic dogmas.[4]

This was not at all how the overwhelming majority of

Catholic Churchmen in the nineteenth, and early twentieth, century regarded the French Revolution. They, by contrast, considered the Revolution's attack on both Church and Gospel to be the logical outcome of its ideas, and not merely the psychological outcome of its antecedents. A declaration of the rights of man, shorn of any accompanying statements of the duties of man, derived from and led to, they maintained, a wholly different anthropology from that of Catholicism. In a theocentric universe, as the Church envisaged it, a human being is defined, first and foremost, in terms of his or her reasonable service to the law of God, a law expressed both in the creation, as natural law, and in revelation, as the law of Christ. The early Jacques Maritain, in his *Anti-moderne*, expressed the traditional view to perfection.[5] He came to define it over against the work of three reformers: Luther, Descartes, and Rousseau.[6] With the Protestant reformation, the world beyond the Church became religiously anthropocentric: exalting the I of faith, *das Ich des Glaubens*, to which all the statements of faith must be referred and by which they must be privately judged. With the rise of Cartesian philosophy, it became cognitively anthropocentric: finding the absolute foundation of all knowledge in the thinking self's thought of self. Finally, with the French Revolution, it became ethically and spiritually anthropocentric: in a manner which would have horrified both Luther and Descartes, the Revolution deified man, throwing over the salutary limitations which authority, tradition and historic order set to his capacity for hubris. If the Goddess of Reason were enthroned on the high altar of Notre Dame de Paris, this was only the prelude to the manufacture of an entire 'religion of humanity' by a child of revolutionary France, Auguste Comte.

The aim of the liberalism which the Revolution spawned in both Catholic Europe and its colonies overseas was the apostasy of the masses from the Church, the destruction of traditional Catholic culture, and the establishment of an omnicompetent State, presiding over a naturalistic morality and disseminating, through secular education, an atheistic or at any rate agnostic concept of society and of personal life. By reaction, the papacy, wherever feasible, hoped to strengthen traditional régimes wherever these had endured the Revolutionary and Napoleonic Wars or undergone subsequent restoration, encouraging Catholic rulers not only to guarantee the Church her freedom of action, *libertas Ecclesiae*, but also to defend her faith and moral teaching by pursuing the common good as defined in an ensemble of moral truths and values both natural and revealed. In this way, the papacy, and the episcopate at large, sought to sustain and be sustained by counter-revolutionary elements in European society, irreconcilable as the Gospel could only be with the Revolution's Luciferianism, its declaration *Non serviam* – 'I will not serve.'

The principal reason why Chesterton did not accept this account of the Revolution, nor the prescriptions for the post-revolutionary situation which it implied, was that he believed Rousseau's concept of the general will to house a great moral truth. He believed that once the common man was allowed his say, once he was made into a creative subject of social action, then, at least in a moral culture shaped by Christianity, such as Europe (including the British and Irish islands) possessed, the majority of men would choose that which is decent (*decens*), right and fitting to humankind. Though he did not believe that a mere majority of a parliamentary kind, a party majority, could be such a lodestar in the pursuit of practical goodness, he considered that some wider and more deeply-held consensus, on matters where all human beings simply by virtue of being human were empowered to judge, that is, on *fundamental* matters, could only be sane and sanitising.

Only in the last years of his life did Chesterton come regretfully to the conclusion that the general will 'is an uncommonly weak and wavering sort of will, without the Faith to sustain it.'[7] In *The Well and the Shallows*, he felt that the truths of that nineteenth-century emancipation which had come to Europe in the Declaration of the Rights of Man and to England in the novels of Charles Dickens, had become isolated and irrelevant, when sundered from the dogmatic tradition of a living orthodoxy which contextualised them and gave back to human living what he called 'fullness, richness, and ... variety.'[8] Nor was this simply a collapse of human confidence leading to the invocation of ecclesiastical authority in a spirit of despair. In one of his earliest essays, 'Art and the Churches', in 1902, Chesterton had applauded the wisdom of past societies in putting religion first, morals second, and art third:

> All the schools of morality have as a fact come out of some agreement about the government of things [religion], and all art has come out of the exultation and excitement of that agreement.[9]

That Chesterton's social Modernism in no way involved theological Modernism but, contrariwise, required the repudiation of doctrinal Modernism for its own survival, is made clear in an interesting exchange of articles between him and the Roman Catholic convert, Robert Dell, a minor journalistic figure of the Modernist movement, in the *Church Socialist Quarterly* for 1909. Chesterton, in his own contribution, calls himself, as we should now expect, 'both Catholic and Democrat,' adding, 'if there were a specially democratic wing of Catholicism I should be with that wing.'[10] But he goes on to say that Dell, in his outburst against Roman Catholic obscurantism, has successfully decided him against the Modernist movement. How did Dell thus succeed in prejudicing Chesterton against the Modernist reform of doctrine? Partly by ineptly presenting Catholic Modernism as a long overdue Protestantisation of the Church, what Chesterton calls, with the freedom of an Anglican High Churchman, 'nothing but old Protestant clap-trap.' Here Dell was a misleading advocate: it might be more accurate to call the teaching of Alfred Loisy and Tyrrell a would-be paganisation of the Church, a pseudo-emancipation of spiritual creativity from the burden of the original apostolic deposit, now deemed irrecoverable, lost in a jigsaw of documentary fragments and in the visionary raptures of the ancient Semitic mind. Further, Dell accused Roman Catholicism not only of an unjustified intellectual and spiritual complacency, but also of indifference to the condition of the poor. Chesterton replies that, whatever the personal sins and shortcomings of Catholics,

> the Catholic creed is committed to the three great rational and eternal roots of altruistic energy [whereas] ... none of the other creeds now disputing its throne are committed to them while most are committed against them.[11]

These three principles turn out to be: first, the principle of justice, for there is a moral law before which all men are equal, so that I ought to help my neighbour to his rights; second, the principle of charity, since I owe, as Chesterton puts it, 'infinite tenderness to any shape or kind of man, however unworthy or useless to the State'; and third, the principle of free will, by which I can really decide to help my neighbour, and be truly disgraced if I do not do so. To this, he subjoins the idea of a 'definite judgment,' that is, of the Last Judgment, for the action in question 'will at some time terribly matter to the helper and the helped.' And Chesterton goes on to claim that the choice is not between the religious complacency and social indifference of Rome on the one hand, and the intellectual curiosity and ethical compassion of Paris on the other, but rather between 'the great European tradition of piety and pity of which both Rome and Paris are co-centres, and that other outer spirit of which Berlin is the centre',[12] the modern spirit which idolises force and materialism, and openly praises evil. In other words, to be really modern is to be a pragmatic practitioner of *Realpolitik*; to commit oneself either to the Catholic Church or to the French Revolution or, preferably, to both, is to declare oneself anti-modern, to engage oneself on the side of forces that, though the home of the good, are diminishing in their effective impact on the contemporary world.

In a final assessment of Chesterton's social Modernism, it must be borne in mind that, in combining a dogmatically orthodox vision of man with veneration for the founders of the First French Republic, Chesterton escaped any easy categorisation as a 'radical Christian.' He insisted that things must be 'loved first and improved afterwards':[13] hence it was necessary to be, in turn, both a reactionary and a revolutionary. This attitude, founded on the two concepts of divine creation and human sub-creation, expunged all trace of anarchism or nihilism from his political ethics and gave him, indeed, a sympathy for those ancient institutions which were bound up with the sheer givenness of the human world in time and space – our 'old ideas of loyalty,'[14] of which examples might be: loyalty to ancient territorial sub-divisions of the earth; loyalty to venerable patterns of familial and social relationship; loyalty to a royal house. His work, then, is not only an early example of an orthodox and natively English liberation theology but is, too, an appeal, cognate with that in Pope John Paul II's social encyclical, *Sollicitudo rei socialis*, for the restoration of the creative economic subjectivity of the citizen.[15]

This appeal has been termed by *The Times* religious correspondent 'papal Thatcherism', but it would be better called 'papal Chestertonianism', for neither the pope nor Chesterton would have made Mrs Thatcher's apparent mistake of reconstructing society in terms simply of the citizen and the State, without giving due weight to the vital intermediate level of cooperative institutions and concerns.[16] But more than this, Chesterton's particular version of social Modernism points to a possible synthesis of Revolutionary and non-Revolutionary values which Maritain so desired both at the time of the condemnation of *Action Française* in 1926, and during the Spanish Civil War. For Maritain hoped that

> after the terrible purifications now being undergone, certain historical values will appear complementary which today, mixed up as they are with so many faults, are setting unfortunate and exasperated men at each other's throats.[17]

The 'Catholic synthesis' of 'tradition and revolution' spoken of by Maritain is still as far from achievement as when he wrote of the Right-wing 'pharisaism' that had undermined the virtue of charity, just as Left-wing Modernism had undermined the virtue of faith.

In moving from Chesterton's social Modernism to his theological anti-Modernism it is important to note Chesterton's complete lack of interest in modernity for its own sake. Quite apart from his somewhat negative analysis of contemporary *mores*, of the state of the arts and of philosophy, it obviously seemed to him quite absurd that one should manifest a *parti pris* for one's own age, merely because it happened to be present. He identified, in what John Coates has called the circumambient 'Edwardian cultural crisis',[18] a 'fear of the past' which played into the hands of the philosophical Gypsy fortune-tellers, Huxley, Nietzsche, Shaw, Wells and others, gazing hopefully as they did into the clouded crystal ball of the future. In Chesterton's words:

> The last few decades have been marked by a special cultivation of the romance of the future. We seem to have made up our mind to misunderstand what has happened; and we turn, with a sort of relief, to stating what will happen – which is (apparently) much easier. The modern man no longer preserves the memoirs of his great-grandfather, but he is engaged in writing a detailed and authoritative biography of his great-grandson.[19]

Chesterton's case for sympathetic *Einfühlung* with the past, over against either preoccupation with the future or exclusive concentration on the present is that, first, I can make the future as narrow as myself, whereas the past 'is obliged to be as broad and turbulent as humanity,' while, secondly, the present has scarcely scratched the surface of the rich ore of good ideas in the past. Just as the strength of the Jacobins lay in their appeal to the republics of antiquity, and the power of the Catholic party in Anglicanism in its reference to the golden age of the Fathers, so Chesterton himself claims the right to reconstruct society on any plan that has ever existed: clocks *can* be turned back, beds need *not* be lain upon as one has made them. With such attitudes, it was hardly surprising if Chesterton were deeply unsympathetic both to Anglican and Catholic Modernism. For part of Modernism was the belief that Catholicism must needs become a 'Church of the future,' by adapting itself in radical ways to the world in which it was set. Such adaptation struck Chesterton as supine: he did not oppose change in itself, but only change argued for on such insufficient grounds. Thus after his conversion to Rome, in *The Thing*, published in 1929 he recalled:

> When I became a Catholic I was quite prepared to find that in many respects she [the Catholic Church] is behind the times. I was very tolerant of the idea of being behind the times, having had long opportunities of studying the perfectly ghastly people who were abreast of the times or the still more pestilent people who were in advance of the times.[20]

But if Chesterton's concern with the total *humanum* rather than with the segment of it living now, gave him something of an *a priori* prejudice against Modernism, his love of the Latin middle ages confirmed that pre-judgment. For, despite von Hügel's sustained interest in the fourteenth-century mystical theologian, Catherine of Genoa, the Modernists by and large set their faces against what they considered to be the too heavy burden of the mediaeval inheritance in the Church of Rome. Not for nothing was George Tyrrell's impassioned reply to Cardinal Mercier's pastoral letter against Modernism entitled: *Mediaevalism*. As Tyrrell wrote: 'I feel my work is to hammer away at the great unwieldly carcass of the Roman communion and wake it up from its mediaeval dreams.'[21] For Chesterton's own concept of the value of mediaeval achievement we have, of course, his own trilogy: *St Francis of Assisi, St Thomas Aquinas*, and *Chaucer*. The three belong together: in Francis, Chesterton found the Christianisation of the troubadour, the idea of courtly love, and – more widely – of romance; in Thomas, he found the baptism of appeal to reason and the authority of the senses; and in Chaucer, he saw a combination of the two, for in Chaucer's world the common people and the intellectuals are interrelated, Chaucer's comic irony containing both the simplicity of the people and the sophistication of the clerks.[22] Given Chesterton's appreciation of the achievement of St Thomas, it is hardly surprising if he regarded Christian Scholasticism with a less jaundiced eye than did Modernists like Tyrrell. While the sage of Storrington looked to the voluntarism of William James and the vitalism of Henri Bergson to provide the philosophical underpinning of the religion of the future, Chesterton prophesied that it would be through Thomism that Roman Catholicism, alone among the Christianities of the West, would resist the seductions of relativism, giving form to chaos, defining moral truths, and maintaining the proportions of the mind of man. In 1988 a letter from the Dean of Philosophy of the Catholic University of America to just this effect was indeed published in *The Times*,[23] the day before the last report of that newspaper on the World Congress of Philosophy meeting in Brighton concluded that what philosophers achieve is not so much a consensus on truth as 'a fruitful unending dialogue about talk.'[24]

When we come to the substance of Chesterton's attack on

theological Modernism, we will not find it very different in his Anglican and Catholic periods. Just as he had, in his Anglican period, rebuffed Catholic Modernism in the person of Robert Dell, so, as a Catholic, he will take on Anglican Modernism in such persons as E. W. Barnes, the Bishop of Birmingham, and W. R. Inge, the Dean of St Paul's. It followed from both the very general and auto-didactic character of Chesterton's theological formation and from his choice of a middle-brow public as the proper audience for a convincedly democratic author that Chesterton could not confront scholarly Modernism on its own terms. This was not the disadvantage that it might seem, however, since a number of the Anglican Modernists were themselves *haute-vulgarisateurs*, anxious to create a widely-based party within the Church of England, a party that would inherit the admittedly feeble Erasmian element in the English Reformation, the mantle of the Cambridge Platonists of the seventeenth century with their sitting loose to divisive doctrines, the legacy of the eighteenth-century Latitudinarians, who were little more than deists in religious outlook, and finally, the nineteenth-century Noetic or Oriel school of which Thomas Arnold, with his desire for a broad Church capable of incorporating all Protestant dissenters, was the most notable representative.

What Chesterton criticised in the Anglican Modernists was, in the first place, their general ethos: the studied vagueness of their doctrinal outlook. He cited with approval Ronald Knox's caricature of their manner which 'tempering pious zeal,/Corrected "I believe" to "one does feel".'[25]

More serious, and less Oxonian in courtesy, were the attacks of E. W. Barnes on the Catholic doctrine of the Eucharistic Presence as magical, a recrudescence of fetish worship, little better than the devotion of the 'cultured Hindu idolater'. Chesterton took Barnes to be Manichaean in his repugnance at the continuation of the life of the Word Incarnate in the sacramental signs, and had little difficulty in disposing of his demand for a laboratory experiment to distinguish between consecrated and unconsecrated wafers. The insistence of Barnes on the absolute profanity of the Eucharistic elements was hardly compatible with even the pre-Catholic Revival Anglican ideas of receptionism (a presence in the receiving of the sacrament) and virtualism (a presence of the power (*virtus*) of Christ); and there would, in time, be talk of an enforced resignation on the part of Barnes. H. Hensley Henson, the Bishop of Durham, spoke therefore only partly in jest when at a crowded Lambeth gathering, with no chair free for the newly arrived Barnes, he hailed him with the words: 'Ah, my Lord of Birmingham, come in; sit on the fire; and anticipate the judgment of the Universal Church.'[26] Henson's own consecration had been delayed, however, by a controversy over his apparent rejection of the Virgin Birth and of the Gospel miracles; indeed, the Jesuit invited to preach at a Mass of Reparation, attended by 1,500 of the faithful, for the attack Barnes had made on the Real Presence ascribed Chesterton's reception into the Roman church to his disgust at the 'unchecked Modernism and heretical teaching' of Henson and Inge, for whom Christianity was, patronisingly, the poor man's Platonism. 'His logical mind,' Father Woodlock wrote, encomiastically, in his booklet *Modernism and the Christian Church*, 'drew its conclusions about the alleged Catholicity of Anglicanism from its complacent toleration of heresy in its dignitaries and official teachers.'[27] Since Chesterton contributed an approving preface to Woodlock's booklet, it must be assumed that he acknowledged the truth of this biographical claim.

Chesterton's preface allows us a glimpse of what he took Modernism in the Anglican Communion to be. He confined himself to three topics. First, the higher criticism of the New Testament, and especially the allegation that the portrait of the divine Christ painted in the Fourth Gospel is historically valueless; second, the concept of miracle; and third, the need for a Church which will teach with authority and not as the scribes. On all three points, Chesterton's ultimate focus is Christology; and, in this, he shows himself to be a peculiarly English and even Anglican writer by background, for the defence of the doctrine of the Incarnation has been the principal theological concern of orthodox Christians in England since the mid-nineteenth century. The Christological implications of Chesterton's concern with the Fourth Gospel are obvious. And despite such recent work as J. A. T. Robinson's *The Priority of John*[28] and the entirely refreshing *Jésus savait-il qu'il était Dieu?* by the Dominican Père François Dreyfus,[29] we still stand in need of reminders that only the transcendent Saviour Christ, coming from the Father in full consciousness of his own divine Sonship and mission, can satisfy the demands of the Church's doctrine and devotion. The master-work of Chesterton's Catholic period, *The Everlasting Man*, will present this Word Incarnate against the background of the ascent of man, in which Jesus' coming is not an evolutionary stage but a revolutionary rupture. On the second point, miracle, Chesterton responds to a passage in the book that he is prefacing which draws on Cardinal Newman's mature understanding of miracles. In his *Essays on Miracles*, Newman, without whittling away the supernatural and objective character of the miraculous, argued that, irregular as miracles must be in terms of the order of nature, they may be altogether regular when seen against the *moral* order of the world.[30] Chesterton proposes that the denial of miracle, which is bound up with a reductionist Christology that holds Jesus to be merely a spiritual teacher, his saving death and its eucharistic sign endowed with merely psychological causality, turns on a faulty concept of the will, both divine and human. He seems to mean, for the point is over-concisely expressed, that miracles belong to the freely-entered covenant drama of personal relationships between God and man and are, moreover, the best attestation of its freedom. Chesterton's final point is that if Christian truth is to be 'seen as a whole and loved like a person,' loved in Christo-centric fashion, then it must be simple in its mode of communication:

> The Modernist has to be always talking about schools of thought and stages of enlightenment, about people who have read this and studied that and the other in a particular sense, until we lose the very notion of bringing his 'simplified' theology to anybody as news, let alone good news.[31]

So Tyrrell had written in his early orthodox stage:

> It is perfectly evident to us that Christ came to teach the masses of mankind, and not to argue or plead with the doctors of the law; and that for the masses dogmatic teaching is a necessity.[32]

Not that Chesterton denied, in a-historical fashion, all development in the understanding of the deposit of faith. But he insisted, at all points when he touched on the topic, from a debate in the year of *Pascendi* and *Lamentabili* (1907) to the writing of *St Thomas Aquinas* in 1933, that such development must be homogeneous with its own principles: digesting and transforming external things, but continuing 'in its own image and not in theirs.[33] He wrote:

> When the great flowers break forth again, the new epics and the new arts, they will break out on the ancient and living tree. They cannot break out upon the little shrubs that you are always pulling up to see how they are growing.[34]

Cecil Chesterton, in the first study ever written of his more famous brother, made him stand for

> the hunger of a perplexed age for the more lucid life of the ages of faith, for the revolt against Modernity, in a word, for what may legitimately be called 'reaction'.[35]

On the other hand, as P. N. Furbank writes, 'he was a refugee from the *fin-de-siècle*, and yet he borrowed almost all his

equipment as a writer from it.'[36] There is, of course, a concealed paradox here in that Chesterton was apparently
indebted for the means in which he stated his vision to those
whom he regarded as its enemies or at least rivals. Like Sir
Robert Peel he caught the Whigs bathing and walked away
with their clothes; or, in the more decorous metaphor of St
Augustine, he despoiled the Egyptians of their gold and silver.
As this reference indicates, he was doing something which
Christian apologists, rhetoricians, poets, and philosophers
have done through the ages, for there is an inevitable give-
and-take between the culture in which the Church finds herself and the manner of her expression of the Gospel which she
preaches. Chesterton thus bore witness implicitly and despite
himself to a truth that he would have suspected if not com-
bated: namely, the essential relatedness of the Church to its
own age.

How may we leave Chesterton and the Modernists?
Perhaps, in true Thomistic fashion, by drawing a distinction.
Insofar as men sought a re-expression of Catholic truth that
would allow a given age to make its own contribution to the
refinement and enrichment of that truth without impairing it,
they ventured well; in the words of the Psalmist, they 'will
not fear the evil hearing'. But insofar as they sought a re-
expression of Catholic truth which would slough off the
faith, worship, and order of the age of the Fathers, Christianity's definitive moment of crystallisation, as if it were simply
one garment among many with which the Gospel might
clothe itself, they ventured ill; and against them, Chesterton,
Pope St Pius X and even (for his virtues, not his vices) Monsignor Benigni, stood out for our spiritual gain. But we must
not let Chesterton be controlled by the anti-Modernist
polemic which is but one strand, albeit a vital one, in his
work. He was, as Dorothy Sayers wrote in 1952,

> a Christian liberator. Like a beneficent bomb, he blew out of the
> Church a quantity of stained glass of a very poor period, and let

in gusts of fresh air, in which the dead leaves of doctrine danced with all the energy and indecorum of our Lady's Tumbler.[37]

As an apologist, Chesterton's posterity was found more in the Communion he left than in that which he joined. It was found in Sayers herself, in C. S. Lewis, in Charles Williams; in a word, in the Anglo-Catholic party for which he continued to show a healthy respect, considering their position a possible one and revering many of its representatives. Catholics need to re-learn from Chesterton the value of apologetics of his dramatic and lively kind.

XVII
The Rise and Fall of
Liberation Theology?

Liberation theology emerged gradually in the period following the Second Vatican Council.[1] At that Council there were
present, as influences on the conciliar process, a wide variety
of theologies: Neo–Scholastic, Neo–patristic, anthropologico
–transcendental (alias Karl Rahner), as well as the interrelated theologies of the 'signs of the times' and of 'earthly
realities', the latter soon to be dubbed 'secularisation–
theology' and chiefly worked out, like its brother movement,
by the French. As succeeding events have demonstrated, the
resultant compound was unstable. So far as the Americas
were concerned, although the Latin American Episcopal
Council (CELAM) had functioned since 1956, the Latin
American influence at Vatican II, whether of bishops or theologians was negligible, with exception of one or two individual voices like the Brazilian Helder Câmara, Archbishop of
Recife, who contributed to the making of the Pastoral Constitution on the Church in the Modern World.

Very different, during the Council's closing sessions, was
the state of affairs in Latin America itself. There a veritable
theological ferment was brewing, as became clear from four
meetings of theologians held at, successively, Petrópolis
(Brazil), Havana (Cuba), Bogotà (Colombia) and Cuernavaca
(Mexico) in the course of 1964–65. What transpired from
these pan–Latin American theological assemblies was the
need for a new theology whose nature would be determined

by the conciliar 'renewal' – but also by confrontation with the often cruel human reality of that continent. Such men as the Uruguayan Juan-Luis Segundo and the Peruvian Gustavo Gutiérrez looked towards a new kind of evangelisation whose agents would be, when compared with their predecessors, at once more critical of contemporary culture and more engaged within it. The name originally bestowed on this prospective new theology was 'historic theology' – selected because it was intended to provide a Christian interpretation of Latin American history, and an attempt to influence that history's direction.[2]

However, these streams of thought or, at any rate, aspiration, soon encountered other currents whose source lay in the sociological analysis of regional economic patterns of dependence and under-development. Dependency theorists argued that true development in Latin America required a socialist breakaway from world capitalist domination. The principal analytic resource of such accounts, as these terms indicate, was Marxism. Accordingly, the form taken in the concrete by the new 'historic theology' in its interpretation of Latin American history was *marxisant*, including as it did such major themes as class confrontation and the need to make an explicit option for socialism, over against capitalism. The experience of Cuba, a Marxist–Leninist political society since 1958, became a general reference-point, and credit was given to wide-ranging aspects of the Marxist analysis of social reality, albeit in varying degrees.

In such circles, though Pope Paul VI's social encyclical of 1967, *Populorum Progressio*, was well received, not least for its emphasis on the limits set by the common good to the rights of private property, that letter's social doctrine was soon regarded as insufficient. More heavily criticised still for faint-heartedness, long-term ineffectiveness and even counterproductiveness in terms of the generation of greater equality between and within societies, was the philosophy of development urged on the governments of Central and South

America by the presidential administration of John F. Kennedy.[3] By contrast, there was general support for a manifesto launched by Archbishop Câmara in late 1966 at Mar del Plata, Argentina, on the occasion of the tenth reunion of CELAM; its key idea was that of structural transformation as liberation from under-development, itelf seen as the true 'collective sin' of Latin America.

In 1967, at the eleventh reunion of CELAM in Lima, the Latin American bishops issued an appeal for a new pastoral strategy, the start of the process that would produce the epoch-making Medellín statement in September 1968. Various bodies contributed to the shaping of this strategy; prominent among them was the Society of Jesus whose Latin American provincials, together with their General, Father Pedro Arrupe, published an influential letter on the topic from Rio de Janeiro in the May of the crucial year; though important, too, was the reunion of theologians held at Chimbolé, Peru, in July, a month before the Medellín congress opened. The Jesuit letter spoke of the need for a sociological analysis which would lead to a courageous denunciation of injustice and a preferential option for freeing others from every form of servitude in the name of Christian evangelisation: the origin, apparently, of the celebrated phrase, 'option for the poor'.

The Medellín congress turned out to be a crucial moment in the history of Latin American Catholicism. One of its participants, the Spaniard Pedro Casaldáliga, Bishop of São Felix in the Brazilian Mato Grosso, summed up its results as nothing less than the provision of a new identity for the Church by, on the one hand, shaking its excessively hierarchical structure, and, on the other, galvanising a 'popular Church', whose growth points would be basic communities, themselves characterised by a process of continuing social re-education, designed to raise the consciousness of their members about their situation and its causes, and to transform that situation through engagement in political struggle.

To animate this process, Medellín gave an impetus, so Casaldáliga reported, to the creation of a new theology which saw the Latin American poor as Israel in Egypt, prior to the exodus to the Promised Land.

Between the reality of a text, and the perception of that reality by various interested parties, there always lies some kind of gap. For the historian of theology, to read the Medellín statement is not to be made aware of anything innovative.[4] The document, rightly, minces no words about the economic, educational and political shortcomings of Latin American society. But it moves within the familiar terrain of Church social teaching, and has nothing of its own to say about doctrine, much less about theology. Bishop Casaldáliga, however, found in it irrefutable evidence of the presence of the new 'theology of history'. The bishop who, by the 1980s, would gain a certain celebrity, or notoriety, thanks to his refusal to go to Rome for the triennial visit of local bishops *ad limina apostolorum*, as also for his enthusiastic support for the Sandinista government in Nicaragua, despite the entreaties of the episcopate there, called this new theology of history 'captivity theology'. That we now speak of LT, 'Liberation Theology', and not of CT, 'Captivity Theology', is owed in fact to the post-Medellín meetings of Latin American theologians. At Cartigny, Switzerland, in 1969, and then in 1970 at Bogotà, Buenos Aires and Oruro (Bolivia), they drew their own inferences from the Medellín congress under the title, soon to become so famous, 'the theology of liberation'.

The first fruits of liberation theology were two large books published in 1971 and 1972 respectively, Gustavo Gutiérrez's *Teologia de la Liberación* in Lima, and the Brazilian Franciscan Leonardo Boff's *Jesus Christo Libertador* at Petrópolis.[5] While their perspectives were distinct, these two works possessed a common aim and used parallel methodologies. As to the two fathers of liberation theology, for they are no less, Gutiérrez was born in Peru in 1928 and studied at

Louvain, Lyons and Rome. Influenced by his discovery of the sixteenth-century Dominican defender of the Indians, Bartolomé de las Casas, he was a fellow student of the Colombian priest Camilo Torres who died on active service with a guerrilla movement in that country. Gutiérrez's book broke with what would soon be called a 'European' concept of theology. Theology is not, or is not only, a kind of understanding, whether spiritual and sapiential, like that of the Fathers and many mediaevals, or systematic and scholarly, like that of the Scholastics and moderns. It is also, or should be, in the light of the signs of today's times, an eminently practical affair, placed at the service not of the ecclesial magisterium but, rather, of the poor and oppressed. Gutiérrez was preoccupied not so much with orthodoxy as with 'orthopraxy'. He insisted that Scripture, the ultimate theological source-book, could not yield 'right action' unless its interpreters were continuously aware of their own situation – their interpretative vantage point – in social and political terms. Theology for Gutiérrez is 'critical reflection on historical praxis' and its greatest early monument is Augustine's *De Civitate Dei*, itself based on a true analysis of the late antique signs of the times, and the challenge which they posed to the Church of its day. For the modern reader in Latin America, socially situated self-awareness could only mean, Gutiérrez continued, awareness of Latin America's history as, in a phrase borrowed from biblical apocalyptic, a 'mystery of iniquity'. The Bible's message, as Gutiérrez saw it, would envisage three levels or stages of liberative activity: first, socio-economic liberation; second, the conquest of certain political freedoms, essential if a people is to construct its own history; and third, the making of a human brotherhood or communion, founded on faith. Whereas, classically, theology has been defined as the 'science of God', in Gutiérrez's portrait of the theologian the divine mystery is to some degree displaced from the centre of the picture so as to be replaced by the mystery of the neighbour – since it is in the neighbour, in his needs, and in his potential, that the structure of redemption is disclosed. This anthropocentric tendency was in part rectified, it is only fair to add, in Gutiérrez's later work, *We Drink from Our Own Wells*, a title taken from Bernard of Clairvaux.[6] There Gutiérrez affirmed the abiding necessity of a life of prayer as the foundation of all Christian activity worth the name. However, in *A Theology of Liberation*, evangelisation concerns not so much the proclamation of a doctrinal message about God as it does the animation of the temporal order by criticism and prophecy – at once denouncing the way things are and suggesting how in the future they should be. Gutiérrez looked in part to a 'this-worldly' resolution of the problem of evil, presenting faith as entailing an option for justice, and filling out what justice involved by an account of social interrelationships drawn from the evidence of the Gospel, interpreting the life and ministry of Jesus on the model of those of the Old Testament prophets namely, as a challenge at once social and religious to the established disorder.

Boff is Gutiérrez's junior by a decade. He was born in Concordia, Brazil, in 1938, and entered a minor seminary at the age of ten. He studied at the major seminary of Petrópolis, where he subsequently taught, being a pupil of his later critic the Franciscan bishop Bonaventura Kloppenburg. Boff was himself ordained to the priesthood as a Franciscan in 1964, and completed his theological studies at Munich where his supervisor was a second later critic – the then professor of dogma there, Dr Joseph Ratzinger. Boff's thesis was published at Paderborn in 1972 under the somewhat doctoresque title, *The Church as Sacrament in the Horizon of World Experience*. In his first contribution to a distinctively liberation theology, Boff adopted what he saw as a new hermeneutic, a lens of a novel kind through which to look at the Gospel data. Like Gutiérrez's innovatory picture of theology as a whole, this new hermeneutic was, Boff believed, made not only desirable but necessary by Latin American reality, which he described with the help of sociology, especially the theory of dependence, and, to some degree, of Marxism. The Boff hermeneutic was to have four features: first, the primacy of anthropology (concern for man) over ecclesiology (concern for the Church); second, the primacy of the Utopian (the future of society) over the factual (the Church's past and present); third, the primacy of criticism over dogma; and fourth, the primacy of the social over the personal. 'Jesus Christ the Liberator', as Boff presents him, preaches a conversion of fundamental mentality whose power revolutionises both the social order and the human being whose life that order houses. Like Gutiérrez, Boff insisted that his starting-point was not something original to himself, but reflected a widespread experience in the Latin American Church, arising out of the rediscovery of the Saviour's 'option for the poor', now representatively embodied in the exploited classes of contemporary societies.

These theologies, once launched, aroused very different reactions. On the positive side, the emergence of liberation theology's founding fathers was seen by some as timely. Even at Rome, it was widely held that Catholicism's centre of gravity was shifting away from Europe to other 'younger' churches, especially in Latin America. At the second General Synod of Bishops, in the autumn of 1971, the Latin American bishops' conferences, some twenty-two in all, began to make their weight felt in the context of a new preoccupation with situations of injustice in those parts of the world where, it was believed, Catholicism's future lay. Again, it was generally recognised that, throughout Western society, the Church was afflicted by a crisis of relevance, and to this liberation theology might be heaven's answer. Indeed, it was at a 1972 meeting of the Jesuit institute of 'Faith and Secularity', founded as a result of Paul VI's appeal to the Society to come up with some answers to the spread of atheism and religious indifference, that *European* theologians first encountered liberation theology. In the improbable surroundings of the

Escorial, Philip II of Spain's palace-monastery, all the chief
representatives of liberation theology foregathered, and were
observed to include an inordinate number not only of Jesuits,
but also of sociologists, socialists and the European-trained.
The point of this remark was to indicate the comparative
absence of members of the basic diocesan priesthood, of
economists, of politicians sympathetic to, at least, some
middle way between socialism and capitalism along the lines
of a 'partnership economy', and of theologians whose formation had been exclusively in Latin America itself. It would
remain a difficulty with the liberationist claim to represent
the spontaneous voice of the Latin American poor that it so
clearly betrayed the intellectual ancestry of its main practitioners in such backgrounds as: the French and German
theology of secularisation associated with Marie-Dominique
Chenu and Johann Baptist Metz; the idea of religionless
Christianity linked to the prison writings of the Lutheran
Dietrich Bonhoeffer, the theology of hope founded by his
fellow Evangelical Jürgen Moltmann, and that widespread
phenomenon of *bien-pensant* Europe, the Christian–Marxist
dialogue. At this conference, then, liberation theology for the
first time projected its own self-image on the European stage.

What was this image? Essentially that of a new, global –
that is, all-encompassing – theological project, whose source
lay in political activity regarded as itself a spiritual experience. The departure point of this project lay in a rejection of
social history in its local reality, while the political activity
engendered by this 'great refusal' was held to challenge the
traditional understanding of the Christian life and to rupture
the (supposedly) otherwise continuous fabric of Christian
culture inherited from the past. The new theology was to be
done by the people, of whom the professional theologians,
issuing from the people and constantly referring back to their
experiences, were the spokesmen.[7] The prime authority
recognised by such theologians, in their scanning of the Word
of God would not be Church tradition but the historical

process itself. They would reinterpret the content of the faith on the basis of historical situations, although such situations were themselves also to be interrogated and interpreted by the fundamental act of faith.

The Escorial conference had a second effect. It exacerbated the negative reaction to liberation theology beginning to be expressed not only by theologians of a mere traditional stamp,[8] but also among the episcopate and by the papacy. The second General Synod of Bishops decided to forbid priests from accepting political office or becoming militant in political parties, a determination later canonised in the new Code of Canon Law of the Latin church. This turned out to be a largely ineffectual fulmination, as witnessed by, for instance, the large number of priests involved in the founding of the movement 'Christians for Socialism' at Santiago da Chile in later 1972, as, *inter alia*, a mobilisation of support for the ill-fated Marxist government of Salvador Allende. In the month which followed the Roman synod, November 1972, tension exploded at the fourteenth reunion of CELAM, held at Sucre, Bolivia. Whereas liberation theology was generally supported by the Brazilian episcopate and a number of other individual bishops (mostly members of religious orders), it was energetically attacked by many of the rest. From that moment on, CELAM began to multiply its reservations on the topic.

A source of particular anxiety was the mode of development of the basic ecclesial communities.[9] Usually sited in rural areas or on the edges of the cities these groups were not the creation of liberationism. Their origin lay in the Brazil and Panama, especially, of the 1950s. Aimed at relieving hard-pressed parish clergy by taking over the teaching of the catechism, they were, from the first, connected with such neighbourhood concerns as health centres and schools. In the course of the 1970s, however, they were gradually adopted as vehicles of liberationist exegesis and politics. Many, it is true, remained harmoniously inserted into surrounding parishes, themselves too large for proper pastoral management. But others became so heavily politicised that to all intents and purposes, they eventually ceased to be ecclesial structures at all.

In 1974, the third Roman Synod of Bishops met to discuss the theme 'evangelisation in the contemporary world', something of interest to liberation theology with its conviction that evangelisation is inseparable from the promotion of justice. During the second part of this synod, the problems posed by the very existence of liberation theology were aired in no uncertain terms. The Brazilian Cardinal Alfredo Scherer of Porto Alegre, a personal nominee of Pope Paul, declared that liberation theology was provoking grave dissension in the Church. He was supported by the Jesuit Archbishop of Quito (Ecuador), Pablo Muñoz, who appealed to theologians to remember that they stand at the service of the Church's unity. On the other hand, another Brazilian cardinal, the Archbishop of São Paolo, Evaristo Arns, a Franciscan, thought the most important priority to be the elimination of the dualism between body and soul, temporal and eternal, which, he claimed, had damaged all traditional evangelisation. An especially influential figure at this synod was the secretary of CELAM, Alfonso López Trujillo, at that time an auxiliary bishop in the Colombian capital, Bogotà.[10] Whilst admitting that acceptable forms of liberation theology did exist, he expatiated on the drawbacks of the unacceptable varieties. First, it was intellectually dubious to accept Marxist methods of analysis while disclaiming any indebtedness to the ideological content of Marxism. Second, the refusal to allow for the possibility of reconciliation between social groups, or the harmonisation of group interests was a recrudescence of Manicheanism, demonising certain social classes and writing them off as beyond social redemption. Third, liberation theology, in its unacceptable forms, understood divine revelation in a thoroughly politicised fashion. It presented revolutionary movements as the real carriers of the history of salvation, preparing the coming of the Kingdom of God. It claimed that, to regain credibility, the Church must be transformed into a sign of revolutionary commitment. It held that she must re-define her unity and universality in a commitment to the proletariat in whom the meaning of history is deemed to reside, and it called on theologians, finally, to make a class option, so that theology itself might become an instrument of revolution. Faced with these conflicting testimonies, the synod proved unable to reach any substantial agreement. Its final statement was vague, and Pope Paul was left to sort out the mess, which he did in the apostolic constitution on evangelisation, *Evangelii nuntiandi*. There he underlined the interrelation between what he termed, somewhat blandly, human promotion, integral liberation and evangelisation, but also went on to deny any identification between these terms. A single explicit reference to liberation theology says simply that it can favour attitudes leading evangelisation to deny its own nature, by forgetting that God himself is the ultimate salvation – and so liberation.

Two further events distinguished 1975. Liberation theologians, feeling themselves pushed out into the cold by the growing distance of CELAM in their regard, held an impressive meeting in Mexico City under the title 'Liberation and Captivity'. Still hoping, at this juncture, that Rome might be more sympathetic than were many South American hierarchies, they invited the attendance of the papal nuncio to Mexico. He, however, in a closing speech to the Congress, used the opportunity to appeal for unity of faith within a plurality of theological methods, urged the participants to avoid all impoverishing radicalism, and advised them to link up again with the best theology of all ages, and with what he called authentic catholicity. At Rome, despite the social humanism dear to Paul VI, there was deepening anxiety about liberation theology. Still in 1975, the Holy See entrusted the topic of the relation between evangelisation and 'human promotion' to the Pontifical International Theological Commission. This body, made up of theologians from outside Rome, but ultimately responsible to the prefect of the Congregation for the Doctrine of the Faith, took the view, in its report, that human promotion is less an aspect of evangelisation than it is an analogy for it. In the present context, the commission opined, it is preferable to emphasise the difference, rather than the similarity between the two. One rather subtle ground offered for this judgment was calculated to allay anxiety in more radical minds. The inevitable setbacks which 'human promoters' receive from the world will be less daunting, the Commission suggested, if they are not experienced as defeats of the Gospel of grace itself.[11] It should be noted that these words were written three years before the advent of Cardinal Karol Wojtyla to the papacy, and four years before that of Cardinal Joseph Ratzinger to the Prefecture of the said Congregation.

Despite such blows, or at any rate pinpricks, liberation theology continued its diffusion, not least outside South America.[12] In 1975 it achieved a North American platform at a major conference, 'Theology in the Americas' held at Detroit. In 1976, at an intercontinental meeting at Dar-es-Salaam in Tanzania, it allied itself with the emerging indigenous theologies of Africa and Asia. From that year dates the beginning of its reception in, above all, South Africa, India and the Philippines.

In the later 1970s and early 1980s, liberation theology's library expanded in its home continent, with such works as Gutiérrez's *Fuerza historica de los pobres*, the Spanish-born El Salvadorean Jesuit Jon Sobrino's *Jesus en América latina*, and various works by Boff, whose output soon topped thirty books selling almost half a million copies.[13] At the same time, the bishops of Latin America were gearing themselves up for a new general assembly which would evaluate the experience of the Church in their territories in the decade since Medellín. This assembly, to be held at Puebla de los Angeles in Mexico, would be convened in the presence of the new pope, John

Paul II. Puebla's preparatory documents were notably unfavourable to liberation theology. Various liberation theologians found their names removed from the list of invited
'experts', and in the end they organised a parallel meeting of
their own.

In his opening address, on 28 January 1979, the pope
remarked of the assembly:

> It will ... have to take as its point of departure the conclusions of
> Medellín, with all the positive elements that they contained, but
> without ignoring the incorrect interpretations sometimes made,
> incorrect interpretations which call for calm discernment,
> opportune criticism and clear choices of position.

In his address, but without naming liberation theology
specifically, the pope warned against a politicisation of the
figure of Christ.

> The idea of Christ as a political figure, a revolutionary, as the
> subversive man from Nazareth, does not tally with the Church's
> catechesis. By confusing the insidious pretexts of Jesus' accusers
> with the – very different – attitude of Jesus himself, some people
> adduce as the cause of his death the outcome of a political
> conflict, and nothing is said about the Lord's will to surrender
> himself [to his Passion] or about his consciousness of his
> redemptive mission.

He also spoke against a politicisation of the concept of the
Kingdom of God, now interpreted as

> attained not by faith and membership in the Church, but by the
> mere changing of structures, and by social and political develop-
> ment, and as present wherever there is a certain type of involve-
> ment and activity for justice.

Here the pope was able to cite some words of his short-
lived predecessor, John Paul I:

It is wrong to state that political, economic and social liberation coincides with salvation in Jesus Christ: that the *regnum Dei* is identical with the *regnum hominis*.

And in any case, the pope went on, the understanding of the human being subjacent to such 're-readings' of the Gospel and the 'perhaps brilliant but fragile and inconsistent hypotheses flowing from them' is defective. The Church's faith in man's supernatural dignity and destiny is something greater than the anthropological reductionism now in vogue, what he called 'forms of humanism that are often shut in by a strictly economic, biological or psychological view of man'. At the same time, however, the pope spoke out strongly against violations of human rights in Latin America, urged the bishops to form the social consciences of their people by making known to them the social doctrine of the Church, and spoke of a 'correct Christian idea of liberation' which he described as primarily salvific, but as releasing energies for the liberation of others in the economic, political, social and cultural domain.[14] The final document of the Puebla assembly faithfully reflected these comments to which no doubt, a number of the Latin American bishops had contributed, in advance.

Some months later, at the seventeenth meeting of CELAM, at Los Teques (Venezuela), a new wave of criticism of liberation theology crested with election of López Trujillo as successor to the Franciscan Cardinal Alois Lorscheider of Fortaleza (Brazil) in the post of president of this standing 'conference of conferences'. About the same time, the Jesuit General addressed a letter to the Society's provincials in Latin America on the subject of Marxism. Father Arrupe summed up:

> In brief, if Marxist analysis does not directly involve adhesion to the Marxism philosophy in its completeness, still less to 'dialectical materialism', as understood currently, it does in fact imply a conception of human history which is at variance with

the Christian vision of man and of society, and leads to the adoption of strategies which threaten Christian values and be-haviour.[15]

It is true that Arrupe added some important qualifications to this statement. He insisted on the relationship between liberation from oppression and the Christian project itself (a relation for which his chosen word was 'affinity', perhaps halfway between the terms 'aspect' and 'analogy', as used by other authorities). He denounced liberal or capitalist social analysis as equally materialist and opposed to Christianity. He called for dialogue and even occasionally cooperation with Marxists, though within a clear affirmation of a Jesuit's priestly and religious identity, and urged the members of the Society to resist any manipulation of his letter which might weaken their commitment to the pursuit of justice. Neverthe-less, his attack on the utilisation of Marxism was couched in strong terms.

A further straw in the wind was the condemnation, by an archdiocesan commission at Rio de Janeiro, of Boff's *Igreja: Carisma e Poder* (*The Church: Charism and Power*). Hopeful of a better hearing at Rome, Boff sent the work, and the condemnation, to the Congregation for the Doctrine of the Faith, on his own initiative, in February 1982. That this was a misjudgment on his part became obvious when, late in 1982, Cardinal Ratzinger, the new prefect of that office, communicated to the bishops of Peru ten critical observations on the work of Gutiérrez. These were made public in the course of 1983.[16] In March 1984, the Italian monthly *Trenta Giorni* printed a leaked report by Ratzinger on liberation theology, which he treated with scant respect as a mixture of bad politics and worse exegesis.[17] In September 1984 his Congregation published *An Instruction on Certain Aspects of the Theology of Liberation*, a text which concentrated almost exclusively on the negative features of the liberation theo-logians' work. My own paper, introducing *Libertatis nuntius* in London, suggested that it offered a critique of liberation theology in terms of three principles: a principle of totality, a principle of catholicity, and a principle of theological autonomy.[18]

First, the principle of totality has it that the Church must address herself to the total human being, by bringing to bear the total Christian revelation. The total human being is more than his secular self, and our secular self is more than our political self. Similarly, while the total Christian revelation has social-political aspects or implications, the totality of that revelation is more than these social-political correlates.

Second, the document appeals to a principle of catholicity. The biblical theme of liberation cannot simply be juxtaposed with particular human situations so as to generate a Christian theology while at the same time bypassing the theological tradition of the Church – whether that be seen diachronically, as spread out over time, or synchronically, as manifested in geographical space. A specifically Catholic Christian theology cannot be spun out of Bible plus experience. It needs a reference also to Tradition, a necessary medium in the reception of Scripture, and, indeed to that articulation of Tradition which is found in the formal teaching of the episcopal and papal magisterium.

Third, the instruction invokes a principle of theological autonomy *vis-à-vis* the conceptual apparatus of philosophy and the natural sciences. Since theology is the intelligent expression of divine revelation, it cannot be subordinated to the deliverances of philosophy or the findings of the social sciences. While theology needs concepts drawn from other disciplines to carry out its own reflection in an organised fashion, it treats these concepts as tools and instruments. Were the concepts and hypoteses of philosophy or social science to dictate the content of theology, then, as in the fable of the sorcerer's apprentice, the instrument would have taken over those who thought themselves its master.

Yet the Instruction spoke of the theme of liberation as 'full

of promise' for Christian reflection and practice, and announced a successor document on the positive side of our
subject. Meanwhile, however, the Congregation made it clear
that its role would not be confined to the making of general
statements. That same month, Boff was summoned to Rome
for interview by Ratzinger, and, despite the protective
presence of the two Brazilian cardinals devoted to liberation
theology, his fellow Franciscans Arns and Lorscheider, the
interrogation issued in the publication, in March 1985, of a
series of negative animadversions on his ecclesiology.[19] Two
months later, the Congregation served notice that Boff
should observe an 'obedient silence' by abstaining from lecturing or writing for an unspecified period. Surely the year of
bitterest feeling in this entire controversy was 1985, well
expressed in the response to the first Roman critique of liberation theology by Segundo in his *A Reply to Cardinal
Ratzinger*, sub-titled, somewhat ominously, *And a Warning
to the Whole Church*.[20]

The Holy See's second, positive, critique, *Libertatis conscientia*, dated March 1986, is not only the longest document
ever published by the Congregation but also entailed in its
making an unprecedentedly wide process of consultation,
involving thirty-five episcopates and forty theologians in
different parts of the world. Curiously, *Libertatis conscientia*
hardly ever mentions liberation theology by name. Only once
is there a reference to the 'theology of freedom and liberation'. We can see in this a will to restrict the 'legitimate and
orthodox' liberation theology which Rome desires to the
limited ambit of a sectorial theology – one, that is, which
deals with some particular area of reality, rather than serving
as a global, all-purpose, account of the world in its relation to
God.

In what, then, for this *Instruction on Christian Freedom
and Liberation* does such a 'legitimate and orthodox' liberation theology consist? It consists in relating Catholic social
doctrine to a traditional soteriology – a classically-

understood doctrine of salvation, itself seen as founded on the christological and Trinitarian faith of the ecumenical councils of the patristic age. This linkage has never been properly achieved in the past. A Christianised society was unimaginable for the definitely minoritarian communities of the New Testament. The Fathers after Constantine, the mediaevals, and the sources of the early modern period, offer suggestive hints as to what the ethos of such a society should be. But only with the crisis in European Christendom caused by the upheavals of the Great Revolution of the West, from 1789 to 1815, together with the timely invention of the papal encyclical as a *genre* suited to authoritative comment on major issues of the day, were these hints gathered up into a 'social doctrine'. Even then, from Pope Gregory XV to Pope Paul VI, that social doctrine was expressed chiefly in terms of natural law thinking, increasingly incorporated into Catholic theology as a way of speaking about the created order, since the patristic period. Although this social doctrine of the Church did not lack all reference to the Gospels, and the more specifically Christian virtues taught or exemplified in the New Testament, it was to some degree cut off from the fundamental dogmas of the Trinity, the Incarnation, the Redemption, and the life of grace. This is where, by implication, the document locates the positive significance of liberation theology. That theology can help to catalyse the process whereby the Church's social doctrine becomes more fully integrated with her basic beliefs about the God of salvation. The political economy and the 'economy' of salvation are being reunited, and for this liberation theology can claim much of the credit.

It is true that this linkage was already apparent in the present pope's first encyclical, *Redemptor hominis*. It might have happened anyway, given his personal determination to interpret all the Church's activity in thorough-going Christo-centric terms. It is also possible that this notion of uniting the Church's social teaching to the great dogmas, and notably to

Christology, came to the pope thanks to his own experience of the difficulties which the episcopate faced in the matter of relating evangelisation to human promotion. After all, at the third Roman Synod, the Archbishop of Cracow had been responsible for drafting the working document which, eventually shelved, was replaced by Paul VI's *Evangelii nuntiandi*, a document disapponting to some precisely for its lack of system in interrelating the proclamation of salvation to the work of justice.

Be that as it may, the position of the Holy See in the wake of the second Instruction was clear: liberation theology's task is the construction of a suitable theological ethics for Christian political activity. It is not to offer itself as a total expression of the Gospel, with the concomitant danger that evangelisation will turn itself, naturalistically, into work for human promotion, leaving over no significant remainder. Instead, liberation theology is to show how the doctrine of salvation requires from the redeemed an ethos of a distinct kind in their social acting. As the Instruction puts it in an epitome:

> The salvific dimension of liberation cannot be reduced to the socio-ethical dimension, which is a consequence of it. By restoring man's freedom, the radical liberation brought about by Christ assigns to him a task: Christian practice, which is the putting into practice of the great commandment of love.[21]

Rome's seal of approval of this pruned-back liberation theology was granted during a special synod of the Brazilian bishops, in Rome itself, in the spring of 1986, the communiqué of which followed hard on the promulgation of the second Instruction. At the same time, Boff's enforced sabbatical was brought to an end. Gutiérrez declared the new document epoch-making. The debate about the legitimation of liberation theology had ended with the latter's substantial vindication. Boff took the same optimistic view, though these judgments were, at least in the latter's case, more hopeful than descriptive. (He would, in fact, abandon the Catholic priesthood in 1993.)

Since 1986, liberation theology has remained on the defensive, and even perhaps entered into a period of relative decline, at any rate in its homelands. The reasons for this are fourfold.

First, and most obviously, the Holy See has not lessened its animosity towards those types of liberation theology of which it disapproves. This is expressed not only in matters of preferment, or in the treatment of schemes for Church policy, but also in the continuing criticism of such actual practitioners as Boff. His 1986 study *E a Igreja se fez povo* ('And the Church Became People')[22] with its claim that the Christian people of the poor must assert a 'hegemony' in the constitution of the ecclesial community led to the reopening of the doctrinal process against him. If the American Protestant observer of liberation theology, Harvey Cox, is right, Boff is presenting a doctrinally innovatory version of the 'four marks of the Church' as given in the Creed (one, holy, catholic, apostolic): apostolicity, now defined as a certain praxis or lifestyle; holiness, now defined as service of the poor; catholicity, now defined in terms of a de-centreing to allow Catholicism to exist in radically diverse ways in a variety of cultures; and unity, now defined in what Cox, paraphrasing Boff, calls 'venturesome love'. Cox, though far more sympathetic to Boff than to Ratzinger, at least gives the latter credit for appreciating the thoroughgoing nature of these proposals, and the need on the side of Rome to offer a coherent alternative picture of the Church of comparable attractiveness, so as to repristinate its doctrinal vision. In this respect, Cox awards Ratzinger higher marks than he does those liberals who simply want to see a happy co-existence on both sides, or, again, those bishops who find in the more radical kinds of liberation theology no more than the expression of an urgent pastoral concern.[23] However, owing to dislike of Roman intervention (often based on a doctrine of the local church not too high, for there can be none such, but faultily constructed), Roman disapproval is currently to some extent counter-productive, which does not mean to say that the wisdom of her overall policy may not be recognised in time.

Second, and more important, is the fact that the opponents of liberation theology in Latin America have passed from the condition of critics who take pot-shots from the sidelines to that of constructive organisers, out to create an alternative theology which will take over the ground liberation theology has, in the past, made its own. This became apparent in February 1988, at a congress of the opponents of liberation theology in Caracas, Venezuela, with participants from ten Latin American countries, as well as from the United States and Europe, including not only a variety of theologians but also two cardinals, five archbishops, nine bishops and two rectors of Catholic universities. Paid for by the theologically conservative charitable organisation Aid to the Church in Need, this congress was addressed by the new president of CELAM, Dario Castrillon Hoyes of Pereira (Colombia). Although at the Extraordinary Synod of Bishops to consider the Church since Vatican II (October 1985), Castrillon Hoyes had remarked that a Church with a machine gun is hard to mistake for the Church of the crucified Christ, his paper was the mildest given. The assembly called for the replacement of liberation theology by what it termed a 'theology of reconciliation'. Moving from an initial 'theology of marginality' (a recognition of the social problem in its Latin American form), this would move, through a 'theology of development' (thus rescued from the obscurity into which the later 1960s had cast it), to a call for the reconciliation of all classes via mutual accommodation within the framework of a reformist social democracy. Although the name, and some of the content, of this would-be successor to liberation theology derives from the papal constitution *Reconciliatio et paenitentia*, promulgated after the Roman Synod of 1983 on the sacrament of confession, Ratzinger cancelled his initial acceptance of an invitation to attend. This may be because, at the congress by contrast with the Roman documents, liberation theology was hung, drawn and quartered without mercy. The Gutiérrez and Boff of the new movement are the Peruvian Luis Fernando Figari and the Ecuadorian Julio Tearn Dutari.

The third cause of the decline of liberation theology is the general disorder into which socialism of a Marxian, or any systematic, kind has fallen since the collapse of the Marxist-Leninist system in the Soviet Union and eastern Europe. In terms both of diplomatic and military assistance and ideological succour and inspiration this collapse has dealt a serious blow to the fortunes of 'tropical Marxism', which has been officially abandoned in Ethiopia and Mozambique, as well as defeated at the polls in Nicaragua. Such a domino effect is not universal: China, secure in her centuries-long policy of isolation from the outside world, will doubtless continue as she is for many a long year. But commitment to the introduction of democratic accountability and acceptance of, at any rate, many free-market mechanisms, are now generally *de rigueur*. In Latin America, as in Africa, civilian régimes and multi-party representative democracies are increasingly the order of the day.[24] Cuba, still held up as, implicitly, the model of a socialist community in the Brazilian Dominican Frei Betto's best-selling book interview with Fidel Castro in 1982,[25] is generally regarded as a somewhat quaint relic of bygone days. Haiti, it is true, may be on the point of re-acquiring a liberationist priest-president, but that unhappy country's political culture is so primitive that it is difficult to regard this as anything other than a sport. Marx himself will remain an important figure in the history of sociological thought, though among some Parisian *universitaires* there is a tendency to take intellectual delight in standing Marxist theses on their head: for instance by treating cultural trends as the true causes of social and political patterns.[26] Academic

Marxism is reported to be alive and well only in the more privileged universities of the United States where it may hang on as the preferred philosophico-political position – just as, throughout the seventeenth and much, even, of the eighteenth century, Jacobitism did at Oxford University. The declining appeal of Marxism or of any systematic socialism is certainly relevant to liberation theology's fortunes, even though liberation theologians have varied greatly in the extent of their appeal to Marx. Meanwhile the question of land reform, round which most violent conflict in Latin America revolves, is still as grave as ever.

In the Latin American church itself, however, the agenda is changing. Twenty years ago, the Catholic Church was still secure in its religious hold on the masses of the population who were, therefore, available to be mobilised by liberation theology should the latter succeed in its aims. Today – and this is the fourth and final cause of the relative decline of liberationism – we are facing a quite different situation: the dramatic advance of Protestant sectarianism, which bids fair to reduce the number of the Catholic faithful (or not so faithful) by as much as a third, in some countries, by the early years of the next century. The reasons for this massive departure from the Church are controverted. The *Catholic Herald*, as part of the liberal Catholic press's relentless campaign for the abolition of the law of priestly celibacy, ascribed this phenomenon, perhaps inevitably, to the lack of a married priesthood.[27] A more plausible explanation would take the form of an inference from what it is that Protestant sects offer: namely, certainty about salvation. Thanks to the Council of Trent, Catholicism can hold out no subjective certainty of salvation for any named individual (short of some private relevation). But the Church can offer the reality of the God of salvation, present through Christ and the Holy Spirit, in her mysteries, just as she can offer an objectively certain teaching about salvation, and how men and women enter upon it for their true and definitive 'liberation'.

XVIII
The Story of *Praxis*: Liberation Theology's Philosophical Handmaid

To reach an understanding of the philosophical underpinning of liberation theology, the primary task is to come to terms with the idea which crops up so frequently in the writings of its exponents: *praxis*. To grasp, in turn, the concept of *praxis* as found in Marxian-influenced thought, some acquaintance with the history of this word, and idea, is necessary.

Praxis *from Aristotle to Hegel*

The foundation, as with so much of our philosophical heritage, lies in ancient Greece. Whilst Aristotle can use the term *praxis* to cover all kinds of activity, such as making things or contemplating the eternal realities, his more characteristic tendency is to keep the word for more specific purposes: to denote men's free activity in political life. Life in the *polis* combines ethics and politics (as later understood). It requires some kind of understanding, but only that modicum of knowledge which is needful for *eupraxia*, doing things well. Aristotle concurred with Plato's position in the *Statesman*: owing to the irregularities, *anomoiotêtes*, of men and actions, there cannot be universally valid rules in politics. In political science we must be content with presenting what applies, in approximate fashion, to most cases, and to reach conclusions proportionate to such premises.[1]

Political understanding, for Aristotle, is counterposed to philosophical, since only the latter, in contemplating things divine, attains familiarity with what cannot be other than it is – and so enjoys the status of knowledge strictly so called. In the course of time this distinction between philosophy and politics was gradually converted into a contrast between theoretical thought and human activity, notably productive activity. It should also be noted that, while Aristotle had a very positive view of the shared life of the *polis*, such that, for him, the pre-political is hardly more than the pre-human, his philosopher is nevertheless to strive for something which radically transcends the political order as a whole, for there is in man an element which is divine: *nous* or intelligence.[2] The conviction that there are legitimate philosophical concerns which go beyond the realm of social creativity would be integral to Christian thinking in the West in the *philosophia perennis*.

The fate of these ideas in the subsequent history of ancient philosophy turns on what individuals thought about epistemology, but also on the development, or regression, of institutional life. For the Stoics, *theôria* seems to have been a wisdom concerned with practical behaviour: but then they showed little confidence in the capacity of mind to explore the intelligible order of the world as such.[3] For Plotinus, politics is an occupation for the herd: its value lies simply in the opportunities it offers to grow in those virtues which contemplation requires. Such contemplation is, for him, not *theorising*, producing theorems, theories, in propositional form and demonstrating them to be true, but a living and immediate contact and union with the Source of all things, and, in an especial way, of mind itself.[4]

The first Christian theologians, the Church Fathers, were obliged to take up some position *vis-à-vis* these notions, not simply because they were current in the philosophy of late antiquity, but because analogues to them, often expressed in non-technical form, as maxims, narratives, parables, were found in the Bible itself. St Luke's story about Jesus as a guest in the home of busy Martha and adoring Mary is a case in point.[5] Translation of Greek patristic writings into English and other modern vernaculars has obscured the fact that the Fathers' discussions of the respective roles of 'contemplation' and 'action' in the Christian life are, so far as language goes, discussions of the relation of *thêôria* and *praxis*. Thus Origen, taking up the remark of the Book of Proverbs that 'the starting-point of the good path is doing what is just', explains that *to praktikon*, the dimensions of doing, will probably occupy most of a Christian's biography, yet *to thêôretikon*, contemplation, is the 'end' of the path whose beginning is just action. Such contemplation is for Origen the completion of all doing, in the *apokatastasis* or ultimate reconciliation of all things in the transfigured world of the Age to Come.[6] In Augustine, the debate is about the relation of contemplation and *charity*. The exiled Czech historian of philosophy Nicholas Lobkowicz, to whom my account is indebted, wrote that Augustine's ideas on this subject

> surround the notion of 'practice' with peculiar existential ambiguities unknown to the pagans. Even in this world, contemplation is man's greatest achievement, and yet charity may demand that one temporally give it up. Actions are bitter necessity, and yet the Christian should pursue them without bitterness whenever charity demands it.[7]

In his earlier, lay, period, Augustine seems to have held that charity includes not only meeting our neighbour's needs but also contributing to the values and works of culture. But, under the stress of his duties as a bishop, as the pastor of, predominantly, North African fisherfolk, he later restricted the *vita activa* to, on the one hand, helping our neighbour in his most fundamental necessities of life, and, on the other, carrying out the works of religion, meaning, primarily, the liturgy.[8] His influence can be detected in the discussion of these issues by St Thomas, for whom a whole range of activities from administering the sacraments to governing a city fall under the common rubric of *necessitas praesentis vitae*, to be distinguished from the prayer, wisdom and contemplation which anticipate the life of heaven.[9]

The first theologian to ask, *Quid sit praxis?* was the Franciscan scholastic John Duns Scotus. Although his successors, like the Thomist Capreolus and the Nominalist William of Ockham, answered his question in a way which allowed them to defend intellectual activity as a kind of *praxis*, Scotus himself, because of the privileged place given to the will in his theological doctrine of man, defined *praxis* in a resolutely non-intellectual way which is uncannily prophetic of Kant, or even of Marx. It is, for him

> the act of a faculty other than the intellect which, by its very nature, succeeds intellection, and may be elicited in accordance with right intellection so as to become right.[10]

In other words, *praxis* is deliberate post-theoretical human action of a kind that can be morally right or wrong, yet does not belong to ethics *tout court*.

Other mediaeval developments relevant to our topic are, first, the conviction of the Islamic Aristotelian thinker Ibn Sina (Avicenna) that sound ethical and political decisions may not be, as Aristotle himself considered, the work of prudence, but rather the practical applications of sheer theoretical insights,[11] and, second, the massive extension of technological control over nature which mediaeval inventiveness produced.[12] Thus Avicenna's rejection of Aristotle's belief that ethics and politics are founded on the ethical and political experience of virtuous men, in favour of the view that they are essentially the realisation of axioms, was confirmed by the emerging image of man as artisan, *homo faber*,

a figure with a well-designed master-plan which he subsequently proceeds to carry out.[13]

If, as E. Zilsel has argued, the origins of the idea of scientific progress are to be found in the mentality of European
artisans at the close of the mediaeval epoch,[14] then the
spokesman for that idea was Francis Bacon whose *Novum
Organon* declares the purpose of all theoretical knowledge to
be power: that is, the mastery of nature.[15] Whilst Bacon's
anti-theoretical attitude was fuelled by the radical scepticism
of late mediaeval Nominalists towards our capacity to grasp
the truth of things, the natural scientists of the early modern
period attempted to reinstate the notion of 'absolute truth' in
the study of nature – but in mathematical, not metaphysical
form. For Descartes, the mathematical method is the paradigm of what human reason is like. One single self-identical
method should be applied in every aspect of knowledge: but
in morals and politics, where the decisions facing us cannot
await the acquisition of a mathematical kind of certainty, we
must opt by a determination of sheer will, appealing to a
provisional ethic which alone can serve our turn until a
greater state of educated enlightenment supervenes.[16] Similarly, Locke held moral and political ideas to be, in principle,
as incontestable as those of mathematics, while for Leibniz
they were as theoretically scientific; Spinoza worked out a
'geometrical ethics', and, on the very eve of Kant's
'Copernican revolution' in philosophy, Christian Wolff used
a 'mathematical method' in his *De philosophia practica
universali.*[17]

Kant's ethics are, paradoxically, even more divorced from
experience than are his mathematics. While, for Kant, intuition (in a somewhat technical sense) is relevant to the
latter, the ethicist has rigorously to disregard both the nature
of man and circumstances in the world around him, so as to
concentrate on *a priori* concepts of pure reason. Kant, in a
step of enormous consequence for the future, identified the
'practical' with the 'free' in the sense of the 'self-

determining'.[18] In so doing, he gave to the term 'practical' a wholly new connotation. Although Thomas, for example, could define free will in terms (merely) of the moving of self to a definite action by way of rational deliberation, Kant makes the characteristically modern claim that it belongs to man's essence that he is free to define his position in the world for himself. All laws save those of physics, are, in the last analysis, imposed upon man by himself. In this sense, Kant's philosophy represents the final unveiling of the main hidden presupposition of humanism since the Renaissance. Peculiar to Kant, however, is the notion that since freedom is not among the objects that show themselves to intuition in the world of appearance (it is 'noumenal'), theoretical philosophy must have as its sibling practical philosophy. For Kant, the need for practical philosophy is due entirely to the subjective constitution of our mind. If a genuine theoretical knowledge of intelligible realities became possible, practical philosophy would evaporate – which it does in Kant's successor, Hegel, whose 'practical' philosophy, *The Philosophy of Right*, is itself theoretical from start to finish.

Praxis *from Hegel to Marx*

The key to an understanding of Hegel's project is that he wishes at one and the same time to preserve the autonomy of reason, as discovered by Kant, without abandoning the claim to objectivity typical of pre-Kantian philosophy. Hegel's solution to the dilemma – autonomy or objectivity – is to declare thought infinite. Autonomous thought must be boundless thought, and if boundless, then the subversive opposition between (knowable) *phenomena* and (unknowable) *noumena* resolves itself into a harmless contrast between what is already known and what still awaits the knower. The objects of sense are appearances whose imminent truth it is to lead us on beyond them, to what lies behind them: to the point where, for Hegel, even God himself ceases to be the 'unknown God'. He invites his readers to share with him an effort of intellectual understanding that culminates in a vision of all reality as the self-manifestation of the Absolute. As Hegel understands it, this vision transforms the whole of man's being; at the same time, insofar as it is expressed conceptually in his own philosophy, it reproduces something that has actually happened in the historical process, the ultimate goal which history has reached.[19] For Hegel, the aim of all willing, all action, is the satisfaction of thought. Our actions in and on the world would leave our thirst for rationality unsatisfied were we unable to contemplate the rationality achieved. Moreover, the importance of will and action dwindles as history progresses: as desire, will disappear when its thirst, of which action is the product, is slaked. And this it is in the contemplative acceptance of the rationality of reality. At a certain point, human history has unfolded all its main potentialities, and after that point the task of the wise man is not to teach the world what it *should be* but to help it contemplate the rationality that it *is*.

Hegel's belief that this unsurpassable goal had been reached in his own time, the Prussia of the early nineteenth century, is scarcely intelligible, psychologically speaking, without adding further premises not mentioned in his philosophy itself. The young Hegel had been brought up, in fact, in an atmosphere of religious and social expectation, eschatological in its intensity. Religiously, the Lutheran theologians dominant in the Swabia of his birth, and notably Friedrich Christian Oetinger, taught a version of Christianity in which history was the process whereby the Absolute realised its own potential, with the 'Spirit' at once God himself and a force emanating from him, and penetrating history.[20] Socially and politically, the experience of the Great Revolution of the West, beginning in 1788–89, led to a dizzy sense of liberation, combined with a more sober feeling of bewilderment at the disapperance of familiar landmarks. People rationalised the experience of the revolutionary upheaval by putting forward, in somewhat crude form, a dialectical theory of history: from naive harmony, through disturbance, confusion and tension to a final stage where all contradictions are resolved in a new and better harmony which incorporates all previous values.[21] It was, in this respect, a convenient coincidence that for the New Testament, the advent of the Kingdom is heralded by a crescendo in the machinations of the powers of darkness. To Hegel's eyes, the French Revolution was the incarnation both of freedom and of terror: because the absolute freedom whose reign it declared was not rooted in objectivity, it was self-destructive. Again, he speaks of it as at once the expression of terror and of virtue: for subjective virtue, working on mere sentiment, brings in its train 'the most dreadful of tyrannies'. Convinced, however, that the Prussian reformism of the years of the war of resistance against Napoleon constituted a transition to a genuinely new stage in the working out of Spirit or Reason, Hegel concluded his *Philosophy of Right* with the statement of belief that:

> Presence has discarded its barbarity and unrighteous caprice, while Truth has abandoned its beyond and its arbitrary force so that the true reconciliation which disclosed the State as the image of actuality and reason has become objective. In the State, self-consciousness finds in an organic development the actuality of its substantive knowing and willing; in religion, it finds the feeling and the representation of this its own truth as an ideal essentiality; while in philosophy, it finds the free comprehension of this truth as one and the same in its mutually complementary manifestations; i.e. in the State, in nature and in the ideal world.[22]

Here we find Hegel attempting to marry Christian theology to secular self-confidence. The Protestant State in its constitutional, law-regulated form, as experienced by Hegel, is nothing other than the reign of the Holy Spirit promised by Jesus Christ, the Son, the Father's Chosen, and become self-aware, and in that sense complete, in Hegel's own philosophy which is thus the finished presence of the glorified Christ, the Spirit, among men.

Marx's thought takes its rise from the debate among Hegel's pupils which followed his death from cholera in 1831. Whilst disagreeing about what, practically speaking, was to be done with the rest of world history, those pupils agreed that, conceptually, in the master's thought, the incarnation of the Logos was now complete.

> This outlook accounts for the almost insane presumption which many of Hegel's pupils displayed whenever they explored what 'ought to be done'. Since they were absolute knowers, their critical, 'transformatory' or revolutionary deeds could no longer be considered a mere groping in the complex universe of things, values and ideals. They were salvific acts paving the way for a New Jerusalem already present at the level of thought. 'Practice' from now would always have a salvific connotation.[23]

While the 'Right Hegelians' held that the existing order was basically sound, simply needing a little developmental tinkering here and there, the 'Left Hegelians' found that, in the light of Absolute Knowledge, it was so wanting as to warrant nothing less than outright abolition. For a Hegelian like the Germanophile Pole August Cieszkowski, the only philosophical endeavour which remained after Hegel was to lay out the future plan of history.[24] And here, according to Cieszkowski, post-theoretical practice is king. Absolute Spirit find its ultimate realisation in *praxis*, in which being and thought, art and philosophy will perish to be reborn as social existence. Pre-Hegelian practice is simply factual, what people happen to do; post-Hegelian practice, by contrast, is incarnated Absolute Knowledge, ultimate wisdom becomes real life. The *praxis* of the future is the action of the Absolute Knower. To realise this programme, Hegelianism had to be made the ideology of the masses. Cieszkowski thus announced the Kingdom, but what materialised was Marx.

Marx was deeply influenced by three Left Hegelians, Bruno Bauer, Arnold Ruge and Moses Hess, whose common interest was: how to translate absolute theory into practice. Bauer contributed the idea of critique: criticism unmasking the irrationality of what must disappear before the world enters on the age of salvation.[25] Ruge stressed the need for reason to return to itself at the level of brute existence, the 'nasty ought of *praxis*'.[26] Hess, mixing a *pot-pourri* of Jewish Messianism and French Socialism, argued that, to reach freedom, humanity must project itself into the future through self-conscious action. Action, as the synthesis of self-consciousness with the future, constitutes the ultimate realisation of freedom. The future it brings about will consist, according to Hess, in a process of social equalisation, ushered in after the conflict of wealth and poverty has reached its zenith, and issuing in the recreation of the equality of paradise. In this utopia, a religion of universal love will reign; the Church will wither away from inanition, and the State whittle down to a mere administrative function.[27]

Marx, who shared Bauer's conviction that nothing of moment was to be expected from the German middle class despite its high culture, sought, and found, in the proletariat, an agent capable of the act of *praxis* required to propel humanity towards its final salvation. For Marx, the Hegelian State, whose task is to reconcile the individual with society, to enable particular social atoms to transcend themselves into something universal, is an illusion – comparable to the religious illusion of a transcendent God denounced by Ludwig Feuerbach. The existing civil society must be transcended, not by the erection of a political superstructure but historically, by the coming into being of a new social order. Accepting Feuerbach's naturalism, which found the 'really real' in matter (not spirit), in the senses (not reason), in living (not philosophising), Marx was led to emphasise the importance, in the constitution of society, of economic factors. Some months after completing the *Critique of the Philosophy of Right*, he turned, accordingly, to the serious study of economics. The critique had to be given historical efficacy. To do this, it must become a material force – for material forces stood over against it in the shape of the State, the churches, and a 'philistine' bourgeoisie which, however delusory their self-description, were, unlike God, real enough at the social level. This the critique could do if it were able to become the dominant consciousness, and so the guide, of a social group which was already a material force to be reckoned with even before it embraced the fledgling Marxian theory. Marx proposed, therefore, that *praxis* is, in Lobkowicz's words,

> the deed of an extra-philosophical humanity, or a part of it, which meets the theory half-way (later Marx even will feel that this humanity fulfils its task without at all needing theory). In short, whereas all other Left Hegelians considered *praxis* as an effluence of Absolute Knowledge, Marx discovered that it also might be an almost 'ontological' development on the part of history. If present society contained a group powerful enough to transform the world, and if this group was to accept the critique as its programme of action, then it was possible to argue that history had destined this group for being the world's ultimate saviour. In that case, however, real history rather than Knowledge was the true principle of salvation.[28]

What Marx sought was a group who could, through the operation of historical laws of a fundamentally economic kind, become agents of saving *praxis* without even, necessarily, being aware of the fact. Social salvation was certain if it happened through those who acted by virtual necessity.

Since the sixteenth century, the term 'proletariat', especially in its French guise, had referred to the lowest social class: beggars, vagrants, in a word, the poor. But in the early nineteenth century, it found itself transferred, thanks especially to the Saint-Simonian economists in France, to the industrial wage-earning class, seen as the modern version of the antique slave, or the mediaeval (or contemporary Russian) serf.[29] But, as a German commentator on French affairs, L. von Stein, himself a contemporary of Marx, pointed out, the distinctive feature of the modern proletariat lay in its awareness of the significance of revolution – as its rôle in the First French Republic had shown.[30] For Marx, the proletariat embodied the negation of the existing social order; it attracted his attention not so much because its members suffered but because they could constitute the 'material weapon' of his critique.

The concept of *praxis* continues to be of the greatest importance for classical Marxists. As one contemporary Marxist theoretician, Adolfo Sánchez Vásquez, has written,

> Marxism is above all a philosophy of *praxis* and not a new philosophical praxis ... The very fate of Marxism as theory (as a new theoretical arm of the revolution) depends upon the role accorded to praxis within it.[31]

This same author provides a succinct provisional definition of *praxis*: it is the 'material activity of social man'.[32] He goes on to explain that writers of his school produce their philosophical work – that is, the theory of revolutionary *praxis* – in order to meet two ends. Their first goal is the overcoming of the 'instinctive and spontaneous point of view of ordinary proletarian consciousness'.[33] The second is the countering of that unenlightened consciousness by a correct understanding of *praxis*, something desirable both for theoretical reasons (the proper understanding of Marx's achievement), and for practical ones (the advancement of the revolutionary process). Sánchez Vásquez himself stresses that a true philosophical consciousness of *praxis* cannot be arrived at until certain necessary theoretical premises have matured in the history of ideas (we have traced schematically such a progress in the foregoing) and until, furthermore, the history of actual *praxis*, of socially transformative activity, has itself reached a point where such a new level of consciousness becomes imperative. Imperative for what reason? Imperative because from this point on men can no longer act upon and change the world 'creatively', that is, in a revolutionary way, without first gaining a true philosophical consciousness of *praxis*. Marx has made his essential breakthrough by creating an original synthesis of English political economy, classical German philosophy and French socialist thought, a synthesis which was not merely a summation, but a revelation of new dimensions and implications. The result, as Sánchez Vásquez makes clear, must involve the total re-casting of all future philosophy:

> The fundamental problems of philosophy have to be posed in their relation to practical human activity, which is central not only from the anthropological standpoint, because man is what he is in and through *praxis*, but also from the standpoint of history (since history is the history of human *praxis*), cognition (since *praxis* is the basis and the end of knowledge, as well as its sole criterion of truth) and ontology (since the problem of the relation between man and nature, or between thought and being, cannot be resolved without reference to practice).[34]

In this perspective, Lenin emerges as the saviour of the Marxist tradition. For by emphasising, over against the ethical revisionism of the Second International, the decisive role of practical revolutionary activity (albeit only when integrated in the movement of objective factors, namely, social and economic forces) he restored the centrality of a theory of *praxis*, with its twin pillars: the primacy of the practical, and the unity of theory-and-practice. Marxism-Leninism is a 'scientific theory of the revolutionary praxis of the proletariat'.[35]

In such a philosophy of *praxis*, while productive *praxis*, in its two main forms of labour and artistic creation, retains an importance of its own, it is political – that is, revolutionary – *praxis* which holds the key to the humanisation of man. Such revolutionary *praxis* is, in one sense, the end of all theory, since it conceives of philosophy in function of *praxis* itself, 'at the service of, and integral to, the actual effective transformation of the world'.[36]

To carry out that transformation, however, philosophy is not simply to deny its own theoretical character, but to transcend itself, seeking suitable 'mediations' between theory and *praxis*, the better to give direction to practical activity: that is, to clarify the content of *praxis*, not to justify that *praxis*. For in Marxism, it is social practice which reveals the truth or falseness of all theory. Even though practice is effective only to the extent that it is informed by theory, yet theory itself is limited by its status as an ideal anticipation of an activity that cannot yet be seen in action. Nonetheless, the primacy of practice does not remove a certain limited autonomy from theory. Though *praxis*, as practical social activity transforming reality in obedience to practical needs, implies some degree of knowledge of the reality it transforms and the needs it satisfies (*praxis* is not wholly blind, in some measure it already sees), it cannot, for all that, explain itself. It is not directly theoretical; nor can it generate theory in some automatic way. As Marx, in his *Eighth Thesis on Feuerbach* (1845), points out, beyond practice lies a further stage: the comprehension of practice, without which its rationality remains hidden. It is that comprehension which calls for the development of an adequate theoretical framework.

Praxis *in Liberation Theology Today*

With these concepts in our possession, we are now in a position to discuss their appearance, and modification, in the work of the liberation theologians. Most importantly, the relation of theory to practice as described above throws light on the insistence of such theologians that theology must be, in terms of the concrete social situation of the theologian concerned, 'engaged', 'committed', 'partisan' and even 'classist' as the Brazilian Servite friar Clodovis Boff – brother of the Leonardo of the last chapter – notes.[37] For the 'engagement' in question, though made not to the sociologically quantifiable 'proletariat' of Marx's use, but rather to a more diffuse, messianic 'poor', reproduces in formal terms the stance of its secular rival.

Boff sees that political engagement functions here as an antecedent epistemological condition for the development of an appropriate theology in a given setting. He records, fairly enough, two difficulties attached to this approach. First, the refusal to justify the 'engagement' of a theologian in a movement for liberation – on the ground that the 'truth' of the condition of the disadvantaged masses of the Third World stands in no need of theoretical 'proof' – renders that engagement intellectually vulnerable. It has no basis in any prior analytic evaluation of what is at stake in such struggle. Second, the logic of politics and the logic of theology, so far from being identical, are in themselves strictly incommensurable. And yet theology, as any discipline, can develop only on certain conditions, and where what is being attempted is a theology of the political as such, then the likelihood is that these conditions will include political ones. Thus Boff, the most sophisticated methodologist among the liberation theologians, speaks of a suitably argued for political engagement as 'permitting' the emergence both of pertinent theological themes, and of a rhetorical style suited to the needs of a particular social conjunction.

> Political engagement in a given cause within a defined group or class, although failing to guarantee the intrinsic quality of a theological theory, nevertheless constitutes a necessary condition for the selection by this theological theory of a determinate and adequate theoretical object, or thematic, as well as that of a style proportioned to its task of communication.[38]

Boff is trying, evidently, to reach an understanding of the

relationship between theory and *praxis* which will at one and the same time resemble that of Marxism, in requiring the theologian to situate himself epistemologically within a given *praxis*, and yet depart from Marxism by limiting the significance of such practical engagement *vis-à-vis* other epistemological factors in the making of good theology. For unless these other factors are also recognised, liberation theology removes itself from the commonwealth of the great theologies of the past which certainly did not conceive of a theory-*praxis* relationship of any such kind.

In his survey of the difficulties facing liberation theology, Boff speaks with some acidity of its

> strident, demanding manifestoes on behalf of *praxis*. It exalts the 'epistemological destiny' of *praxis* to the point of threatening the autonomy of theoretical practice – to the detriment of *praxis* itself.[39]

The 'unelaborated formulation' of the thesis that '*praxis* is the criterion of truth' is, he protests, 'ambiguous' and even 'erroneous'. From what we have seen of the total claims of Hegelian speculation, and their mirror effect in Marx's hopes of revolutionary *praxis* as the agent of total (secular) salvation, such excesses, on the part of theologians who see themselves as standing, philosophically, within the Marxist tradition, are hardly surprising.[40] Even where the initial act of engagement in *praxis* is seen as a commitment to the poor as *God*'s poor, made on the basis of the Gospel, and so in Christian faith, the unique place occupied by the concept of *praxis* in Marxism – unique in importance, unique in comprehensiveness – cannot but threaten the primacy of theology's own source – divine revelation in its two forms, Scripture and Tradition, interpreted under the watchful care of the 'magisterium' or teaching authority of the church.[41] Liberation theology, to maintain its own orthodoxy – which means, in the last analysis, its evangelical authenticity – must, as Boff himself writes, accept the criteria of revealed faith and that distinctively Christian 'practice' which is charity, and not rest content with the theoretical or political 'mediations' of its own social hope. Yet at the same time, as he also rightly notes, both believers and unbelievers do ask of the church today that she will put forth practical *corporate* 'signs' of the credibility of her own doctrine. Her doctrine is quizzed about its capacity to shape forms of human 'conviviality' – life together – that can give fresh hope to society's victims and history's losers.[42]

But this is not to say, *pace* Marx, that all the contradictions of the human condition can be resolved here below, nor, *pace* Hegel, that the rational understanding of how we are as we are (the 'rose of reason in the cross of the present') can ever be complete. If it is the task of philosophy to arouse and sustain questions about all the dimensions of human living, one of the blessings which theology confers on her philosophical handmaid is a sense of the limitations of human thinking, and of human action. Theory may instruct the world, and *praxis* improve it, but only a 'beatific' vision, and the advent of a different kind of Agent, can redeem it.

XIX
Rex gentium: History, Nationalism, Christ

The Church's liturgy calls on Christ as *Rex gentium*, 'King of the nations', the One whom they all 'desire', the cornerstone who unites them. It appeals to him, therefore to 'come and save man whom you made from clay'.[1] In this celebrated antiphon, the Church affirms the relevance of Christ to world history and, more specifically, to the fate of the many peoples of the world whose histories contribute to the single history which is that of the world as a whole. The text intimates that this history constitutes an implicit call for his Coming, and it states quite explicitly that only Christ can unify their different and (presumably) divergent histories, and make them one.

Introduction

This text indicates an absolutely vast subject which – it is probably fair to say – historians and philosophers in England (even when believers) would by and large regard as taboo. In this they would doubtless be joined by the majority of theologians. The relevance of Christ to world history, and, in particular, to the fact of its multiple national differentiations, is, they would say, simply too large a subject to talk sense about. English historians, with occasional exceptions like Arnold Toynbee, do not think it a proper part of the historian's task to identify the structure of the historical process as a whole.[2] The philosophy of history is not, in England, the study of the wider meaning of that process but, rather, the justification of any limited statement about the past.[3] English philosophers of history avert their gaze in horror from their Continental counterparts, whose vaulting metaphysical ambition has produced schemes like: history as the coming of Reason to self-consciousness (Hegel); or as the formation of a socialist society where the specific essence of humanity will be realised in uncoerced labour (Marx). Nor is theology in any very different condition. Theologies of history available in English tend to be translations from French or German of works by 'Neo–Patristic' authors.[4] These figures – and here Jean Daniélou of the Society of Jesus,[5] and Hans Urs von Balthasar[6] were especially notable – saw themselves as following in the footsteps of the Church Fathers and early ecclesiastical writers who realised that the Bible tells a story from Genesis to Apocalypse, the Beginning to the End, and wished to fill in some of the blank pages.[7] But the bulk of their more fastidious modern successors have not wished to emulate such dogmatic *naïvëté*.

Although, in this perspective, liberation theology may be regarded as a theology of history, since it is concerned with the relationship of 'material praxis' (that is, the historical transformation of society) to the Kingdom of God, and hence to Christ, the vogue for literature from Latin America has not generated any large-scale reinterpretations of the story of English society, nor of the history of the West at large.[8] It may be surmised that this state of affairs will continue. For in the first place, the by now centuries old empiricism of British culture militates against the liberationist grand scheme, as against all others. And secondly, liberation theology draws its passion from, and finds its relevance in, a situation which is not ours, namely, the enormous strains created by the massive and high-speed industrialisation of traditional agrarian societies. Although the Neo–conservative reform of British society may produce analogous tensions among limited sections of the population, the very limits of the scale of these problems – comparatively speaking – will probably prevent the rise of an indigenous liberation theology of the ocean-going Latin American model.

The English, it seems, are not natural practitioners of the philosophy and theology of history: not, at any rate, since the seventeenth-century Civil War in which conflict such wider interpretations of British history as there are – the Whig, and the Tory – took their rise. The monument to this incapacity is the library of the Victorian historian Lord Acton at Aldenham.⁹ There his projected 'History of Freedom' lies scattered in a thousand fragments, a card index 'system' that no one, starting with himself, could put together.¹⁰ Would Acton, indeed, even have *begun* the 'History of Freedom' had he simply been a Shropshire squire, and not also half German, and born in Naples? The cultures which put forth Hegel, Marx and Gianbattista Vico could at least suggest to Acton his project, whereas left to himself, tramping his acres, he would probably have conceived history only as a set of limited, and thus manageable, frames – like the *vignettes* of A. E. Housman's poetry in *A Shropshire Lad*. But do the frames need a framework? Will they suffer one? Can such a framework assist exploration of the title, *Rex gentium*, relating history, the nations and Christ? These are our questions.

A philosophical history

Acton was Regius Professor of History at Cambridge. Another Cambridge professor, resembling Acton in his capacity to see the conventional limits of historiography through an oblique angle lens, is Ernest Gellner, whose *Plough, Sword and Book: the Structure of Human History*, was published in 1988.¹¹ Gellner's Jewish background, Central European birth and Parisian upbringing give him contact with a more speculative tradition of historical writing, enriched, in his case, by philosophical and social-anthropological expertise.

The combination of Gellner's gifts and interests makes for

an important book, for several reasons. First, *Plough, Sword and Book* suggests a suitable method for writing a philosophy of history, as distinct from a history of philosophy. Second, it enables us to take stock of the present state of play in world affairs – *toutes proportions gardées* in a work of scarcely more than two hundred pages. Third, it might provide a model for a Christian version of itelf, such is the sanity of its underlying doctrine of man, just as Augustine and Eusebius found models for their overall interpretations of historical development in the pagan writing, both chronicle and philosophy, of their time. I hasten to add, however, that, as it stands, Gellner's study provides little but cold comfort for Catholic Christians, since its author holds that Catholicism, in its fundamental patterns as a belief system, a hierarchical ordered religious governance, and a liturgical or sacramental community, is the characteristic religious form of an 'agro-literate' society whose heyday is now long past. It will, he thinks, prove unable, in all probabilty, to survive, except in pockets or in a thoroughly diluted version, the advent of distinctively modern society in its full-blooded form. Only Islam, as the most consistently 'Protestant' of the world religions – unitarian (without mysterious dogmas), egalitarian (without, at least in principle, a clergy) and scripturalist (communicated by texts, or by information about texts) has much chance of living on in strength to represent the pre-industrial faiths in the post-industrial world to which the explosion of production in contemporary technology is leading us. *Plough, Sword and Book* is thus to be read critically, not least with the criticism of faith, rather than fallen upon with a glad cry. But this is ever a necessary *caveat* when despoiling the Egyptians.

First, let us hear what Gellner has to say about the legitimacy of the general enterprise on which we are engaged. He writes:

We inevitably assume a pattern of human history. There is

simply no choice concerning *whether* we use such a pattern. We are, all of us, philosophical historians *malgré nous*, whether we wish it or not. The only choice we do have is whether we make our vision as explicit, coherent and compatible with available facts as we can, or whether we employ it more or less unconsciously and incoherently ... The great paradox of our age is that, although it is undergoing social and intellectual change of totally unprecedented speed and depth, its thought has become in the main unhistorical or anti-historical ... The joint result of our inescapable need for possessing some backcloth vision of history, and of the low esteem in which elaboration of global historical patterns is at present held, is a most paradoxical situation; the ideas of nineteenth-century philosophers of history such as Hegel, Marx, Comte or Spencer are treated with scant respect and yet are everywhere in use.[12]

One can only agree. Gellner goes on to describe the method which he personally proposes to use in setting about this 'inescapable' task. It cannot be a matter of simple description. The richness and diversity of historical reality are such that a non-selective description could not be begun, much less completed. Instead:

One chooses the crucial and elementary factors operative in human history, selected to the best of one's judgement, and then works out their joint implications. If the resulting picture fits the available record and highlights the relevant questions, well and good ... The method is in principle very simple; its implementation is not.[13]

In other words, the method involves three steps: *induction* of key factors in change from the imaginative scanning of particular historical narratives; *deduction* of possibly illuminating implications from the concurrent operation of these factors; and the *comparison* of the resulting schema with the empirical record. In other words, one returns to the starting-point with a fuller grasp of the original historical materials: in my (epistemological) end is my beginning.

What Gellner claims to have identified, using this method,

is simply the fundamental principles of all historical development. He does not think of these principles in a deterministic
way. History contains certain steps. Earlier ones are pre-
conditions of later, but they do not necessitate the emergence
of their successors. His key terms in describing these fundamental principles are: production, coercion, cognition, that
is, labour, power, knowledge – the 'plough, sword, book' of
Gellner's title.

What I have called the 'sanity' of Gellner's underlying doctrine of man turns both on his integrated balance of determination and creativity in the relation of historical laws to
human subjectivity, and on his selection of these key factors.
For him, as for the Christian doctrine of post-lapsarian man,
humankind is engaged in transforming the earth through
labour, involved in a mesh of power relations, and yet open,
through intelligence, to the understanding of the real.
Gellner's trio may also be expressed as: economy, governance, culture. But while 'these three are one', his interest is
focused on culture, which he defines as a constellation of
concepts or ideas which guide thought and conduct. Much
of his argument takes the form of consideration of the kinds
of concept that are possible or likely in various sorts of social
condition. Changes in the social economy and the political
order will probably, though not certainly, bring about and
transmit to the future certain transformations of culture.
From these transformations there result fresh understandings
of the world, and of human living. (Better, such transformations *are* such fresh understandings.) Apart from the
unwarranted omission of the realm of aesthetics – for understanding is also carried by symbol and by concept – this
account seems unexceptionable.

A theology of history

Gellner's work is an exercise in philosophical history: and
how would a theology of history draw on its findings? Any

philosophy undergoes baptism if it submits to the illumination of its own materials by faith in redemptive activity of the triune God. A philosophy of history becomes a theology of history if it accepts that the source of history is the Father, that the norm of history is his Son, Jesus Christ, and that the fulfilment of history is the work of the Spirit, whom the Father and the Son send forth.

In a *Theology of History* Balthasar wrote of the Spirit's work in world history:

> The work which he undertakes, the shaping and fashioning of what the Son bequeathed to him, is a work of supreme divine freedom. He is presented with two data: the life of Christ, and 'world history'; and it rests with him to dispose of the infinite wealth in the life of Christ that it can blossom out in the variousness of history, and that at the same time history, thus made subject to this norm, shall be able to discover the fullness within itself.[14]

As this account suggests, Balthasar stresses in the first place the transcendence of the Son and Spirit *vis-à-vis* history. They do not simply uphold the structure of history as it develops, via nature, from the Creator's hand. As divine persons, they are capable of relating history in a new manner to the God who is not only its Source but its Goal. As Balthasar puts it:

> The Spirit ... makes history into the history of salvation ... prophetically oriented towards the Son...

while the latter's

> action is what history is for; his uniqueness sets it free to attain its proper character.[15]

Yet at the same time, Balthasar is careful to underline that, in this, the redemptive action of the Holy Trinity does not just disregard, much less ride roughshod over, the natural pattern of history. The Spirit

> leaves history its own immanent laws and structures, but orders it and all its laws in subjection to the laws of Christ.[16]

The relation of history's natural structure, the 'structure' of Gellner's sub-title, to its supernatural structure, the structure disclosed by Christian faith, is like that of nature to grace at large. Grace builds on the historical expression of nature, elevating it in the process. It does not overthrow it. The Spirit operates in the order of created spirit not, Balthasar insists, as 'another', but rather, echoing some words of Nicholas of Cusa, 'as one exalted above all otherness'.[17]

The Spirit, that is to say, is so transcendent that he can be wholly immanent, his divine creativity so utterly indifferent to maintaining its difference from our human creativity that his sovereign work can go undetected by the secular historian. Yet what he achieves is a real transformation, for he uses the natural structure of history as a means by which to attain his own goal.

The key to an appreciation of that goal is, for the Christian, the life of Jesus, since the Son made man is history's 'norm'. To cite Balthasar once again:

> A situation in the life of Jesus must not be regarded as a closed, finite thing, delimited by other historical situations, previous, contemporaneous or subsequent. Since it is the manifestation in this world of the eternal life of God, it always has a dimension open to that which is above. Its meaning, the number of its possible applications, is, even at its own historical level, something limitless ... The richness of reference in each particular ... christological situation is so great that it can give birth to further situations of extreme diversity, sharply distinct from each other, yet not ... established in a relativistic autonomy, but finding their norm and governing principle in that particular Christ-situation which is their source and their context.[18]

If the distinctive form of Christ's temporality, his participation in history, lay in his unique receptivity to the will of the Father for the world, something which enabled history to reach its anticipated fulfilment in him as its personal norm, then the proper content of that norm lies in those exemplary responses to the human challenges of Christ' environment, in which the divine will was concretely expressed.

Jesus and foreigners

The 'Christ-situations' most pertinent to his role as 'King of the nations', are, perhaps, Jesus' dealings with those who were, to a Palestinian Jew such as himself, aliens or foreigners. The Gospels contain a number of such allusions, from the Syro-Phoenician woman in the Synoptic tradition[19] to the woman of Samaria in John;[20] from the Roman centurion whose servant is at death's door in the Synoptics,[21] to the Greeks, that is, Hellenistic diaspora Jews, who seek to speak with Jesus in the Fourth Gospel.[22] While it would be out of place here to attempt a detailed exegesis of these passages,[23] it is possible to offer one general comment about this entire set of situations. Jesus treats foreigners with a sense both of their *difference* from those whom the Johannine prologue calls 'his own', and of their *unity* with them. He does not treat them in a universalistic way, as though their differences from Palestinian Jewry, or, for that matter, between themselves, counted for nothing – as though they were simply human beings, with no significant further specifications worth adding. And yet Jesus also incorporates them, in ways suited to each representative individual or group, into the outreach of his own mission. It was, then, with sense of identity-in-difference; or solidarity-in-distinctiveness; or of *differentiated unity*, that Jesus approached the Gentiles who stand around the edges of his mission to Israel.

These representatives of the nations are a significant penumbra in the Gospels, even though the Light of the

World, as shining there, falls first and foremost on and for the Jews. They foreshadow the turning of the Church to the Gentiles after Pentecost, and help give that turning its justification. These foreigners, these non-nationals, frame the Gospel tradition: they appear at its beginning with the Magi, and at its end, with that other pagan centurion who, in the midst of the portents which follow the death of Jesus in Matthew, calls out, 'Truly, this was a son of God'.[24]

The principle of identity-in-difference

The identity-in-difference approach, which is such a hallmark of Jesus' attitude to people of divergent origins, has its most important continuation in the structure of the Church, the community of Jesus' disciples. In the words of the Letter to the Ephesians, the 'middle wall of partition' has been brought down.[25] The Gentiles, who until then were far off, being strangers to the covenant of the Promise, are now brought nigh, since Gentile and Jewish Christians form one body, although, as we see from the Acts of the Apostles, the unity of that body is itself of a differentiated kind. Whilst, unfortunately, such Jewish Christian churches as that to which the Letter to the Hebrews was addressed did not long survive the Roman Jewish wars of the later first century, the same fundamental pattern of unity-in-difference can be seen in the further development of the *Catholica*, the Great Church. For it is a characteristic of that Church to hold in the communion of a single doctrinal faith, governing order and sacramental life a multiplicity of distinct cultures, whether liturgical, spiritual, intellectual or linguistic. In this, the Church reflects its own nature as a network of local churches each of which, however, can only be fully 'the Church' by opening itself to the rest, in a process of reciprocity and exchange, of initiative and reception (and sometimes, when the needs of communion in the one faith, order and life suggest this, of *non-*

reception), over which the local church of Rome, with its Petrine office-holder, presides as guardian.[26]

But now the question arises: Does the form of the Church as such an identity-in-difference, have anything to contribute to the future pattern of human history – that changing constellation of cultures or conceptual interlinkings for the guidance of thought and conduct, themselves assisted in their rise to hegemony by changes in the social economy and political order in approximately the way that Gellner has charted? If the norm of history is the incarnate Son, whose attitude to others this principle of identity-in-difference describes, and if what the Spirit brings about, ultimately, in history is the sovereignty of this same norm, though respecting history's own principles of development as he does so, then we should expect that the Church's experience will offer a key to the resolution of relevant tensions, concerning identity and difference, in *secular* history. Nor is this simply a matter of the Church as a model; it is also a question of the Church as an agent. For since Christ, all history is, at the most fundamental level, sacred, because of the presence and testimony of the Church of the Word Incarnate in the single, all-inclusive history of the world. As Balthasar writes:

> The Church, transcending history but acting as its content and medium, is the ultimate gift of the Creator to human history, given to bring it to its own realisation from within.[27]

The particular problem in contemporary secular history to which this one-in-many aspect of the Church's being relates is that of the existence of nations. It is the problem of nationalism.

The problem of nationalism

In *Plough, Sword and Book*, Gellner offers, *inter alia*, a picture of where we are in world affairs at the present time.

Basically, he describes five kinds of societies in different parts of the world.

First, there are Western pluralistic societies. In such societies, the free market extends to ideas and religions. Pre-industrial faiths survive, but are entertained in a 'semi-cognitive' spirit, along a sliding scale of Cupitt-isation. Alternative 'world-stories', intended to re-endow a scientific cosmos, sanitised of value, with moral meaning sufficient for living, come off the ideational production line at a quick rate, but as rapidly become obsolescent. Over against the established culture stands a counter-culture, either 'quietist' (presumably mystical, or ecological, or both) or 'chaotically revolutionary', and patronised by the more prosperous social strata's 'young and less successful members'.

Second, there are a (by now) fast diminishing number of Marxist societies, built on a nineteenth-century system which holds together, after its own fashion, a theoretical description of the world with an ethico-political prescription for history.

Third, there are Islamic societies where, so far at least, a traditional religion, in its orthodox form, has shown a remarkable fit with the requirements of secular modernisation.

Fourth, there are in the Third World a variety of societies, for which that of India may stand as exemplar, where paternalistic modernisation from above is combined with toleration of the ancient folk-culture still in place below, thus giving rise to an uneasy pluralism not unlike that of the West itself.

Finally, in Latin America and sub-Saharan Africa, relatively weak civil societies are dominated by a correspondingly strong State apparatus. Here ideological life is 'opportunist', an attempt to exploit international competition between the Soviet and Western blocs, a phenomenon neatly summarised by Gellner in the axiom, 'Cuius military aid, eius religio'.[28]

Whilst this survey well brings out the mobile, fluid nature of contemporary world society, it is remarkable that Gellner barely mentions what is, perhaps, the single most potent force, for good or ill, in world society: namely *nationalism*, a topic to which he himself has earlier devoted an entire book.[29] From the former Soviet Union to the Middle East, from Latin America to Ireland, there is no one factor in world political history of greater moment today than the nationalist factor. I follow a scholarly interlocutor of Gellner's, Professor Elie Kedourie of London University, in regarding nationalism as a European doctrinal export first marketed in the early nineteenth century. Nationalist doctrine may be summed up in three tenets: humanity is naturally divided into nations; these nations have characterising features whereby they can be known; only national self-government is legitimate government. As Kedourie writes in his study of the topic:

> Not the least triumph of this doctrine is that such propositions have become accepted and are thought to be self-evident, that the very word 'nation' has been endowed by nationalism with a meeting and a resonance which until the end of the eighteenth century it was far from having.[30]

Kedourie traces the genesis of this doctrine to five factors. At the head of his list is the French Revolutionary conviction that the principle of sovereignty resides essentially in the nation, in such wise that no body of men, or individual man, can rightly exercise authority if that authority does not derive expressly from the nation. Second, Kedourie adduces the centrality which Kant gave to the rôle of self-determination, autonomy, in ethics: an individualist anticipation, he believes, of the later slogan, 'Better self-government than good government'. The third and fourth causes featuring in Kedourie's explanation of the rise of nationalist theory derive from another German philosopher of the Revolutionary and

Napoleonic upheavals: Fichte. Fichte had insisted that the State is the creator of human freedom, not merely in an external or material sense but also in an internal or spiritual one, since only by merging their wills in the will of the State do individuals find their true freedom. Fichte also fathered the idea that it is by struggle that humanity ascends the ladder of culture. Conflict between states indirectly promotes the self-realisation of mankind since it demonstrates the superiority of one over the other, thus giving it in practice the leadership it merits in theory. Lastly, there is the notion beloved of Herder and Schleiermacher which takes the nation to be a 'natural' division of the human race, endowed with its own peculiar character which it is the godly duty of its citizens to preserve pure and inviolate.

Once nationalist doctrine has thus emerged from a fateful interplay of ideas, its anthropology and metaphysics are set to work in the reinterpretation of history. Kedourie stresses the ways in which nationalism exploits the loyalties which a common religion has created over time. Moses becomes a national leader in a revolt against colonial oppression; Judaism, accordingly, ceases to be the *raison d'être* of the Jew and transmutes into a product of Jewish 'national consciousness'. Mohammed, similarly, becomes the founder of the Arab nation, while Islam itself is transformed into a political ideology. Nor is Christianity safe from the contagion. Hus takes on the features of a precursor of Masaryk; Luther of Bismarck.

While Gellner's *Nations and Nationalism* succeeds better than Kedourie's work in showing *why* such nationalist doctrine has appealed to so many groups in the nineteenth and twentieth centuries (for Gellner, a modern industrialised state can only function with a mobile, literate, culturally-standardised 'inter-changeable' population of the sort which nationalism engenders), Gellner does not really disagree with Kedourie's assertion that nationalism is necessarily disruptive of human amity. For they concur in the proposition that, on any reasonable calculation, the number of potential nations on the face of the earth is much larger than that of possible viable states. In other words: at any given time, the satisfaction of some nationalisms must necessarily mean the frustration of others. The significance of this within, say, the North Atlantic archipelago (Britain-Ireland) is obvious, while in terms of international diplomacy the plight of Israel-Palestine, the tragic *imbroglio* of Bosnia or the situation of the peoples of South Africa are other pertinent examples which spring at once to mind. What is less well known is the scale, worldwide, of the difficulties caused by the triumph of nationalist doctrine for parts of the earth's surface where two or more quite distinct communities cohabit. A recent survey of international human rights has concluded that the two hundred million people belonging to minorities and indigenous peoples are 'without question still the most deprived and ill-treated'.[31] Kedourie, indeed, concludes his own account of the actual effects of nationalism in these words:

> The attempts to refashion so much of the world on national lines has not led to greater peace and stability. On the contrary, it has created new conflicts, exacerbated tensions, and brought catastrophe to numberless people innocent of all politics. The history of Europe since 1919, in particular, has shown the dangerous possibilities inherent in nationalism. In the mixed area of Central and Eastern Europe, and the Balkans, empires disappeared, their ruling groups were humbled and made to pay, for a time, the penalty of previous arrogance. Whether these empires were doomed anyway, or whether it would have been possible to preserve them is mere speculation. What can be said with certainty is that the nation-states who inherited the positions of the empires were not an improvement. They did not minister to political freedom, they did not increase prosperity, and their existence was not conducive to peace; in fact, the national question which their setting up, it was hoped, would solve, became, on the contrary, more bitter and envenomed; it was a national question, that of the German minorities in the new nation-states, which occasioned the outbreak of the Second World War. What may be said of Europe can with equal justice

be said of the Middle East, or of South-East Asia, wherever the pressure of circumstances or the improvidence of rulers or their failure of nerve made possible the triumph of nationalist programmes.[32]

What matters for Kedourie is not *national* government, but whether rulers are just and merciful. That is 'the only criterion capable of public defence'.[33] In the light of our theological reading of history, seen in the radiance of its norm, Jesus Christ, we can, however, take one further step. The criteria for the public defence of governments are not restricted to justice and mercy. They include also the promotion of identity-in-difference: the recognition of the solidary unity of human groups even in and through their differentiated distinctiveness. But, given that the triumph of such identity-in-difference is one important specification of the 'christifying' of all history, does the natural structure of history's secular unfolding, drawn upon in the economies of the Son and the Spirit, permit us to hope for advance in this regard in our time?

The social economy which is so vital a precondition, via the political order, for the moulding of culture cannot be fully described today without invoking factors which make for greater international cooperation. The revolution in communications and transport, and the emergence of such global problems as the interrelated issues of environment, population explosion and diminishing resources make not only possible but imperative an overcoming of the nationalist ethos. The 'book' which 'plough' and 'sword' need today is the ethical and spiritual patrimony of the human race in so far as these subserve the principle of solidarity-in-difference, the foundation of any lasting international order.

Our common European home

It is the recognition of this principle which governs, to come closer to home, the attitude of the Holy See at the present time to the development of the European Community. Thus, in his address to the European Parliament on 11 October 1988, Pope John Paul II declared:

> A common political structure, springing from the free will of all European citizens, far from endangering the individual identities of the peoples of the Community, will be a fairer guarantee of all rights, cultural ones in particular, of all the regions. These united European peoples will never accept the dominion of one nation or culture over the others, but they will uphold the right, equal for all, to enrich each other through their differences.[34]

And the pope went on to say that this Europe must include its own Eastern half, without whose presence Europe cannot have the 'dimensions which history has given it'. He also suggested that the experience of such reconciliation (between divided European nations and blocs) would be an education in, for example, generosity to foreigners, and to refugees (of whom there are at present some twelve to fifteen million worldwide), as well as in openness to the spiritual wealth of peoples in other continents.

The pope used the same occasion to make an impassioned appeal in favour of the continued public relevance of Christian revelation. Insisting that the sins of historic Christendom were abuses, not uses, of its own beliefs, he remarked:

> It is my duty to stress emphatically that if the underlying religious and Christian fabric of this continent were to be denied as an inspiration to morality or as a positive factor in society, not only would the entire heritage of our European past be negated, but the future dignity of European humanity – and here I am talking about all people, followers of Christ or not – would be gravely endangered.[35]

In other words, the principle of identity-in-difference (as one salient principle in the reconstruction of Europe), though it emerges from supernatural revelation, is necessary for the future of the *natural* structure of history in its European, as no doubt in other, forms.

If the movement towards European integration is, in such a way, one of those 'signs of the times' of which the Second Vatican Council spoke – symptomatic manifestations of the work of the Spirit in world history – then a considerable revision of historical understanding must be set in motion.[36] A re-evaluation must be undertaken of those pre-nationalist polities which, for all their limitations, embodied the principle of identity-in-difference in some recognisable form. Kedourie is principally an historian of the Ottoman Empire, but a more obvious candidate in a European Catholic perspective is that of the Danubian monarchy, brought to an end by a coalition of factors, among which Woodrow Wilson's doctrinaire nationalism was one, in 1919.[37] Balthasar wrote:

> It may well be that the *kairoi* [opportune moments] produced in Church history by the Holy Spirit – such as the appearance of a great saint or some other important spiritual mission – do contain within them the answer (in advance) to some pressing problem in secular history.[38]

Is it a coincidence that just this particular *kairos* in the history of Europe, constituted jointly as it is by the formation of the European Community in the West and the ending of the Soviet system as we have known it in the East and the consequent prospect of what Mikhail Gorbachev has called 'our common European home', is also the moment when the authorities of the Church are preparing to raise to her altars the servant of God Charles of Hapsburg under the title 'patron of peace'? The *Rex gentium* needs his mediations, whether in ecclesial history, in the *universalis papa* who, precisely in his fostering of fundamental self-identity within the protection of legitimate diversity, deserves the controverted title of *vicarius Christi* bestowed on him by St Bernard, or in general history, in the form of statesmen who will comport themselves as saints in the secular.

Coda

Yet at the same time, so as to avoid an implausible exaltation of the significance of individuals over against wider movements in history, as well as a false Prometheanism in which we would look to man, not God, for salvation, we must add that these human mediators of the 'King of the nations' point to him by their failures as well as by their successes. For as the liturgy proclaims each year in Advent, even though the Spirit is at work in the world to raise up natural history to the level of the Kingdom of God, the final coming of the Kingdom, howsoever much prepared, is sheer grace, the free Parousia of the Lord, the appearance of the King, the Desired of the peoples, to raise up man, this poor potsherd and immortal diamond whom he formed from the clay. He is the *lapis angularis*, the stone of the corner who alone can make them finally one.

Imbued with this 'catholic' hope, English Roman Catholics will not resent the continued aspersions cast on the quality of their patriotism. They can look to an older England, where a nation was neither so sovereign nor so competitive, as well as to an older Europe of which that England was part. They can look as well to that *patria* which is the Kingdom of God, in which heaven, the locus of our most fundamental *politeuma* 'citizenship',[39] descends to earth, and that common City is set up where stands the Tree of Life whose leaves are 'for the healing of the nations'.[40] The goal of history is a universal spiritual society. The Catholic Church will fulfil its own historical rôle by leadership in overcoming the divisions of humanity, and drawing the nations into that spiritual unity which is, we believe with theological faith, their destiny.

Part Four

Theology,
Literature and Art

XX
Dante's Way: Poetry and Grace

How does the speech of the poet differ from that of the theologian? The poet's language, his 'wruning' of the world, is not that of the theologian in our modern academic sense – someone who has information to offer about the history of reflection on God's revelation, together with a speculative grasp of his own, brought to bear on a contemporary world of thought. Nor is the poet's language that of the theologian in the Western mediaeval sense of the *doctor catholicae veritatis* – someone who orders teaching received from prophetic minds, those of the prophets, apostles, and, above all, of Jesus Christ, the 'chief prophet', in that phrase of St Thomas which harks back to a primitive Christological theme of the New Testament. The speech of the poet is not like either of these. We cannot ask of it the rationality, systematic coherence and even, proportioned dogmatic coverage of themes which we expect from the professional theologian.

One possible move would be to contrast poet and theologian by affirming that, in situations which both would see as significant – for example, a man suddenly aware of a subtle violence attaching to some moral act of his, and in that moment regretting it, disowning it – the theologian would have recourse to general principles of *understanding* (conscience, sin, human existence, and the like), while the poet would draw on the vocabulary of sensibility, of *feeling*. But here we must be careful not to set feeling over against thinking. The poet is concerned with the complete act of human response, in which affective and intellectual elements are in interplay, and 'describe' each other in the sense we might use that word of the steps of a dance.[1] In Dante's *Commedia*, for instance, there *are* moments of well-nigh pure evocation of feeling – chiefly of innocence, of an innocent in-breathing of the natural world in the mode of a child, for, as Dante remarks in his *Convivio*, the child desires God unconsciously in and through all things.[2] But far more of the artistic weight of the poem is invested in a multitude of subtle distinctions in the evaluating of spiritual experience. Dante holds together these distinctions by means of his sense of the enormously complex articulation of the real, its variety in unity. Although this sense is religious as well as metaphysical, trembling constantly as it does on the brink of awe at the Creator's majesty, it never lets go of conceptual clarity. The *Paradiso*, Dante's account of heaven, swims with the dynamism of spiritual life. It is filled with metaphors of motion, of dancing, swaying, revolving, drawn partly from the mystical theology of Denys the Areopagite. But never is it mere immersion in a vague ocean of being – for Freud the dubiously valuable root-experience which underlies religiosity. In aspiring towards the *trina Luce*, the threefold light of the Trinity for which the mind in all its questings unknowingly thirsts, Dante apprehended God's life so vividly in created analogies that this apprehension could become one with his delight in the clarities and interrelations of substances in the created order.

> O abounding grace, by which I dared to fix my look on the Eternal Light so long that I spent all my sight upon it! In its depth I saw that it contained, bound by love in one volume, that which is scattered in leaves through the universe, substances and accidents and their relations as it were fused together in such a way that what I tell of is a simple light.[3]

May we try a second tack and suggest that what character-

ises a poet is his acutely *individual* vision, whereas the con-
fessing theologian takes his stand on the *shared* experience
implied in Church teaching and worship, and the academic
theologian approaches his work via a methodology which he
and others have worked out by, so to say, standing back, and
trying to take in the structure of their subject matter from
without – through, then, a *common* enterprise. Yet just as
poetic language is never creation *ex nihilo*, so poetic vision is
never exclusively personal. Dante's, certainly, was sustained
by the faith-tradition of the mediaeval Catholic Church and –
scarcely less important – by the web of meanings held in the
wider culture of Christendom.

Any adequate list of the latter would have to include
Dante's spiritual and humanist inheritance from the ancient
world, from Statius, Cato and, supremely, Vergil, who represents for Dante an outpost of antiquity where the Incarnation
almost comes into view; his debt to the common life of the
city of Florence, the home loved and cursed as he ate the
bread of exile; the shared literary world of poetic tradition
and innovation found among the Sicilian and Tuscan chival-
ric poets of the *dolce stil nuovo*, those 'makers' who aroused
Dante's poetic gift, and whom he left behind. This said, it is
true that Dante's vision of the Christian life was as deeply
personal as the scope of grace it manifests is universal. But is
not the theologian worth his salt always in some way a
sapiential theologian – one who has experienced, in some
shape or form, the realities spoken of in Scripture and liturgical confession? We should like to think that the theologian
is someone who has allowed Christ's revelation to appropriate him or her, enabling them not simply to repeat the words
of the sacred authors, and the Fathers, but to recast them
from the mould of personal experience.

Let us try a third time. Is it perhaps the case that the poet
theologises through symbols? Does he not discern and
express the divine dimension of a situation through his work
of image-making, so that his teaching is inseparable from a

gift of symbolic structures that bestow on us – if we but inhabit them – new insights and fresh qualities of response? We are close to our goal here, and for that reason must tread more carefully. Biblical revelation is itself, in Austin Farrer's phrase, 'a revelation of images'.[4] Although the dogmatic theologian is concerned to display these revealed images (Son, Spirit, Kingdom, Lamb of God, Vine, and the rest) by way of a more systematic determination of the God-world relationship, the main task of the biblical theologian is their careful explication – linking him in this to the literary critic. What distinguishes the poet, in the Christian context, is that he generates new or reborn images in which the terror and splendour contained in those of the canonical revelation can be re-expressed in a fresh perspective.

In speaking of symbols we must take care that no covert contrast of symbol and reality, the merely symbolic and the fully real, lurks at the back of our minds. To cope adequately with his point we would have to launch out on an almost limitless sea, but we must at least touch its shoreline. All beings that can enter into self-communication are of their nature symbolic in that they necessarily 'ex-press' themselves in order to attain to their own essence.[5] Above all, symbol is the medium in which another being comes to the knowledge of anything sufficiently high on the scale of creation to be inwardly selved. As Léonid Ouspensky affirmed in his study of Orthodox iconology: 'To understand a symbol is to participate in a presence.'[6] 'Symbol' is a way of speaking about the possibility of communication between beings, about the 'open' texture of reality.

It is true that much of Dante's symbolism is highly formal. Not only does it tend to typology, which is generally regarded as respectable. More, its typology frequently turns into allegory, which is not. Yet we should not be too fearful of the term 'allegory', for, as Pierre Mandonnet pointed out: 'When the type enters into action, its action is allegorical.'[7] Nor, in any case, would the relation of Beatrice, Dante's childhood love and lifelong lady, to the revelatory power of grace be adequately stated by the bald formula, 'Beatrice = revelation'. The typological and allegorical significance of, respectively, her being and action, are more internally complex. Following Mandonnet's analysis: in the order of *ars* (the *ratio factibilium* of the Scholastics), she symbolises the divine beauty of Christian revelation, surpassing, as in *Paradiso* 27, the beauties of nature and art. In the moral order (the *ratio agibilium*), she represents grace, raising human activity into the supernatural realm so that, by virtuous living, human beings may merit life everlasting. In the order of *scientia*, knowledge (the *ratio speculabilium*), she stands for faith, and the light of glory which it ushers into human intelligences: her smile is in her *eyes*, for God is encountered, ultimately, in the *beatific vision. However, none of this is to be sundered from Beatrice's own flesh-and-blood individuality.* Her grace-bearing beauty can function effectively as a symbol – in Dante's poem, and in his life – because it is in itself an epiphany of the real, a shining-forth of her true inwardness of reality. This inwardness is both transformed by and rooted in God's grace – Beatrice is 'a miracle, whose root is solely the wonderful Trinity' – and it has the capacity, therefore, when expressed, to throw light on what is not itself. She becomes the image whereby Dante perceived all other 'God-bearers': the mystery of the Church, the Blessed Virgin, Christ himself. Her very function is to bring Dante to that condition where he can perceive these realities directly. St Thomas Aquinas would have called her form *quaedam irradiatio* – someone or something presenting herself, or itself, by luminosity, the shedding of light.

Although, philosophically speaking, Dante was a Scholastic eclectic, rather than a strict Thomist, the admiration and love he expresses for Thomas would justify interpreting the poet with help from the theologian.[8] However, the phrase I have used to speak of the Dantean symbol, an epiphany of the true inwardness of reality, is actually more indebted to another student of Aquinas, the spectacularly innovatory Irish prosist James Joyce, whose *Finnegan's Wake* is an attempt, like Dante's, to celebrate the unity of creation, though without Dante's passionate evangelical, moral and political purpose.[9] In *Finnegan's Wake*, Joyce's arch-druid Balkelly tells us that he

> savvy inside true inwardness of reality, the Ding hvad in idself, id est, all objects (of panipiwor) allside showed themselves in trues coloribus resplendent with sextuple gloria of light actually retained untisintus, inside them.[10]

A veil of illusion, of blunted sensibility, hides the 'hueful panepiphanical' world, for, as Daedalus remarks to Cranly in 'Stephen Hero', even the clock on the Ballast Office is capable of an epiphany. But for Dante, with his less aesthetically centred universe, this 'veil' is, in the last analysis, the sinful condition of humanity, given over as human beings are to the dimming, or even blinding, power of sin, and notably to Dante's cardinal sin of spiritual pride.

Pride expressed most typically (as with Satan) in the refusal of another's love is a rejection of the divinity that shows itself in the goodness of nature and reason. In its deceitful character, pride corrupts human reason and betrays the bond of trust which should link human beings in the specifically human good, the *bonum commune*. Hence the dominant role played in the *Inferno* by *tradimento*, the breaking of trust, which ruptures the unity of both the city and the Church. Its result is blindness. In their splendid isolation and congealed understanding, the damned have no more grasp of the meaning of their own lives than they had on earth. Satan is a parody of Aristotle's God, lost in self-contemplation. In Purgatory, by contrast, the meanings revealed by the encounters Dante describes are as clear to the characters as they are to the readers. The gesture most characterisic of the *Purgatorio* is the embrace – learning to see again means growing in charity which in turn renovates vision.

For Dante, to have one's vision rectified and illuminated is to see reality, in the concrete and the particular, as (in principle) redeemed by Christ and (in practice) in process of redemption. This involves the presentation to the mind of epiphanic moments; but these are of no use unless to interpret them we have the benefit of graced understanding, 'prophetic' knowledge. Beatrice, Dante's girl and *donna*, had been during her earthly life such a moment for the poet. But he had not understood then the extraordinary drawing power he felt in her. That discovery was the work of her sainthood when, by God's enabling grace, she gave him the light with which to see the epiphany she is.

In all this, language is vital, as no Christian poet, a servant of the *Word* of God, could fail to grasp. In *Finnegan's Wake*, Joyce's St Patrick cries out in praise of language

the sound-sense symbol in a weed-wayed-wold of the fire-there the sun in his halo cast.[11]

The 'sound-sense symbol' of poetic discourse can concentrate much of the sunlight of reality, the blaze of being, in the wold of words. Even if the paths of the wold (compare the 'dark forest' in which Dante's *Commedia* opens) are weed-grown, yet the light of Being may still be trapped between wold and weeds.

Aristotle remarks in book alpha of the *Metaphysics* that the philosopher must marvel at Being, just as the poets do, and be himself a lover of myths and poetry.[12] That at any rate is the sense of the *Aristoteles Latinus* that Dante would have used when studying with Dominicans and Franciscans at their centres in Florence. St Thomas comments on Aristotle's text that, to make it possible for us to rejoice either in the representation or the discovery of the real, poets must use metaphors. For ...

... metaphors or symbolic locutions are, as it were, the poetic vestures of the truth of things as they are, from which wonder arises.[13]

The distinctively poetic way of communicating Christian truth might, then, be summed up as follows. The poet travels in the vehicle of metaphor. His task is, namely, to carry meaning across from one reality so as to illuminate another. In so doing, he lights up relations which, without him, might long have remained unsuspected, unexplored.

But the *Commedia* is not simply a poetic exploration of being. More christianly: the creation of the poem and its gift to the reader, is an act of grace. The question, Was Dante a mystic, and, if so, how did his mystical experience enter into the making of his poem?, resembles the question, Did Paul have a strictly mystical experience on the Damascus road, and, if so, how could a private experience ground his public apostleship? Both Paul and Dante believed themselves to have been experientially touched by One who could be identified historically thanks to the saving history of God with man which is public, ecclesial. Their precise subjective state under grace is of only secondary interest. Dante speaks of a momentary *raptus* into God's glory, itself the source and term of all epiphanies. In the opening canto of the *Paradiso*, and the *Letter* to Can Grande, he records that from this he retained what would be useful of the salvation of others as well as his own. According to Thomas, to suspend contemplation for the sake of saving others belongs to the highest perfection of charity. Dante has such a saving work to perform. This word about God made poem is an evangelical proclamation, a ringing cry from God's mercy and justice as these are disclosed in the poet's life and in the whole spiritual and physical world. The *Paradiso* contains several hints that Dante may be a type of Paul.[14] His holy poem, mighty with the power of heaven as well as that of earth, may transfer those living now from the Wrath to the Mercy, from a state of *miseria* to one of *felicitas*.[15] For Dante, to open the *Commedia* is, then, to stand at a *kairos* a moment of judgment, in the history of sin and grace.

But if the poem is an act of grace, it also offers a vision of grace. The *Commedia* enacts a personal vision of the universal attracting and recreating power of grace, intensifying as Dante moves from the *Inferno* through the *Purgatorio* to the *Paradiso*. In this process, the awareness of grace, welling up in us as God's communicated life, turns gradually into an adoring understanding of God's life as a process of eternal communication: the blessed Trinity.

Within the New Testament, the Letter to the Colossians chimes with the *Commedia* by implying that the world of grace is a total ambience, environing everything that is and transforming it at its roots. Jesus Christ, whose coming constitutes the primary meaning of 'grace' for Christians,[16] is

> the image of the invisible God, the first-born of all creation; for in him all things were created, in heaven and on earth, visible and invisible, whether thrones or dominions or principalities or powers – all things were created through him and for him. He is before all things, and in him all things hold together. He is the head of the body, the Church. He is the beginning, the first-born from the dead, that in everything he might be pre-eminent. For in him all the fullness of God was pleased to dwell, and through him to reconcile to himself all things, whether on earth or in heaven, making peace by the blood of his cross.[17]

For Dante, the concealed work of Christ in history and the cosmos – at once creating, recreating and reconciling – flares into epiphany at privileged moments in our experience. The poem itself is one such epiphany. Like the Letter to the Romans, it declares at once God's wrath and his grace. The *Inferno* shows man's distance from God, a distance which exists in God as the pathos of wrath. The *Paradiso* shows how, by means of the transforming effect of the union of God and man in Christ (imaged in canto 32 of the *Purgatorio*), human existence can become sheer praise, pure grace.

In this unfolding event of salvation, Dante's share receives its unity through Beatrice.[18] Mediating both grace and glory, she is invoked in Messianic salutation, in language reminiscent of the Song of Songs. Beatrice is 'she who imparadises my mind'. She 'in-Christs' Dante's mind and heart; she is for him a God-bearer, another *Theotokos*. While she comes to meet him in judgment on his sinful condition, she also acts as an image of grace, of the redeemed life. In her eyes, Christ's humanity and divinity are alike reflected ...

> ... the Eternal Joy that shone direct on Beatrice satisfied me from the fair eyes with its second aspect.[19]

But Dante's spiritual possession of Beatrice is not the consummating end. His love of her, though it is a divinely grounded self-giving and beatifying love, must be enlarged further until it becomes the love of God. Similarly, Beatrice is not herself God's revealing action, but only a focusing of the *stelle*, the lights of heaven, that central metaphor of the poem which ends each of its parts on a note of hope and radiance. Dante is faithful to her only if he looks with her, in the direction to which her being points him. There is a sense in which he must die to her. As she gently chides him ...

> ... with the light of a smile, she said to me: 'Turn and listen, for not only in my eyes is Paradise.'[20]

As Fr Kenelm Foster justly remarked, the moments when Beatrice, as Dante's guide, detaches him from herself 'are among the most exquisite in the Paradiso'.[21]

We can recall here the warning of St John of the Cross, that none of God's gifts may be identified with God himself. Nevertheless, God is truly known in them: Beatrice can never be reduced to a mere occasion in Dante's actual salvation.

We might say, then, that for Dante the Christian must be sensitively alert to the extended sacramentality of experience. Such a statement must not be taken, however, in a non-dogmatic (much less anti-dogmatic) sense, as a covert introduction of a humanism with a religious tinge. The chief locus for such extended sacramentality, indeed, is the humanity of Jesus Christ, whose divinity we can touch by faith, and who gives the theology of grace its centre. And so, in *Purgatorio* 32, when the tree of the moral order of the cosmos flowers again, Dante is suddenly awakened by splendour and a cry, like the disciples at the Transfiguration. He is at once reminded of the *melo*, the 'apple-tree' which is Christ, and whose blossom, Christ's humanity, is both the sign and the pledge of the apple-fruit, his Godhead. Here Dante invites us to recognise an incarnational principle. All created things have an outward *bellezza* and an inward *bontade*, but the latter is, in its turn, outward with regard to a mystery that lies beyond human understanding yet is suggested, prompted, throughout the created order.[22] That is true not only of Christ's flesh, but also of the smile of Beatrice, and the dream of a just empire and its coming to be.

The pattern of the Christian life of grace is not, therefore, as Charles Williams believed, one either of the affirmation of images, or their negation. For Williams, there are two Christian ways: the *via negativa* of the deliberate denial of images, 'asceticism', and the *via positiva* of their wholehearted acceptance, 'sacramentalism'. Though there are traces of a more nuanced presentation of this theme in the work of Williams, his exploration of *The Figure of Beatrice* led him to see the *Commedia* as, above all, a celebration of the sacramental way.[23] Yet the sacraments are always to be related to Christ's Cross, the source of their sanctifying power – and that divine Death makes the *via negativa* cut through the very sacramental terrain from which Williams would exclude it. The pattern of the Christian life, as revealed by the *Commedia*, is, rather, one of death-and-resurrection. In going down to Hell on Good Friday, and emerging on the morning of Easter Day, Dante 'sub-fulfils' the Passover of Christ. He shares in that past Death and Resurrection which makes possible his present experience of grace, living by these signs as promise of something even greater still.[24]

The centrality of the Paschal mystery in the grounding of the *Commedia* makes Dante a poet of universal significance for the Christian *oikoumenê*. True, in no obvious sense was he a bridge-builder across the greatest ecclesial divide of Christian history — that between West and East. In his cosmology, his politics, his piety, he was, evidently, a mediaeval Latin Catholic. For Dante, when Constantine, in moving his capital to Byzantium, 'made himself into a Greek', he did something regrettable, if also well-intentioned.[25] He cut himself off from that providential divine guidance which ties the destiny of the human race on earth to the fortunes of the city of Rome, its empire and its papacy.[26] It is true that Dante wished to see the humbling of the papacy in its political power, in order to return it to apostolic simplicity and poverty; that he consigns the most hierocratic popes of the Gregorian Reform to Hell; that in the *Purgatorio* he presents the tree of the moral order of the cosmos, ravaged by Adam, restored by Christ, as once again assaulted by contemporary Christendom over which the papacy presides;[27] and that in the *Paradiso*, he puts into the mouths of the saints quite scathing attacks on the *curia romana*.[28] None of this alters the fact that, for Dante, Rome is that 'Rome where Christ is Roman'.[29]

Nonetheless, Dante's vision of things is a privileged point of awareness from which both Western and Eastern Christians alike can review their sense of reality in faith. Catholics speak much of 'Tradition', the Orthodox, indeed, of 'Holy Tradition'. Yet Tradition is holy only because in it the Holy Spirit discloses to us the relation between the Lord of Tradition and the world to which he is present, in which he is involved. Tradition is holy because it reveals the union of

God and man, the reality of grace. Dante's *Commedia* makes clear that the Latin Christian sense of grace is not primarily a matter of the formal analysis of Scholastic theology – liberating grace, habitual grace, operative grace, cooperative grace, operative-cooperative grace; actual grace, prevenient grace, prevenient-subsequent grace, sanctifying grace; healing grace, elevating grace, *gratia gratis data, gratia gratum faciens.* These analytic terms have their place, so long as they are used with a proper Thomist feel for distinguishing in order to unite.[30] They must be housed within a sense of the whole mystery, which is God's initiative in eliciting from his creatures a new kind of freedom in the consent of love, a freedom for communion and transfiguration in our destiny with him. If these words mean little to us, we should read Dante's *Commedia.*

XXI
Imaginative Eschatology: Benson's *The Lord of the World*

The advent of the end of the second millennium is unlikely to be greeted, in the historic Christian churches, with the mixture of enthusiasm and alarm which heralded the end of the first. Quite apart from the inroads of 'de-mythologising' and 'existentialising' before which traditional eschatology has lost ground, the number symbolism of biblical apocalypticism simply does not lend itself to *two* thousand years in the way believers with misplaced literalism applied it, in fear and awe, to the completion of the first thousand years of the *agôn* between the Gospel and the world. On the other hand, consider some presumptive 'signs of the times': the possibility, admittedly controverted, of eco-catastrophe; the ever-present threat of nuclear war – the more pressing as smaller powers, with less to lose and weaker traditions of rational policy-making, acquire weapons of mass destruction; the victories of secularist materialism which, it seems, only the Islamic powers will challenge – courageously as to substance, injudiciously as to mode; the creation of a medical technology that can encompass, at the ends of the life process, the manufacture of some human beings and the safe disposal of others; the new disparity between the technical means to feed the hungry, never before present, and the political will to do it. These provoke thought, and, in any case, the ending of a millennium reminds the Church of her faith conviction that, in this world, the human project is essentially limited in time. *In this world.* The transfer of representative colonies from a dying earth to the planets of other solar systems, as science fiction, may become in science fact – but, for man-in-the-world at large, nothing can chip away that massive doctrinal truth. Hence the importance of keeping alive eschatological thinking: and, since concepts here are of only limited usefulness, the importance, especially, of an eschatological *imagination.* Here there are few modern masters, or monuments. They include Robert Hugh Benson and his novel, *The Lord of the World.*

Benson was born on 18 November 1871, the son of an Anglican clergyman of moderately High Church views, Edward White Benson.[1] The latter was at the time headmaster of Wellington College (a royal appointment), and would become, successively, Dean of Lincoln, Bishop of Truro and Archbishop of Canterbury. Robert Hugh received the conventional education of a son in such an Establishment family: Eton, and Trinity, Cambridge. Though at first unaware of any strong vocational compulsion, he was ordained to the Anglican ministry by his father. Gradually, however, his religious soul unfolded. He gravitated towards the Anglo-Catholic wing of the Church of England, becoming in 1898, a member of the semi-monastic Community of the Resurrection at Mirfield in Yorkshire. At the same time, equipped with the cultured literacy of his family circle, and his own talents, he began to acquire a certain celebrity as preacher and writer. In 1903, he underwent a crisis of denominational belonging. Convinced that Christian discipleship required one to enter into communion with a divinely given centre of unity, he accepted, under the influence of Newman's *Essay on the Development of Christian Doctrine*, the papacy's 'Petrine claim'. It lies in the scriptures, he wrote, 'like a great jewel, blazing on the surface, when once one has rubbed one's eyes clear of anti-Catholic predisposition'.[2] Accordingly, he was received into the Catholic Church at Wood-chester (Gloucestershire), the noviciate house of the English Dominicans. Ordained to the Catholic priesthood at the English church of San Silvestro, Rome, he made the Cambridge parish of Our Lady and the English Martyrs his base for an itinerant ministry of conferences, retreats and sermons (1903–08), as well as a stream of novels and devotional and controversial literature. In 1908, he created his own ambience in a refurbished house, 'Hare Street', with a person-ally designed chapel, in the Hertfordshire village of Bunt-ingford, where he followed a horary originally inspired by his admiration for the Anglican community of Nicholas Ferrar, at Little Gidding, in the time of Charles I. Benson died in the house of the Bishop of Salford, from angina complicated by pneumonia, on 19 October 1913, at the early age of 42, and was buried at Hare Street, under a slab inscribed as he had directed: 'priest of the Catholic and Roman Church, a sinner, looking unto the revelation of the son of God'.[3]

The Lord of the World was written in Cambridge in the course of 1906–07, and it is, like Benson himself, a study in contrasts. Within Benson's own personality, the artist and the priest lived in tension. But, since both art and priesthood are gifts of God, the two vocations were eminently capable of integration. However, the world of the late twentieth cen-tury, as Benson imagined it in this novel, was divided by a conflict which, of its nature, could admit of no pacification.

The Antichrist of *The Lord of the World* is one of Benson's most brilliant literary creations – bearing in mind that in this work he wished to display not character but the incarnation of types and ideals.[4] Based, according to Benson's bio-grapher, Cyril Martindale, on a combination of the person-ality of Napoleon I and that of a contemporary English Socialist politician (unnamed by Martindale in 1916 for obvious reasons – Philip Snowden might be in biographer's, and author's, mind), Benson's 'Julian Felsenburgh' is a personification, not of evil for its own sake, but of a human culture which has set itself up as self-sufficient, and therefore over against God. The great theme of the novel is the defiance of the Supernatural by a purely natural civilisation. The future it describes is one where the unity of mankind is virtually achieved, without reference to the claims of a personal God. A humanistic naturalism does not need to be affirmed for it is everywhere assumed – absorbed, Benson remarks, as priests absorb God in communion. The man of the future is the crown of a world where the divine is immanent, evolving pantheistically through nature. This man of the future recognises in the Antichrist his own corporate Godhead, and falls down in adoration before the one in whom man's divinity has at last become transparent. His world is a world of high technology, where speed and precision reign, and whatever escapes the order of a rational, humanitarian socialism must be removed from view. This means, above all, the dying, the depressed, the desperately ill, all of whom are despatched by the ministers of euthanasia, the new clergy. The religion of Humanity is like a new revelation. Thus an old Catholic lady, sinking into death at the moment when the Antichrist is proclaimed as Lord of the World, is compared by an unbeliever to a Jew dying on Easter Monday.

In sharpest contrast, the Church of Benson's novel has all the supernatural novelty of authentic Catholicism in its difference from the world. Benson's Church has an acute sense of what is important: it exists so that the supernatural virtues of faith, hope and charity may flourish, and that, through them, human beings may enter, by obedience and sacrifice, into the very life of God. The author is equally concerned with the *interior* and the *exterior* expression of these virtues, and so of that life. Interiorly, the hero, Percy Franklin, later the last pope – his name taken from the last day of the year – Silvester III, is a mystic; indeed, the novel contains one of Benson's finest descriptions of the Prayer of Quiet. This mysticism, nourished as it was in Benson's case by the mediaeval English sources of Mother Julian of

Norwich and the hermit-priest Richard Rolle, is, at the same time, warmed by a tender Christocentrism.[5] Exteriorly, the same inspiration, in Benson's imaginative vision, leads the last Catholics to create a particular kind of society. It is found in papal Rome, once again under the civil rule of the successors of Peter, and, along with Ireland, all that is left of the old Christendom. In this Christian Rome, human beings are allowed to live individualistically, picturesquely.[6] They are not tied up to be the State's pattern men. Compassion and generosity replace the planning of a new revolutionary man. Capital punishment, though rarely practised, is in force, since, though human life is holy, human virtue is holier still. Advanced technology is deliberately shunned, because it distracts the human imagination from its main task, the living of life in relation to God. Between the invitation of grace, and the resistance of a falsely autonomous nature, there can be no compromise, no peace. The destruction of Rome by an uncanny anticipation of nuclear power is the answer of the Antichrist to Catholic protest when Westminster Abbey, place of the crowning of Christian kings in the house of prayer of Christian monks, is turned into a pagan temple. But the end of Rome only presages the end of the papacy itself, as the refugee pope, who has fled in the steps of his Master to Palestine, is finally obliterated, with his clergy and faithful, at prayer before the Blessed Sacrament, in his refuge by the plain of Megiddo – Armageddon.

The message of Benson's novel is complex. It is a plea for the internationalism of Christ over against a godless internationalism, just as Benson's earlier novels[7] contrasted the internationalism of the Catholic Church with the nationalism of the Anglican Reformation, the patriotic ideal of Elizabethan England. It is also the evocation of a Christianity which will take the form of an incarnate mysticism.[8] Hence his concern for a ritual capable of expressing divine revelation, and his preoccupation with a spiritual power that manifests itself in service and humiliation. But, most importantly of all, it is a statement of the true relation between nature and grace. Grace builds on nature and perfects it, yet it demands from nature a profound, though gentle, transformation. According to Benson, the most successful form that evil can take is its most subtle form: opposition to grace in the name of the all-sufficiency of natural perfection. Benson's warning is that if we cease to be able to distinguish happiness from holiness, we shall have succumbed to Antichrist. However, he also faced with equanimity the prospect of a massive, neo-pagan apostasy from the Catholic Church, for he saw that the Church's only lasting victory lies in Jesus' Parousia. Thus he ends his novel with the Second Coming of Christ, a meta-historical event so super-positive that it can only be expressed in the language of negation. 'Then this world passed, and the glory of it.'

Though the idiom of *The Lord of the World*, its stylistic organisation in images and atmosphere, will vary in its appeal to different generations, it is difficult to see how its meaning can cease to be relevant to any of them. History is constructed on the basis of, fundamentally, three factors: wealth, power and knowledge.[9] With the Fall of man, we must expect all three to be distorted, and human beings to become parodies of him who was rich in glory and understanding. Unlike the life of the incarnate Son, our economics, politics and science do not always proceed in obedience to the Father, in the loving service of mankind. And whilst in the last decade of the twentieth century the Marxist caricature of the Kingdom of God is fading away from our gaze, there are not lacking those who proclaim a neo-capitalist 'end of history' in the paradisal pleasures of an all-satisfying consumer materialism.[10] Benson reminds us that the Church has her own theology of history situated, like her life itself, between the lightning flashes of the Resurrection and the thunderclap of the Parousia. History is not evolving towards its own perfection; rather is it in the hands of its crucified Judge who will come at an hour that we do not know. Benson has no triumphalism save that of the Easter mystery: the Christ who reigns from a tree; the Church who is queen because she is suffering Mother; and a Petrine ministry whose rôle reaches its climax in its last officeholder: 'vicar of Christ' *par excellence* because, like the faithful ones of the Letter to the Hebrews – 'destitute, afflicted, ill-treated, wandering over deserts and mountains, and in dens and caves of the earth, of whom the world was not worthy'[11] – he stayed loyal to God's commission, encouraging a remnant with words of hope, until the Lord's return.

XXII
On Baptising the Visual Arts: A Friar's Meditation on Art

I owe this chapter's sub-title to Winefride Wilson, one of the last members of that remarkable English Catholic experiment in the uniting of art, worship and life, the Ditchling Community. That was how she rendered the German name of an important manifesto for the revival of Christian art: Wilhelm Heinrich Wackenroder's *Herzensgiessungen eines kunstliebenden Klosterbruders* (1797) ('Heartfelt Outpourings of an Art-loving Cloister-brother').[1]

Wackenroder's impassioned appeal for a renaissance of Christian art, so moribund in his period as in our own, has lost nothing of its relevance today. In this chapter I propose, first, to indicate the significance of this subject; second, to place this discussion in its contemporary secular context; and third, to make some proposals for retrieving, and enhancing, the lost riches of the Church's iconography.

The significance of the subject

The Second Vatican Council instructs all Catholics that 'those decrees of earlier times [the reference is to the Second Council of Nicaea, 787, and the Council of Trent, 1545–64] regarding the veneration of images of Christ, the Blessed Virgin and the saints be religiously observed'.[2] And this bare statement of *Lumen Gentium*, the Dogmatic Constitution on the Church, is filled out in its sister text on the Holy Liturgy, *Sacrosanctum Concilium*. In the latter, we find a distinction (to which I shall return) between 'religious art' (*ars religiosa*) and 'sacred art' (*ars sacra*), seen as the high-point of religious art at large. According to the Council, the two types share a common orientation:

> By their very nature, both of the latter are related to God's boundless beauty, for this is the reality which these human efforts are trying to express in some way. To the extent that these works aim exclusively at turning men's thoughts to God persuasively and devoutly, they are dedicated to God and to the cause of his great honour and glory.

The distinguishing feature of *sacred* art, however, lies in its intimate connexion with the liturgy itself. Sacred images are, the Council fathers explain, designed expressly for use in worship; they are fashioned 'for the edification, devotion and religious instruction of the faithful'. And so these images above all must be 'worthy, fitting, beautiful', since they are *rerum supernarum signa et symbola*, 'signs and symbols of realities beyond this world'.[3]

Behind these statements there lies, in the first place, a whole *anthropology*, or teaching about man – and since, in Catholic Christianity the primary doctrine which the Church possesses about man is his *imagehood of God*, this must mean an understanding of the human being in his or her relation to God. St Thomas, in his discussion of religious activity, asks whether religion necessarily involves any 'external actions'. He replies that it does: for, while our perfection consists in the due ordering to God's glory of our *mens* ('spirit' or 'the feeling mind' may be the best translation of this word), nonetheless:

> The human mind needs to be led to God by means of the sensuous world (*sensibilium manuductione*), since – as St Paul

says – the 'hidden things of God are manifested by those things that are made'. Hence, in divine worship the use of corporeal things is necessary so that, by using signs, man's mind may be aroused to the spiritual acts which join him to God.[4]

Man is an *embodied* soul, or, better, an ensouled body; body and soul do not merely meet in him, but are immanent, indwelling, one in the other, the spiritual with the 'carnal'. I do not mean this term in Paul's sense of the 'fleshly' – that which is hostile to the Spirit of God, but in the French poet Charles Péguy's sense of *le charnel* – his favoured word for all our solidarity with the visible world, at once as humble as the dust and radiant as the most splendid epiphanies of finite beauty. We move to God in no other way than from, within, and by the medium of this incarnate order wherein we are situated. We reach out to him through the matter which is not defined over against God's Spirithood for he is the *Creator*-Spirit, related to us as origin and goal of body and soul alike. In the words of the too neglected French theologian Eugène Masure, man is

> the living sanctuary of an uninterrupted encounter between the visible and the invisible.[5]

Nothing is more natural, then, than art, and especially religious art. The spirit of man expresses its own desire for, and striving towards, its Source, by means of art works, themselves stimulated by the material milieu where the Creator Lord signals to us through all *his* works of creation.

The Council's allusions to sacred art in particular require, however, a second context also if we are to do justice to their importance, and that is the *biblical economy of salvation*. In the Old and New Testaments, the exchange between God and man is not confined to the *word* of God – if that term be understood simply of language rather than, against its own Semitic background, as the dynamic energy of Israel's Lord.

Instead, the divine Glory shows itself in a variety of scenes or *tableaux vivants*, from Exodus and Sinai to Calvary and the Resurrection appearances, all interrelated in the developing narrative of the divine Action. And while the prophets, as recipients of the divine Speech, were told to act out their messages in the form of special gestures or signs (*ot'*), when the personal Word of God himself assumes our flesh, prophecy in its last representative, John the Baptist, yields the centre stage to a Figure whose *whole human being* is a sign. Jesus' humanity discloses in visible form the divine person of the Son, and the Son from all eternity is in the image of the Father. Both the Gospels and the liturgy find the supreme self-revelation of God, therefore, in those visual scenes – the mysteries of the life of Christ – where the pattern of our salvation was first made known. From the Nativity to the Ascension, from the Baptism to the Cross, God in stooping down to us in his Son has shaped a path for us to return to him – which we do in self-identification with the meaning and grace of these archetypal moments in both sacramental, and ordinary, living. The instinct of Christ's faithful was from early centuries to portray these scenes in art, so that, tutored and moved by the image, Christians could apprehend their salvation not in name only but in very truth. Though the possibility of superstitious abuse of images has caused hesitation (Erasmus, and before him, the theologians of the court of Charlemagne), or even rank iconophobia, the Church – and not least the Church of Rome – has held firmly to the view that sacred art is entailed by the Incarnation itself.[6]

Our context

We must turn now to the situation in which – in terms of the general culture – we find ourselves today. It is true that, at the start of this century, there arose in France, in the work of Cézanne, van Gogh, Gauguin, an art concerned with transcendent reality – over against both the empirical impression *tout court.* or the mere reveries of the personal subject.[7] Again, in German-speaking central Europe an art with metaphysical and spiritual claims on the viewer continued in vigour, notably among the Expressionists, thanks to the still potent energies there of the Romantic revival, so that secular art could have recognisably religious themes.[8] Moreover, in the course of this century, a variety of artists not themselves Christian, have looked back for guidance and inspiration to earlier Christian forms – to the Russian icon in the case of Malevich, with his lost modern icons 'The Orthodox' and 'Head of the Peasant', and Chagall, with his illustrations of Old and New Testament scenes, or to the more modest Western icons of the folkloric Bavarian *Hinterglasmalarei* ('painting on the back of glass'), which interested the Blaue Reiter school, and notably Vassily Kandinsky with his own 'Sancta Francesca' and 'Saint Vladimir'.[9] Yet these are only dots in a kaleidoscope. The *overall* situation of the practice of art in the twentieth-century Western world, and especially today, is disoriented in the extreme. One witness must suffice, the American art critic Susi Gablik. She takes as her theme the shift from 'modernism', the later nineteenth-century profusion of new styles and ideologies, to the current 'post-modernism', where modernism itself is left behind in a pluralism so radical that it can no longer chart intelligibly the historic development of styles, and abandons, moreover, the very task of relating the texts of the intellectuals to the stuff of the world. The world of the visual artist now

is a world complicated by changes without parallel. Models and standards from the past seem of little use to us. Everything is in continuous flux; there are no fixed goals or ideals that people can believe in, no tradition sufficiently enduring to avoid confusion. The legacy of modernism is that the artist stands alone. He has lost his shadow. As his art can find no direction from society, it must invent its own destiny.[10]

Not that this loss of a transcendent point of reference –

both for individual action in a genuinely *common* life, or for the common life in a goal truly capable of integrating nature and history because lying beyond them – is in any way surprising. As Gablik remarks, the circumambient culture in which modern art came to be stands on four pillars: secularism, individualism, bureaucracy and pluralism. In a despiritualised world, where the numinous, the mythic, and the sacramental are progressively eliminated; in a bureaucratic or managerial culture which has snapped the roots in tradition of an individual now seen overwhelmingly as economic agent and above all as consumer – is it any wonder that art has lost its moral authority, and finds itself deprived of any coherent set of priorities, or persuasive models from the past, or even criteria for self-evaluation?

The strain of commitment to a spiritual vision in an unspiritual society has proved too much for modern art. For such early modernists as Kandinsky and Malevich, the artist was the last active carrier of spiritual value in a materialised world: and such Abstract Expressionists as Rothko tried to perpetuate such an understanding of vocation. But, on the whole, by the 1970s, 'the aesthetic' meant no longer an aesthetic spirituality (Malevich claimed to see in his black squares the face of God – perhaps a vestige of the 'negative theology' of the divine mystery found in the Christian East). Instead, it signified an exclusive concern with the demands of the painterly medium. Despite such exceptions as Dorothea Rockburne with her Angel series and the Annunciations of Brice Marden, the artwork was conceived increasingly as nothing more than a painted surface. To ask after meaning became the new philistinism.

In the context of the 'secular fundamentalism' of the contemporary West – with its rejection of all cognitive beliefs about the nature of reality (save the belief that we cannot know what that nature is) and of all understanding of ethics as formed within a common life, in response to values and goals established in relation to a transcendent Truth and

Good, the artist can no longer take as his own the corporate ends of society (for it has none worth the name), but must distinguish himself through his singularity.[11] But the removal of all inhibitions from individual freedom simply removes the artist from the social substance. As Peter Fuller, the trenchant English critic not only of art but, even more, of criticism, pointed out, if art can be anything that the artist says it is, then it will never amount to anything more than that.[12] Fuller, who before his early death in a car accident in 1990 was deliberately seeking out Christian theologians in an attempt to come to grips with the mystery of *being* which artistic *meaning* must presuppose, likened the freedom of the contemporary artist to that of the insane. They can do whatever they like, since whatever they do, they will have no effect at all. Thus, for example, the anti-commercial and anti-art establishment gestures of the pioneers of such things as 'Minimal', 'Conceptual', 'Performance' and 'Body' art have secured both market value and establishment status: the *avant-garde* is co-opted; the business world has met it, and embraced.

Gablik, in her survey of our present winter, has appealed for a renaissance of the sense of artistic tradition, without which there can be no generation of stable and lasting criteria for art. Her appeal for a counter-insistence to that of modernism, her stress on the need for preserving 'certain continuities', echoes Fuller's last contribution.[13] What she has in mind, more clearly than he, is a high doctrine of cultural continuity with historic, religiously-founded civilisation.

Our present situation is one in which art, having abdicated any connection with a transcendental realm of being, has lost its character as a world-view – as a way of interpreting either nature or history ... For those who see transcendence as being as vital to the human mind as hope – and as indestructible – the irreverence of modernism is a real threat to the social and psychological bases of human greatness.[14]

The negative lesson is that we must learn to set limits to the exploration of cultural experiences – as much as to the possibilities of biological experiment, and for the same ultimate reason, that the world, before it is an *agendum*, a field for action, is a *factum*, a deed, and not only a deed, but a gift, *donum, donum Dei*.

The recovery of tradition

The positive lesson to be drawn from reflection on the current situation is an invitation to the Church of the West to reconstitute its iconographic resources, and to use its ethos – its ethical teaching on human life in society – to provide some guidelines for the reorientation of a non-sacred art which may, however, still be of religious importance in its orchestration of spiritual themes.

To take first (and briefly) this question of an art which is spiritual yet not believing: the Church's ethical and philosophical concept of the human being as flourishing through the virtues, both a person and, inextricably, a social agent, and in both dimensions – interiority, and the common good, open to a transcendence which he cannot name, is itself of the utmost cultural pertinence. Catholics could learn from the experience of Anglicans about the possibility of sustaining a dialogue with artists who are 'half-way to faith', not least because artists of a sympathetic temper are glad of the opportunity to approach, through the venues of cathedral or parish church, a (hopefully) receptive audience. But Catholics should also learn here from the mistakes of Anglicans, and most recently, in England, the embarrassing controversy about the figure of a 'golden man' – Adam in his primaeval innocence or Feuerbachian man in self-exaltation to divinity? – placed, during an exhibition on the spiritual in art, within the interior of Lincoln Cathedral. An art expressive of a 'spiritual quest' does not belong in the liturgical setting where the mysteries of orthodoxy are confessed and celebrated. But it could certainly have a place elsewhere in a church complex: for example, in a parish hall or room where, let us say, catechumens, or those simply enquiring about faith, are taking their first steps in the context of the Rite for the Christian Initiation of Adults. Such 'religious' (but not 'sacred') art carries within it those questions – Why is there something rather than nothing?; What is man?; What is the good for man, and what his destiny? – which are the meat and drink of all religions.[15]

Moving on to the second topic, which concerns me more, since it is closer to Christianity's dogmatic heartlands, that of sacred art – what do I mean by the urgent need to 'reconstitute' the Church's 'iconographic resources'? In the first place, I mean a willingness to scan the repertory of styles from the past in search of iconographic qualities still desirable in the art-making of the present. To wrench to our purpose a saying of Jeremy Bentham, the question should be not: How long ago did a stylistic feature originate?, but: Can it be of theological use to the Church today? We must have done with the self-denying ordinance that rules out all allusion to the art of the past on the grounds that 'modern man' (that chimaera) wants only the contemporary – and receives as a consequence an often uninspired, and too facile, abstract art, in the windows and on the walls of his churches, an art which of its nature cannot express the Christian fact (for the revelation of the Incarnate is always through *form*), though it may evoke certain dimensions of that fact, such as (a generalised) 'mystery' or 'transcendence'.

If Gablik is right in her fundamental contention that, without rules and standards, innovation becomes meaningless, and criticism a beating of the air, and that, for there to be standards, a tradition must be in place, then we must reconsider the recent disdain of the *bien-pensants* for any recourse to former artistic styles. The rejection of all such recourse as pastiche, or imitative sterility, not only disfranchises the (limited, but real) achievements of Christian art since the

Romantic movement. More than this: had such a veto been generally observed in yet earlier generations their finest creations would never have come to be. Thus, on the one hand, the *Lukasbund* (the precursor of the Pre-Raphaelites, and commitedly Catholic) looked to mediaeval German wall-painting and the Italian primitives; the Beuron school to Egyptian art; the English Gothic Revival to the 'Decorated' or 'Middle Pointed' style of the Middle Ages; Bernard Buffet to the Catalan Romanesque. And on the other, the great styles of historic Christendom involve a series of revivals, as new needs, materials, and techniques, as well as ideas prompt the rediscovery and extension of the basic principles of a tradition. Are we supposed to question the authenticity of the Byzantine art of the 'Palaeologan renaissance', or the International Gothic?

But secondly, the recreation of iconographic means must go hand-in-hand with the evangelical control of iconological themes. The faithful should not be subjected, in what they see in church, to the caprices of a parish priest, or – probably worse still – an ecclesiastical architect. Within the rudimentary limits indicated by the Second Vatican Council, and the Code of Canon Law of the Latin church (can. 1188), a new consensus should be fashioned as to just what images, and in which interrelation, might house aesthetically the Christian liturgy. Basically, the role of sacred images in the liturgical assembly has been to orientate the Christian in theological time and space. First, in theological time: so that, by taking in the church's painting and sculpture he or she comes to place themself in relation to the economy of salvation as it advances from the beginnings, through Israel to Jesus Christ, the founding of the Church, its history of holiness, and the final return of the Lord with all his saints. But theological space is also important here: within the 'now' of the offer of creation and redemption, the Christian belongs to a cosmos, and that cosmos – above all through man who is its priest, is open to the heavenly world which is not so much awaited by us as eternally present to us. In other words: the Bible and the history of the Church, suitably contextualised in a Christian metaphysic, are what must guide the formation of a *scheme* of images – ideally, in every church building erected, or restored.

It should be said at once that the rite best placed in the Catholic Church to carry through these recommendations is that of the Byzantine Uniates – precisely because it has developed a full, organised *scheme* of images, displayed on the icon-screen separating (but also linking) sanctuary and nave, and throughout the church building as a symbolic microcosm of the spiritual universe, and because, also, it has put into liturgical practice the concept of the festal icon, which is to serve as a focus, at once didactic, and devotional, for the high-points of the Christian year. No other Christian tradition in the Great Church has developed not only its iconology (its understanding of sacred images), but also its iconography (its creation and use of such images) with this admirable thoroughness. This is not simply an unfavourable comparison of the Latin church with its Byzantine-Slav sister; the non-Byzantine Oriental rites – whether of the Syrian or the Alexandrian family – are equally lacking in consistency with that of the Latin West. We shall not be far wrong in ascribing the more sustained attention which the Byzantine church gave this matter to the trauma of the Iconoclast crisis. For, although the Seventh Ecumenical Council (Nicaea II), which restored the images, left surprisingly little trace in the way of subsequent theological commentary, the crisis itself made a permanent impression on the Byzantine mind. The idea that the Gospel, as the proclamation of the Word Incarnate, must be made equally and inseparably via the word – language – and the (visual) image, became a pervasive one, both in theory and in practice.[16]

In a sense, then, I am calling for a Byzantinisation – in this regard – of the Latin church (and the other non-Byzantine rites). Nor is this cloud-cuckoo land, for the process of 'reception' of the art of the icon is already well advanced in certain Catholic circles in the West.[17] However, I am not in fact proposing that Western church art should become *stylistically* Byzantine, that we should import Greek or Russian icon-screens to replace our ousted communion-rails. I am simply appealing for the replication, in the different stylistic circumstances of the Western rite, of the quality of iconographic imagination and practice which characterises the Greco-Slavonic church.

In practice, this will not be done without the creation of at least one school of Church art in the territory of every national bishops' Conference. Such schools are absolutely taken for granted in the Orthodox world. In the recent West, an isolated example was the 'school of sacred art' founded by Maurice Denis and Georges Desvallières along the lines of a studio workshop for apprentices.[18] Without a coherent strategy, embodied in suitable institutions, allowing for doctrinal and theological stimulus and control, as well as financial subsidy and moral support – nothing significant will be done. Sacred art will continue to wander in the wilderness, and Christian initiation will remain deprived of one of its most vital dimensions: the baptism of the imagination.

What is it that we lose by such a deprivation? In the first place, the chance to see, and live with, images of transfigured humanity – above all, of the Saviour – which not only cohere with but root in the deepest humus of the psyche the truths contained in the formal doctrine of the Church. Even if the homily, for example, fails to convey a suitable sense of who Jesus Christ is, whether by a defect of doctrine or a lack of the power to move souls, heart and mind can still be touched by the Christ of a Byzantine mosaic, a Romanesque fresco, a Russian icon, or such a twentieth-century image as Rouault's *Holy Face* – itself indebted to a persistent tradition of depicting the Redeemer in this guise, not unconnected, perhaps, with the 'true image' long venerated at Edessa (Syria) and found, in its mediaeval form, in the Shroud of Turin.[19] (And though our grasp of the figure of Christ is, evidently, central to the happy condition of the 'sense of the faith' in the Church, the same basic point about the 'adequate' and potent image can also be applied to the quality of perception of our Lady, and the saints.)

And in the second place, the absence of suitable images means the loss of models, and incentive, for growth in the virtues, both natural and divine. The gestures depicted by the artist can be a moral education in themselves (as with Blake's bowed heads, intimating humility, tenderness, compassion), and a school in how to respond to the crucial events of man's salvation (as in Giotto's depiction of awe, prayer, blessing).

If our Catholicism has become at once too wordy and too fixated on 'structures', then the therapy it needs is to turn from 'problems' to 'presence' — for in any case, it is only by virtue of the saving presences, and their pressure on our minds and hearts, that problems in *this* context can be solved at all. And to mediate the presence of the Holy, the Church must regain her rôle as 'iconifier' — bearer of images, and mother of artists.[20]

Part Five

Theology and Holiness

XXIII
The Spirituality of the Dominicans

The basis of every spiritual way is the search for God. It is a matter of putting God into one's life, or of considering one's life in relation to God. This search for God can take on different aspects. It can be a union with God by knowledge and by love. It can be the concrete realisation of the will of God. It can be cooperation with his creative and redemptive plan. What was the spiritual way of St Dominic, and what is that of the Dominican 'family' – friars, nuns, sisters and layfolk – which has sprung from him?

To answer this question we must have some idea of Dominic's life, work and personality. The life is simply told. He was born in Castile around 1170, and was from boyhood intended for the priesthood. He began his studies early with an uncle who was archpriest in the area, but Dominic was no mere bookworm, as is shown by his selling his books during a famine, to buy food for the poor. The combination of studiousness and charity singled him out in the eyes of an astute observer, one Diego, who was prior of the cathedral chapter of the city of Osma. The chapter had recently adopted the common life as laid down by the Rule of St Augustine. Following the model Augustine had established for his own cathedral in North Africa in the fifth century, they would not only worship regularly together but own all things in common, and seek God together as brethren; they wanted to be, like the Jerusalem community of *Acts*, 'of one heart and one mind'. And all this in the service of the official Church, symbolised in the bishop.

As events turned out, Dominic did not remain a canon of Osma, where in 1201 he had become sub-prior. What put Dominic's life into a wider frame was the request, in 1203, of Diego, now bishop, that Dominic should accompany him on a diplomatic mission, concerning a royal marriage, to Denmark. The first of the two trips which this involved gave Dominic experience of the spreading heresy of the Albigensians, a group of people who, like the Gnostics of the first Christian centuries, denied the goodness of the creation, and understood redemption in a way which bypassed the worshipping life of the Church with its apostolic faith, ministry and sacraments. On the second visit, they found the Archbishop of Lund in the course of organising a great mission to pagans living around the eastern side of the Baltic sea, and were sufficiently impressed by this to go to Rome to seek permission to join him. When the pope refused to let Diego abandon his bishopric, they found another outlet for their desire to spread the faith. In south-west France, where Dominic and Diego had earlier met their first Albigensians, some Cistercians were preaching – as papal legates, but not for all that very successfully – against the heresy. Diego associated Dominic and himself with them, even to the point of taking the Cistercian habit (in his case), but added a new element: they would imitate the apostolic lifestyle of the original disciples of Jesus, just as, for very different purposes, the Albigensian preachers were doing themselves. So began the Preaching: combining the forthright teaching of exact doctrine with a way of life, simple, prayerful, like that of the apostles.

On Diego's death in 1207, Dominic kept it up, this time with the support of Fulk, Bishop of Toulouse. He it was who encouraged Dominic to form a group of preachers, based in the city of Toulouse, with the task of helping the bishop to carry out his own role as teacher of the faith: not just negatively, to correct heretics, but also positively by building up the faithful themselves. Thus the whole doctrinal mission of the Church was entrusted, on a tiny scale, in one local place, to the nascent Order of Preachers.

And so it was until 1215 when Dominic accompanied Fulk to the Fourth Lateran Council to ask the pope to recognise his new community. As the Council was anxious to avoid a useless proliferation of monastic rules, Dominic was asked to take an already existing one. Naturally, he chose the Augustinian, to which he added a 'customary', typical of the reformed canons, making for austerity in food and clothing. At first, the confirmation was for a single local church, that of Toulouse, where the brethren would have a vow of stability, made into the hands of an abbot. But Dominic quickly realised that the need for such apostolically-living teachers of truth was as wide as the Church itself, and the Bull of confirmation was changed to make it worldwide. At Pentecost 1217 Dominic announced to his startled community at Toulouse that he was going to scatter them to the four winds. This is the most striking instance of the way that, in the thirteenth century, as a response to the needs of the Church, a major portion of Latin monasticism suddenly went itinerant, and became a travelling affair. Curiously, in so doing, it harked back, without knowing it, to the origins of the monastic charism, at least in its Syrian (rather than Egyptian) form. (The early Irish monks, and some of the 'black' monasticism of the Dark Ages had also gone missionary, but not on the same scale.)

The rest of Dominic's life, until his death in 1221, consisted in setting up this international Order, with its doctrinal mission (to the highly intelligent, but also to the very simple), its life of study and contemplation, based in a disciplined conventual setting, but one where friars must be ready at all times to go out to meet the needs of preaching. No wonder that the houses of the Order were themselves known as 'holy preachings'.

The members of the Order were known as *'Friars'*: but it would be more correct to say in the first place *'priest*-friars'. And here we come to the question of the different groups of people who belonged to the Dominican household, or family. Although the Roman pope had declared the Order an 'Order of Preachers', and by his universal pastoral authority it was given a place in the local structures of Christendom wherever the special place of the pope in the Church was accepted, what he was doing was to extend to a particular group of presbyters (priests) the function hitherto reserved (in principle) for the bishops – that of preaching the Church's doctrine. Dominic did not intend, however, that those who were to be his spiritual children should be exclusively priests. The lay brothers, to whom he proposed to commit the entire temporal side of the Order's life, were to cooperate in the Preaching, not only by forming domestically the 'preachings', the houses themselves, but by serving the Word, the divine Utterance, in loving devotion, thus becoming – like the Peruvian half-caste of the sixteenth century, Martin de Porres – examples of holiness to inspire the rest. Again, the enclosed nuns, whom Dominic gathered into communities of reformed Albigensian ladies even before his Order was itself fully established, were to be contemplators of the Word, and by their intercession for the Preaching, to serve it evangelically. As time went on, fraternities of lay people attracted by the Dominican spirit also sprang up, and from these groups of 'tertiaries' as they were called, came in the modern period new conventual groupings, mainly of women, but also occasionally of men: 'sisters' and 'brothers', often working in areas, like nursing, very far from the concerns of the original Dominicans, yet hoping to infuse into their chosen vocations something of the Dominican way of looking at things.

What then of Dominic's own spiritual personality, his particular way of being a saint? The evidence we have, mainly from the witnesses called at his canonisation process, gives us the main outlines. The texts stress his radiance and joy, especially in trials and difficulties. They note his accessibility, his readiness to sympathise with others and to console. At the same time, they depict his austerity of life; his speaking only of God or to him; his fervour in prayer and preaching. There is no uniquely *personal* savour about the testimonials as there is in the obvious case for comparison: his contemporary, St Francis. Dominic's *persona* was love of the Word and its diffusion: his *personality* is disclosed only in the shape of his work. His attraction was that of the Gospel completely lived, the 'grace of the Word'. Dominic's spiritual personality is distinctive in that it wants to be a medium for the Gospel which the Church carries, so that, through the Order which he raised into being, the single Word may be refracted in countless human lives. Similarly, he took from the various sources for the religious life available to him what he believed would best serve the mission of the Gospel. Thus we can find echoes of the desert tradition, of the Augustinian common life, of the austerity of the hermits of Grandmont (a slightly older Order than his own), and of the monastic observance of the Cistercians. All have been brought into the service of a new conception, though one which does not waste time parading its own originality: a body of Christian disciples who will 'pass on to others the fruits of contemplation', not as the incidental overflow of such contemplation, but of its very essence, as a ministry of the Word.

In their spirituality the Dominicans were not fussy about where they drew ideas and images from, just as they were open to inheriting bits and pieces of the traditions of other religious orders. What mattered was not where something came from but what was done with it. It became Dominican by being integrated into a life of loving devotion to the Word of God, expressed in the desire to communicate that Word to others. If not quite *everything*, then an awful lot was grist to the Dominicans' mill. Some Dominican authors are highly mystical and metaphysical in their themes and images, like Meister Eckhart and the Rhineland spiritual writers in general. Others are very homespun, like William Peraldus or Humbert of Romans. What makes them Dominican is the putting to service of these materials in a particular way, a way which is at once directed towards God as the Word, the Word of truth, and towards human beings as those to whom the Gospel of truth must be brought.

We see this combination of variety-in-unity in the Dominican saints. Although remarkably different in way of life, in personality, and in the concrete form of their spiritual teaching, they are all servants of the Word, to whom they are devoted in contemplation and whom they bring to others in active mission. The manner in which this is done varies enormously, from a Catherine of Siena, who did it through friendships expressed not least in her correspondence, to John of Fiesole (Fra Angelico) who did it through his paintings. In all of them, the centre is at once the Truth of God, a truth which must, since it is the truth of our Creator and Redeemer, also be *love*, and the doctrinal communication of that truth, a communication which, since it is for our healing and raising up to share through Christ the co-existence of the Holy Trinity, is necessarily also *life*.

This is, naturally, at its clearest in the theologian saints who have greatly influenced our picture of Dominican sanctity as, above all, intellectual holiness, the devotion of the mind to God, the mind in love with God. Such were Thomas Aquinas and Albert of Cologne, figures who emerge as the Order moved from the edges of towns, where it faced towards both town and country (a habitat which well expressed its 'catholic' mission) to concentrate on the university centres. In such academic saints, Christian wisdom clothes the highest forms of intellectual culture with itself. Because ideas are so influential, this will always be a major priority for the Dominican Order; but at the same time, it has not forgotten that Christian wisdom can also exist among the unlettered and the poor, for its own life began in conversations with an Albigensian innkeeper.

What, then, is the significance of Dominicanism for us today? I hope that, from what I have written, it may be clear that the *particular* way of Dominican spirituality is, paradoxically, as it may seem at first sight, a *universal* concern with the Word of God in its totality. That Word is expressed in creation, in all its realms, from the Angels, through man to the world of the animals, and below that to the flora and the inanimate creation. It is also expressed in revelation, in the totality of the doctrinal vision entrusted by Christ to the apostles of his Church. It is this concern for the Word in the wholeness of its self-expression, the wish to contemplate it lovingly and communicate it faithfully, that animates Dominican spirituality, and enables it, as I have indicated earlier, to press into its service all the materials that come to hand. This has the advantage that such a spirituality will not be totalitarian, because it will leave much to be filled in by the individual, according to the temperament, interests and emphases of each. Dominicans have been noted, for instance, for their devotion to the Angels, and to the dead – both myriad sets of beings belonging to the totality of the world, yet easily screened out by our having too narrow a view of man's experience. Again, Dominicans in defending the goodness of the Incarnation and the sacraments have perforce been obliged to see the whole natural universe, from which Christ's body and the ritual signs of the sacraments were taken, as very good – as, in a weakened yet still real sense, the '*sacrament* of the world'. At the same time, when this same concern for the totality of the Word is thought of in regard to revelation, the Dominican spirit, though always situating the life of the Church within the wider whole of the world, is profoundly 'ecclesial' – it is not on the margins of the Church's life and mission but at their heart. Hence the Dominican love of the Bible, the Church's book and the liturgy, the Church's prayer, and Dominican fidelity to the apostolic structure of the Church, to the service of pope and bishops. All of these are formed by the Holy Spirit, who still acts through them. Dominican spirituality wants to make us enter the spaciousness of scripture; to walk about in the vastness of the perspectives which the liturgy offers; and so to enter more fully into the mission of the Church, which is wind and flame on earth, a continuing Pentecost.

'Hoarded grain rots, but it bears fruit when scattered' are words ascribed by an earlier chronicler to St Dominic. The Dominican, and the Dominican-influenced lay person, knows that he or she must first become grain – through study, through devotion in the cell, whether of the priory or of the heart, and through openness to the Spirit who gives Christians speech – what the early Dominicans liked to call the 'grace of preaching'. But at the same time, they also know that they have a mission to spread the Word to their neighbours, whether by a sermon, a letter or a painting, or any of the many other media that may be called 'communication'. In the words of the apostle whose letters (together with the Gospel of St Matthew) Dominic always carried, 'Woe to me if I preach not the Gospel'.

XXIV
Ekaterina Sienskaya Abrikosova: A Dominican Uniate Foundress in the Old Russia

Our story opens in a well-to-do and cultivated merchant family in the Moscow of the 1880s.[1] A son of the house, Vladimir Vladimirovič Abrikosov, born on 22 October 1880, was at once the future husband and the cousin of the central personality of this chapter. When his schooling was finished, Vladimir Vladimirovič entered the Faculty of History and Philology of Moscow University, where he wrote a dissertation on the causes of the Western Reformation. Despite this religious choice of topic, Abrikosov was uninterested in the Orthodoxy of his family tradition. He appears to have had little knowledge of the teaching of the Orthodox Church and did not attend its liturgy. He dismissed Catholicism as obscurantist, and his sympathy for Protestantism was at best lukewarm. Western philosophy, whether ancient or modern, engaged him more, but in years to come he would deplore the manner of his historical studies as formalistic, lacking in attentiveness to history's significance. Such a constellation of attitudes was by no means uncommon among educated Russians in the liberal families of the period.

In 1904 Abrikosov married a cousin, two years his junior, Anna Ivanovna Abrikosova. She was born on 23 January

1882 and had attended the first *gimnaziya* (high school) to be opened in Moscow for the education of girls. In 1899 she won a scholarship to Girton College, Cambridge, electing to read history, assiduously, earning from her contemporaries the nickname 'Deadly Earnest'.[2] Anna Ivanovna was a gifted linguist with, in time, an excellent grasp not only of English but also of French, German and Italian, as well as a considerable knowledge of Greek and Latin.

The household of the newly-weds was free-thinking. God was neither affirmed nor denied. Politically, both supported the current which would lead to the constitutional Revolution of 1905. With what the late Nicolas Zernov called the 'religious renaissance' then beginning among the Russian intelligentsia they had nothing to do.[3] Their inherited wealth enabled them to live a carefree life, devoted principally to European travel and the arts. Thus, with the exception of a single month in 1905, they spent the entire period from 1904 to 1910 in France, Italy and Switzerland. Cultural tourism led them to visit a number of Western art galleries and monasteries, and this encounter with Western Catholicism in its artistic and historic monuments precipitated in Anna Ivanovna a personal crisis of a religious kind. This was by no means unprepared as for some while she had been reading works of philosophy in an unsuccessful effort to find a fuller meaning for life. Probably at the suggestion of her friend, Princess Maria Mikhailovna Volkonskaya, whose family, unable to maintain their Russian domicile after their conversion to Catholicism, now lived in Rome, Anna Ivanovna discovered the mystical *Dialogue* of the fourteenth-century Dominican tertiary Catherine of Siena. She was especially struck by a phrase in its prologue: *virilmente cognoscere e seguitare la verità* ('virilely to know and follow the truth'). The whole passage reads in its most recent, if somewhat insipid, translation:

So it is true that the soul is made one with God by love. Hence this soul I speak of, desiring more earnestly to follow this truth, stirred up in herself that primary desire which aims at the soul's own good, for she well knew that no soul can be of benefit to others, by teaching and example and prayer, unless it has first been of benefit to itself by the acquiring of virtue.[4]

In December 1908, at the fashionable Parisian church of the Madeleine, Anna Ivanovna was received into Catholic communion by the Abbé Maurive Rivière, afterward Archbishop of Aix-en-Provence. Though she had no other thought than to join the Latin rite, Rivière pointed out, correctly, that, for the Canon Law then in vigour, while she might worship in that rite she would belong to that of the Byzantine-Slavs. After a year in Rome studying theology jointly with her husband, he too made profession of the Catholic faith at the Madeleine, in November 1909. Anna Ivanovna's biographer, Fr Ambrosius Eszer, has noted that their conversion was not so much an abandonment of Orthodoxy (which in reality they had hardly known) but more a re-discovery of Christianity at large.[5] In the fervour of their new-found faith, Anna Ivanovna proposed that she would become a Dominican sister, and that her husband should be ordained in some monastic or religious Order. As this plan could only be carried out, as things stood, in the Latin church – for the Dominicans possessed no Uniate branch – the couple appealed personally to the pope, Pius X, for permission to withdraw from the Byzantine rite, which, in any case, as Catholics they had never experienced. The pope, faithful to the spirit of the canons, turned down their request. Shortly afterwards, a telegram inviting their presence at a family occasion caused them to return to Russia, which they did in time for the celebration of the Orthodox Christmas in January 1910. They reoccupied their enormous apartment in the newly constructed 'Jerusalem Court' on the Prečistenskii Boulevard – large enough, so it would later prove, to house a religious community of twenty – and there, that winter, they gave hospitality to a

certain Leonid Fe'dorov, still a seminarian but the future
Exarch of a Russian-rite Catholic church.

At this point I must digress to say something about
Fedorov whose life would be inseparably interwoven with
that of the Abrikosovs, and about, too, the ecclesiastical
entity over which he came to preside.[6] Leonid Fe'dorov was a
few months older than Abrikosov. Born in St Petersburg on 4
November 1879, his mother, a widow, ran a restaurant much
frequented by the religious philosopher Vladimir Sergeievič
Solov'ev.[7] According to Fedorov's biographer, Paul Mailleux
of the Russian College in Rome, it was through boyish conversations with his mother's distinguished customer that
Fe'dorov began to take his faith more seriously and, after
high school, entered the St Petersburg Ecclesiastical Academy,
housed as this was in a portion of the imposing Alexander
Nevsky monastery. But Solov'ev's apocalyptic ecclesiological
speculations included dreams of cooperation between the
tsar, as Christ's representative in his kingly office, and the
pope, his representative in the priestly office. Association
with him unsettled Fedorov's Orthodoxy. By 1902 he had
resolved to become a Catholic, something it was only politic
to do abroad. Quite apart from the unwillingness of the Latin
clergy in the Russian empire, chiefly Polish, to risk the State's
displeasure by receiving converts from the national Church,
such an action was technically (before 1905) a civil offence.
The Polish pastor of the Latin parish of SS Peter and Paul was
ready, though, to accompany the twenty-two year old across
the frontier, with a view to locating, in Austria-Hungary,
some kind of ecclesiastical burse which might enable him to
continue his studies for the priesthood in a Catholic context.

The obvious patron to approach was the celebrated if controversial Uniate Archbishop of Lvov in Austrian-ruled
Galicia, Andrey Szepticky (1865–1944).[8] Like many of the
landed aristocracy in the Hapsburg Ukraine, Szepticky's
family had passed over to the Latin rite, but Alexander (to
use his baptismal name) was intent on reviving for his people

the full patrimony of the Byzantine church. Hence his wide-ranging activities as bishop which extended to the reinvigor-ation of the liturgy and Church music, the rescue of historic objects, the founding of monasteries following the rule of the Constantinopolitan monastery of the Studion, and a pastoral outreach so successful that it soon gained him the dis-pleasure, for its possible political implications, of the imperial governments in both Petersburg and Vienna. In Petersburg they feared an autonomist movement in southern Russia, in Vienna the siren voices of pan-Slavism – though this did not prevent the Archduke Franz Ferdinand and his morganatic wife, the Duchess of Hohenberg (later assassinated at Sara-jevo) from choosing Szepticky as their confessor.

At Lvov, Fe'dorov was warmly welcomed and the arch-bishop provided him with a recommendation to take to Rome, where he became a Catholic amid the Baroque glories of the church of the Gesù. Pope Leo XIII sent him for his studies to the newly-founded seminary of Anagni, a hill-town in the southern Latium where Boniface VIII, promulgator of the bull *Unam Sanctam* on the salvific necessity of obedience to the Roman bishop, had been hit in the face by a supporter of the king of France. Later, Fe'dorov moved into Rome, partly to be nearer to Grottaferrata, the Greek-rite monastery on the slopes of the Alban hills, partly to meet the exigences of the tsar's consular officials, who were incensed at his edu-cation by the Anagni Jesuits. Threatened eventually with the withholding of his re-entry permit should he take Orders at all in the Church of Rome, he repaired in 1907 to the Swiss university city of Fribourg, where he passed himself off as an Italo-American, making use of his workmanlike but not en-tirely watertight hold on the mother-tongue of Dante.

In Petersburg, meanwhile, the liberalisation of the religious legislation of the empire which followed on the constitutional settlement of 1905 was having its effect.[9] A disciple of the Princess Volkonskaya's mother had conceived the idea of founding in the capital a Russian-rite Catholic parish. This was Natalya Sergeievna Utčakova, a high-society *grande dame*, a friend of the empress-mother Maria Feodorovna, and blessed accordingly with the right of *entrée* to government ministries. Although Uniate Catholicism remained illegal, the Minister of the Interior and President of the Council of Ministers, Pyotr Stolypin, promised to turn a blind eye to Mme Utčakova's schemes. A chapel was constructed in her townhouse, and a chaplain found in the person of Fr Alexis Zertčaninov, a former Orthodox priest who had come to Catholicism as a result of patristic research undertaken with a view to refuting the religious claims of the Russian 'Old Believers'. Mme Utčakova had retained Fr Zertčaninov, against the possibility of such a day, in the protective seclusion of her country villa on the Finnish border. By 1909 all was ready. But without authorisation for the actual celebration of cultus, she hesitated about opening shop. A stratagem was shortly found. The curate, Fr Eustafii Soussalev, had previously been himself an Old Believer. At Easter 1909 the following letter, signed by him, was duly despatched to Nicholas II.

> On the radiant feast of Christ's Resurrection, the Russian Old Believers in communion with the apostolic see of Rome, offer to the Most High their prayers for the health of your imperial Majesty, and for that of the Tsarevič.

The reply arrived by telegram:

> His Majesty thanks for their prayers the Old Believers in communion with the Holy See.[10]

And so the die was cast.

Canonically, the parish required an episcopal overseer, and Andrey Szepticky, whose Lvov archbishopric included in its title the defunct see of Kamenec-Podolsk, stranded behind the Russian frontier as this was by the westward extension of the tsarist empire in the eighteenth century, considered himself well qualified to be that person. It soon became clear that strong leadership was going to be needed if the Petersburg experiment were to survive and to extend itself. The Latin archbishop of Mohilev, in whose diocese Petersburg fell, viewed the venture with unease. In particular, he distrusted the ethos underlying the liturgical purism of its supporters, so different from the somewhat bastardised Latino–Orientalism familiar across the border in the Hapsburg Ukraine. In 1912, Fe'dorov, now an ordained monk, arrived back in Petersburg to find an uncertain situation. He had come directly from one of Szepticky's monastic foundations, Kameniza, in Bosnia. There he had acquired the conviction that whereas, to Western Catholics, an Oriental rite was simply a matter of worshipping in another language, saying different prayers and using different gestures, for the East, dogma and liturgy were one. Faith and rite made up together a seamless garment. The former, to change the metaphor, was incarnate in the latter, as spirit is incarnate in the flesh. He was, therefore, much relieved, when the Holy See, under pressure from both sides in the liturgical dispute, finally directed that the new parish's worship should differ not at all from that of the Synodal Church of Russia itself: *nec plus, nec minus, nec aliter*, as the Roman letter briskly put it. Not that the parish simply identified the Christian life with Christian worship. By 1913 it was animating an ambitious movement of assistance to the poor of the capital city, and had also started a modest theological magazine, *Slovo Istiny* ('The Word of Truth'). By this date it claimed in the vicinity of Petersburg some seven hundred souls.

To return to the Abrikosovs: we last encountered them in Fe'dorov's presence in Moscow in 1910. How had they been faring? In the course of 1911 they had developed what may be termed an apostolate of the *soirée*. Seated around the samovar, the couple, still barely thirty years of age, provided for their interested acquaintances an entire theological formation in miniature. Vladimir Vladimovič taught

214 Scribe of the Kingdom

philosophy and dogmatic theology, Anna Ivanovna dealt
with ascetical and mystical theology, and Church history.
Their materials were mostly Western, but, under the influence of their meeting with Fe'dorov, and impressed by his
enthusiasm for the Russian religious tradition, and the
Byzantine rite, their attitude was slowly changing. Little by
little they gravitated towards the idea of opening a chapel of
the Russian rite. Not that this implied any diminution of
respect for the Dominican Order to which they had been
attracted in the West. On the contrary, for in the years 1911–
12 they both sought profession as lay Dominicans in the
tertiary chapter based at the Muscovite church of St Louis des
Français. On aggregation to the chapter Anna Ivanovna,
anxious to honour the authoress of the *Dialogue*, took the
additional name Ekaterina Sienskaya, 'Catherine the Sienese'.
Becoming a lay Dominican can mean, according to choice,
little or much. For the Abrikosovs it meant much. They made
a private vow of permanent continence within marriage, and
drastically simplified their living arrangements, dispensing
with the help of all but a single servant. In the university
milieu to which most visitors to the household belonged, a
number of women students sought reception into the Catholic Church. Their families rarely approved. Anna Ivanovna
was to take them under her roof – literally. With bedrooms in
'Jerusalem Court', and inducted as Dominican tertiaries, it
was among this group, that, over the years 1913 to 1917,
the making of a full conventual sisterhood was gradually
prepared.

The outbreak of the First World War in August 1914 did
not, however, leave everyone's life quite so unchanged. Fr
Leonid, whose name had lain accusingly on the books of the
authorities since his student days, was promptly deported to
Siberia. This could be, but need not be, as bad as it sounds. In
Fe'dorov's case it was, in fact, a perfectly tolerable exile.
Those with sufficient means made the 'stages' across the
Urals at their own expense, travelling in the more comfort-

able carriages of the Trans-Siberian railway. Fe'dorov's destination was, in any case, only just beyond the Urals: Tobolsk, a picturesque town in pleasant countryside whose Orthodox seminary boasted a well-stocked theological library. With the liberal Revolution of March 1917, all restrictions on religious liberty were finally lifted, and Fe'dorov was unconditionally set free.

For the Abrikosovs and for Archbishop Szepticky, the few months' duration of the constitutional Republic seemed a golden time. Anna Ivanovna now put her plan into full operation. She would have a fully-fledged conventual priory of Dominican women, devoted to the intellectual apostolate, in the setting of a Byzantine liturgical life in the Russian tradition. The identity of the prioress was not in doubt. On the feast of St Dominic, 1917, the lady of the house became *Mother* Ekaterina Sienskaya, with her erstwhile fellow tertiaries now her religious subjects. The question of a Russian-rite chaplain had so far proved intractable, but with the announcement by Szepticky of a forthcoming visit to Petrograd, she saw her opportunity. She bundled her husband onto the train and, on the Sunday of All Saints, Metropolitan Andrey raised him to the sacred priesthood. Szepticky felt his own presence in Russia (he had been seized as a prisoner-of-war during the occupation of Galicia by the tsar's army), to be, at this juncture, providential. He proceeded to name Leonid Fe'dorov 'Exarch of the Greek-Catholic Church of Russia'. Summoned from Tobolsk, Fe'dorov arrived at Petrograd on Holy Saturday 1917, being received with full honours at the railway station by A. V. Kartashev, the last Procurator of the Holy Synod, who conveyed him to the archbishop's residence in a court carriage. The provisional government undertook to provide stipends for the exarchate's seven clergy – not that the newly-ordained Vladimir Vladimirovič had need of *that*. More important to the Abrikosovs was the fact that their activity was now public and, above all, officially recognised both by Church law and by that of the State. And in this context it was vital for the future that their aims and ideals should coincide as completely as possible with those of the new exarch, literally canonised as these were at a brief synod, held under Szepticky's presidency, at the end of May.

What were those aims and ideals? In no way were they proselytising, or either hostile to or even critical of Orthodoxy. Fe'dorov's overall objective was the corporate reconciliation of the Catholic and Orthodox Churches via that of their respective hierarchies. The mission of his little community was to be a mission of witness. Using a term from Scholastic philosophy he called it the 'exemplary cause' of reunion.[11] Canon 52 of the exarchate's constitution explicitly forbade priests in their preaching to enter upon controversial matters. They were simply to set forth Catholic doctrine in a positive frame of mind. This reflected the spirit of the Abrikosovs who had embraced Catholicism as agnostics engaged on a spiritual search, and not out of any dogmatic disagreement with Orthodoxy. In historical retrospect one might even venture the judgment that their eirenicism was in some respects excessive. A little more open-eyedness about certain deficiencies in the pre-Revolutionary Russian church might, without any diminution of charity, have better prepared them for the approaching *débacle*.[12] In his 1974 'Letter to the Third Sobor of the Russian Orthodox Church outside Russia' Alexander Solzhenitsyn wrote:

> Truth compels me to say that the condition of the Russian Church towards the beginning of the twentieth century, the long-standing, humiliating position of its clergy, the oppression by the government and the Church's identification with it, the loss of spiritual independence and the consequent loss of authority amongst the majority of the educated class and the mass of urban workers, and – worst of all – the shakiness of this authority even among the mass of the peasantry (how many proverbs there are which mock the clergy and how few which respect them!) – the condition of the Russian Church *was one of the chief reasons why the revolutionary events were irreversible*.[13]

The italics are Solzhenitsyn's.

I have mentioned that Fe'dorov arrived at Petrograd on Holy Saturday 1917. On Easter Monday of that year, a second traveller reached the Finland Station, with what results history records. This was, of course, Lenin. During the first years of Bolshevik rule, however, the unique experiment which Mother Ekaterina had created endured more or less unscathed. The day-to-day context of the sisters' work consisted of an intense liturgical and studious existence. Their worship was almost entirely Byzantine. The only modifications they made to Russian liturgical practice were adaptations of the Byzantine troparia for the invocation of a number of Western saints and *beati*, mainly those of the Dominican Order. They did, however, continue to use the Rosary of the Blessed Virgin, and they sang the *Salve, regina* (Hail, holy Queen) to the solemn Dominican tone, but in Russian translation, at the end of the liturgical day. Their music was of the somewhat operatic kind favoured in the Russian church from the later nineteenth century onwards. In fact a musician from the Moscow Opera House took their choir practices. Their library was meant to serve not only the nuns but also the needs of the parish. They added to it bound typescripts of their own, translations of Western spiritual books considered by them closest in ethos to Russian piety. With assistance from selected layfolk, they provided for young people an entire third-level education, ranging from mathematics, through the study of Russian history, to that of Eastern monasticism, intending thereby to counteract the influence of the new Communist University system. At a more prosaic level, they taught catechism classes, clandestinely after the official banning of religious education for those under eighteen. They also worked in kindergartens until this too was terminated by the State in 1922.[14]

Mother Ekaterina herself, as she entered her late thirties, was an imposing figure with whom other strong personalities found cooperation less than easy. Tall and powerful in build, her face is described as impressive, with a high forehead, a hooked nose, and penetrating eyes. In her relationships with other people, she avoided sentiment and familiarity. She expressed herself briefly and always to the point. For the sake of recollection and study she insisted on the meticulous observance of silence. In a word, she was glacial. Or, as one contemporary observer put it more chivalrously, with her one felt 'the cool of the mountain tops'. This, however, was not entirely a matter of personal temperament. Her two main concerns in governing her community were: first, a striving through *askêsis* and prayer for perfect discipleship; and second, a concentration on the community's goal so thorough that it would shut out everything irrelevant to that purpose. With Mother Ekaterina the decks were always stripped.

The impression of a certain puritan authoritarianism helps to account for the adverse criticism which she and her sisters endured. To the neighbouring Polish clergy she was 'the Russian pope-ess'; to a number of the Moscow Othodox her community was known as 'the Abrikosovian sectarianettes'. A comparison with Mrs Thatcher and her think-tank may not be altogether out of place! That some Orthodox should find her work alarming or at least distasteful is understandable. The reservations of the Polish clergy require further comment. With the creation of the exarchate, Mother Ekaterina had committed herself wholeheartedly to its chief aim: the restoration of communion between the Orthodox church of Russia and the see of Rome. In this new context she turned abruptly against the Latin rite which she had once petitioned a pope to let her enter. Her opposition to the Polish clergy was intensified by the outbreak of war between Russia and Poland in 1920, but of itself it antedated that painful event. Where Polish churchmen in Russia were concerned, she did not mince her words:

Hostility, narrow provincialism, together with an inborn hatred of the Eastern rite [she wrote] and an absurd desire to maintain a leading rôle in the Catholic Church of Russia, as well as the alien fantasy of latinising the Russian people.[15]

She fought this battle with every means in her power, and argued her case with whoever would listen, in Russia, abroad, in Rome. She would tolerate in Russia no Latin missionaries or Orders, unless they went over to the Eastern rite. She would accept no Latin bishops, but only the exarch. She would let no Latin churchman administer the funds of the Pontifical Aid Programme launched by Pius XI in the wake of the Civil War.[16] The Polish presence in Russia, much of it, historically, the creation of deportees, she stigmatised as a 'colonial Church'. And as to the idea of a Russian-speaking Latin rite she wrote it off in a single English word: 'nonsense'. A painful contrast is presented by her rather productive early relations with the Communists. 'What an interesting enchanting personality your little mother is', exclaimed an ideological re-education officer to one of the sisters. 'It's just a shame that she isn't a Communist.'![17]

Mother Ekaterina also enjoyed excellent relations with many of the Orthodox clergy, as indeed did the exarch himself.[18] In 1919, the Orthodox Metropolitan Benjamin of Petrograd, together with the exarch, made a joint protest against Bolshevik attacks on the Church, and they further projected a common course of apologetics to counter atheistic propaganda. Such relations had their analogues in Moscow as well: in June 1922, after the placing under house arrest of the patriarch Tikhon, a presentation was arranged for him on his name-day as a public manifestation of solidarity. Fr Vladimir was invited to take part, not least to compensate for the absence of the many Orthodox clergy who had gone over to the collaborationist body known as the 'Living Church'. The patriarch embraced the Uniate priest warmly, and sent his blessing to his wife's sisterhood. In her correspondence, which mentions scores of Orthodox ecclesiastics, never once does Mother Ekaterina speak of any of them with acerbity.

At the end of that summer, Fr Vladimir was expelled from the Soviet Union along with a distinguished company of Orthodox philosophers and theologians – Berdyaev, Frank, Bulgakov, Lossky – and passes out of our story though he lived on in France well into his eighties dying at Meudon, outside Paris, as late as 1966. In his absence, and in the face of the growing persecution inflicted on Orthodoxy, Mother Ekaterina's sympathy for the Russian church, previously less marked, perhaps, than that of the exarch and the Petrograd parish at large, became noticeably stronger. The official Church was, she declared a 'national bulwark', a 'bastion of all that is best in Russia'. She viewed with mounting concern the development of an anti-hierarchical current, the progress of Protestant sectarianism, and above all, the speedy advance of unbelief, even among children. Her nights were haunted by the spectre of a new generation formed solely on Communist teaching.

Her spiritual counsels became more impassioned, more dramatic, more Dostoevskyan. She interrupted a choir practice to tell her community:

> In Russia Christ wants now only one kind of sacrifice. Only self-sacrifice ... will content him ... An ardent spiritual life, a pure faith, a will of iron ... And I mean by that a love which asks nothing, but which gives everything.[19]

Called on to comfort her sisters and the parishioners, she herself felt the acute loneliness of separation from her husband. An image of the Madonna which reached her from the Princess Volkonskaya consoled her, but at the same time she wrote out repeatedly, almost incantationally, the key-word of the seventeenth-century French Jesuit Jean-Pierre de Caussade's treatise on abandonment to divine Providence, '*abandon, abandon, abandon*'. Financially, the community depended now on assistance from the Pontifical Mission. To begin with, she had deplored the entrusting of this programme to, of all people, an American Jesuit.

> Do they realise at Rome [she wrote] the fear and revulsion here for Jesuits? ... This ... Order ... cannot enter Russia. Its arrival will be the ruination of all our work.[20]

But she soon came to appreciate the worth of the young Bostonian, Edmund Walsh, and he hers. However her initial reaction was thus far correct: the peremptory expulsion of the Mission by the Soviet authorities as a bourgeois-clerical ploy signalled the coming storm which would indeed carry her work away.[21]

In February 1923 the exarch was arrested and condemned to ten years' imprisonment, at first in the relatively mild setting of the Sokolniki prison, where he managed to write two catechisms and to hold ecumenical conferences with the Orthodox, and then in the much severer Lefort prison outside Moscow. In November of the same year, Mother Ekaterina was herself arrested together with eight other sisters, and placed in the dreaded Lubjanka prison, deprived of all human contact, in a windowless cell, with a permanently burning electric light. After four months, the sisters were transferred *en bloc* to the Butyrskii prison, where they could enjoy a degree of mutual contact. There they partially recreated their religious life, singing the Offices from memory, in low voices. On 30 April, the foundress' name-day three sisters made solemn profession into her hands, and the others made an act of self-offering for Russia. In May they heard of their trial, conducted in *absentia*, as of their sentencing under articles 61 and 62 of the then Soviet penal code. These articles covered any relations of advantage with the international bourgeoisie, together with the organisation of sedition, armed uprising and espionage. Mother Ekaterina was convicted on four counts: illegal diplomatic correspondence with foreigners; relations with the Pontifical Aid Mission and the receiving of its monies; maintaining an illegal school; and membership of a religious community whose existence was contrary to the statutes of the Soviet State. The sentence was deportation to Siberia.

Initially, her exile was fixed for Western Siberia, the Tobolsk – no less – where Leonid Fe'dorov had once brushed up on Orthodox theology. She, however, was not at liberty, but incarcerated, though under a mitigated prison régime. Nonetheless, it was harsh enough to take its toll on her physical health, and her activities were hampered by months of illness at a time. Despite her difficulties, she managed to gather information about the whereabouts of the other sisters, and resumed her spritual motherhood by correspondence. She taught reading and writing to those of her fellow prisoners who were illiterate, taking them through Pushkin, Gogol and Tolstoy. They repaid her by sending in fruit to improve her diet and flowers for her cell from their work in the fields. The prison authorities commented on the dignity of her bearing and the condition of her cell: more like a court lady than a prisoner.

In this prison life, her spiritual personality seems to have attained its full flowering, thanks to union with God by assimilation to Christ in his passion. At the end of 1929 she was transferred to Yaroslavl, where she would remain until shortly before her death. Her correspondence ceased, probably from fear of drawing down suspicion on the addressees. Ironically, she was thrown together with a Polish prelate, Teofil Skalski, apostolic administrator of the Latin diocese of Žitomir, but all anti-Polonism had drained out of her system. He wrote later of her 'neat, aesthetic and even festal appearance', and her 'complete simplicity and dignity'.[22] She taught the other inmates the Psalms, and the use of the English language, and copied out newspaper articles she thought important.

Late in 1931 she developed cancer of the breast. Taken to the prison hospital of the Butyrskii she was operated on, but without much hope of success. On account of her serious condition she was now released, though placed under the embargo of the so-called 'régime of minus 12', in other words, with an accompanying prohibition order on residence in the six largest Russian cities, together with the seaports. She was, however, permitted visits of ten days' length to Moscow, and the final testimonies to her come from these excursions. She remained under surveillance, and, at a meeting with women students in the house of a friend, was once again arrested in August 1932. Charged with the dissemination of religious propaganda, she was sent back to Yaroslavl, but to an isolation cell. Her health deteriorated. In the course of 1935 the cancer reached her face. In the spring of 1936 she was brought back to the Butyrskii Hospital, where she died on 23 July of that year. Four days later her body was cremated by order of the prison authorities and her ashes interred at a place unknown. No priest prayed; no friend was present. The exarch was already dead. Having served eight years of his sentence, mostly in the Solovki Islands in the White Sea, he had been released on the condition that he remain in northern Siberia. He had died in March of the previous year at a town of the tundra, Viatka, later renamed 'Kirov' in honour of Stalin's assistant. The fate of only one other member of Mother Ekaterina's community is certainly known.

Although Anna Ivanovna's career (if that is the word) was marked by human frailty, it is not entirely unworthy of a mention in the Church's history. Though she was in high degree a self-willed, headstrong and even impulsive woman, she was also a deeply religious one. Her courage, which existed finally in the mode of sacrifice, her love for the Church, and her concern for her fellow human beings – even, ultimately, for Poles! – were palpable. Her boundless energy and her somewhat domineering temperament were pitfalls –

yet they were also presuppositions for the success of the enterprise she undertook.

Whereas there were many sisterhoods devoted to social and charitable works in the Russian Orthodoxy of the nineteenth century, there was none, or so it would appear, consecrated to the intellectual apostolate which she made her own.[23] At the same time, she was attempting an experiment in ecumenism, the living out of the way of life of an Order of the Latin Middle Ages within the context of an Eastern church, preserving that Order's own ethos and elements of its devotional life, while transplanting these to the setting of the Byzantine-Slav liturgy and its spiritual world. That, as the child of a liberal and even secularised milieu who had found her way to Christianity through Western Catholicism this required of her a further education in Eastern Orthodoxy itself only added to the magnitude of her self-set task.[24]

We know that many Orthodox view with profound suspicion all attempts at Uniatism no matter what the circumstances. Yet not all of Mother Ekaterina's Orthodox contemporaries saw matters in this light. Indeed, the Moscow patriarchate, in the person of its highest officer, saw fit to bless her work. No doubt the menace of the Bolshevik persecution of the churches drew them together. It is a Christian truth of wide application that out of suffering, borne in an evangelical spirit, does the desert bloom. The suffering which both purified and warmed Mother Ekaterina's heart may also provide a valuable education of feeling for those involved in the ecumenical task today.

Notes

Chapter X: Bulgakov and Sophiology

1. On Bulgakov's life, see W. F. Crum, 'Sergius N. Bulgakov: from Marxism to Sophiology', *Saint Vladimir's Theological Quarterly* 27 (1983), pp. 3–26.
2. Cited in J. Pain and N. Zernov (ed.), *A Bulgakov Anthology* (London 1976), p. 3.
3. For Bulgakov's literary output, see K. Naumov (ed.), *Bibliographie des oeuvres de Serge Boulgakov* (Paris 1984).
4. C. Graves, *The Holy Spirit in the Theology of Sergei Bulgakov* (Geneva 1972), p. 3.
5. L. Bouyer, 'An Introduction to the Theme of Wisdom and Creation in the Tradition', *Le Messager orthodoxe* 98 (1985), pp. 149–61.
6. For their inter-connexion, see C. Graves, *The Holy Spirit in the Theology of Sergei Bulgakov* (Geneva 1972), p. 3.
7. S. Bulgakov, *Agnets Bozhii* (Paris 1933), p. 122.
8. C. Graves, *The Holy Spirit in the Theology of Sergei Bulgakov* (Geneva 1972), p. 7.
9. See C. Lialine, 'Le débat sophiologique', *Irénikon* XIII (1936), pp. 168–205.
10. S. Bulgakov, *Svet nevechernii* (Moscow 1917). For example, see p. 212: Sophia is 'a special fourth hypostasis of another order ... the beginning of a new creaturely multihypostaticity.'
11. S. Bulgakov, 'Ipostas i ipostasnost', in *Sbornik Skatei, Posviashchenniikh Petru Berngardovichu Struve* (Prague 1925), pp. 353–71.
12. In the essay, 'Die Lehre von der göttlichen Weisheit (Sophia-Lehre)', in the *Handbuch der Ostkirchlichenkunde* edited by Endre von Ivánka (Düsseldorf 1971), pp. 143–56, sophiology is described as 'neurussiche Gnosis': a confusion of natural, philosophical knowledge with the supernatural knowledge of faith, plus elements of mysticism both natural and supernatural as well. However, sophiology conceived as an 'artistic and intuitive' approach to the eternal beauty disclosed in the creation is treated more kindly.

13. S. Bulgakov, *The Wisdom of God. A Brief Summary of Sophiology* (London 1937), p. 18.
14. B. Newman, 'Sergius Bulgakov and the Theology of Divine Wisdom', *Saint Vladimir's Theological Quarterly* 22 (1978), p. 53.
15. S. Bulgakov, *The Wisdom of God. A Brief Summary of Sophiology* (London 1937), p. 34.
16. C. Andronikof, 'La problématique sophianique', *Le Messager orthodoxe* 98 (1985), pp. 46–7.
17. K. Naumov (ed.), *Bibliographie des oeuvres de Serge Boulgakov* (Paris 1984), Preface, p. 40.
18. L. Zander, *Bog i Mir* I (Paris 1946), pp. 194–5.
19. S. Bulgakov, *Ikona i ikonopochitanie* (Paris 1931), pp. 51–2.
20. C. Andronikof, 'La problématique sophianique', *Le Messager orthodoxe* 98 (1985), p. 56.
21. B. Newman, 'Sergius Bulgakov and the Theology of Divine Wisdom', *Saint Vladimir's Theological Quarterly* 22 (1978), p. 73.

Chapter XI: Balthasar and his Christology

1. On 23 June 1984; an English-language account is provided in *L'Osservatore Romano* for 23 July 1984.
2. H. U. von Balthasar, *Herrlichkeit. Eine theologische Ästhetik* (Einsiedeln 1961–69); *The Glory of God* (Et: Edinburgh and San Francisco 1983).
3. Balthasar's own estimate of his life and work is in *Rechenschaft* (Einsiedeln 1965). The most thorough study of his theology to date is A. Moda, *Hans Urs von Balthasar* (Bari 1976); for his Christology see also G. Marchesi, *La Cristologia di Hans Urs von Balthasar* (Rome 1977).
4. See H. U. von Balthasar, *Romano Guardini. Reform aus dem Ursprung* (Munich 1970): the title is significant.
5. See especially H. U. von Balthasar, *Herlichkeit*, III, p. 1.
6. H. de Lubac, 'Un testimonio di Cristo. Hans Urs von Balthasar', *Humanitas* 20 (1965), p. 853.
7. H. U. von Balthasar 'Die Metaphysik Erich Pyrzwara', *Schweizer Rundschau* 33 (1933), pp. 488–9. Pryzwara convinced himself of the importance of the analogy of being in theology.
8. Balthasar has compared the 'evangelicalism' of the *Exercises* to that not only of Barth but of Luther! See *Rechenschaft* (Einsiedeln 1965), pp. 7–8.

9. See R. Aubert's summary of the *Nouvelle Théologie* in H. Vorgrimler, *Bilan de la théologie du vingtième siècle* (Paris 1971), I, pp. 457–60.

10. Pius XII, *Humani Generis*, pp. 14–17.

11. Stressed by B. Mondin, 'Hans Urs von Balthasar e l'estetica teologica' in *I grandi teologie del secolo ventesimo* (Turin 1969), I, pp. 268–9.

12. H. de Lubac spoke of Balthasar enjoying 'una specie di connaturalità' with the Fathers; but de Lubac has never suffered from that tiresome suspension of all criticism of patristic theology which is sometimes found, not least in England. In *Liturgie Cosmique: Maxime le Confesseur* (Paris 1947) de Lubac points out that the Fathers stand at the beginning (only) of Christian thought, pp. 7–8.

13. H. U. von Balthasar, *Erster Blick auf Adrienne von Speyr* (Einsiedeln 1967), with full bibliography.

14. H. U. von Balthasar, *Parole et mystère chez Origène* (Paris 1957); *Présence et pensée. Essai sur la philosophie religieuse de Grégoire de Nysse* (Paris 1942); *Kosmische Liturgie. Höhe und Krise des griechischen Weltbilds bei Maximus Confessor* (Freiburg 1941).

15. H. U. von Balthasar, *Bernanos* (Cologne 1954).

16. H. U. von Balthasar, *Apokalypse der deutschen Seele* (Salzburg 1937–39).

17. H. U. von Balthasar, *Wahrheit. Wahrheit der Welt* (Einsiedeln 1947).

18. Thus H. U. von Balthasar, *Herrlichkeit*, III, I.

19. H. U. von Balthasar, *Theodramatik* (Einsiedeln 1973–1976).

20. *Theologik III: Der Geist der Wahrheit* (Einsiedeln 1987) completes a study Balthasar begin with *Wahrheit* (Einsiedeln 1947), reissued as *Theologik I. Wahrheit der Welt* at Einsiedeln in 1985, and continued in *Theologik II. Wahrheit Gottes* (Einsiedeln 1985).

21. H. U. von Balthasar, 'Der Ort der Theologie' in *Verbum Caro* (Einsiedeln 1960).

22. H. U. von Balthasar, *Karl Barth. Darstellung und Deutung seiner Theologie* (Cologne 1951).

23. By Professor T. F. Torrance, to the present author in conversation.

24. H. U. von Balthasar, *Karl Barth. Darstellung und Deutung seiner Theologie* (Cologne 1951).

25. Pascal, *Pensées* 449 in the Lafuma numbering.

26. See H. U. von Balthasar, *Schleifung der Bastionen* (Einsiedeln 1952); *Wer ist ein Christ?* (Einsiedeln 1965); *Cordula oder der Ernstfall* (Einsiedeln 1966). The notion that, because Christian existence has its own *form*, which is founded on the prior *form* of Christ, Christian proclamation does not (strictly speaking) need philosophical or social scientific mediations, is the clearest link between Balthasar and Pope John Paul II. See, for instance, the papal address to the South American bishops at Puebla.

27. H. U. von Balthasar, *Herrlichkeit*, I, pp. 123–658.

28. H. U. von Balthasar, *Einfaltungen. Auf Wegen christlicher Einigung* (Munich 1969).

29. Cf. A. Nichols, *The Art of God Incarnate: Theology and Image in Christian Tradition* (London 1981), pp. 105–52.

30. For an excellent analysis of Balthasar's twofold Christological 'evidence', see A. Moda, *Hans Urs von Balthasar* (Bari 1976), pp. 305–410.

31. H. Vorgrimler, *Bilan de la Théologie du vingtième siècle* (Paris 1971), I, pp. 686ff.

32. We can say that, had Balthasar been St Thomas, he would have begun the *Tertia pars* of the *Summa* at Question 36: *de manifestatione Christi nati*.

33. 'Mysterium Paschale', in H. U. von Balthasar, *Mysterium Salutis* (Einsiedeln 1962), III, 2, pp. 133–58.

34. H. U. von Balthasar, *Glaubhaft ist nur Liebe* (Einsiedeln 1963), p. 57.

35. 'Mysterium Paschale', in H. U. von Balthasar, *Mysterium Salutis* (Einsiedeln 1962), III, pp. 227–55. Balthasar speaks of a 'contemplative Holy Saturday' as the centre of theology, in contra-distinction to G. W. F. Hegel's 'speculative Good Friday'.

36. See J. Chaine, 'La Descente du Christ aux enfers', *Dictionnaire de la Bible Supplément* II.

37. G. Marchesi, *La Cristologia di Hans Urs von Balthasar* (Rome 1977), p. 351.

38. The French translation of *Herrlichkeit* is entitled 'La Gloire et la Croix'.

39. Newman's affirmation in Verse Four of the angelic chorus in the *Dream of Gerontius* that what refined flesh and blood in the Incarnation and Atonement was a 'higher gift than grace' recalls Balthasar's insistence that the divine Son did not come primarily to teach (*verum*), or to help us (*bonum*) but to show us himself (*pulchrum*).

Chapter XII: Adrienne von Speyr and the Mystery of the Atonement

1. H. U. von Balthasar, *First Glance at Adrienne von Speyr* (Et: San Francisco, Calif., 1981), p. 19.
2. Ibid., p. 23.
3. Ibid., p. 33.
4. Ibid., p. 35.
5. A. von Speyr, *Kreuz und Hölle I. Die Passionen* (Einsiedeln 1966). These texts are the fruit of her experiences on Good Friday and Holy Saturday in the years 1941–63.
6. For a full bibliography, see H. U. von Balthasar, *First Glance at Adrienne von Speyr* (Et: San Francisco, Calif., 1981), pp. 104–10.
7. Ibid., p. 36; pp. 87–90.
8. Ibid., p. 67.
9. B. Albrecht, *Eine Theologie des Katholischen. Einführung in das Werk Adrienne von Speyrs. I Durchblick in Texten* (Einsiedeln 1972).
10. Ibid., pp. 90–2.
11. Ibid., pp. 92–3.
12. A. von Speyr, *Confession: The Encounter with Christ in Penance* (Et: London 1964).
13. B. Albrecht, *Eine Theologie des Katholischen. Einführung in das Werk Adrienne von Speyrs. I Durchblick in Texten* (Einsiedeln 1972).
14. Ibid., pp. 93–6.
15. Ibid., p. 96.
16. Ibid., p. 97.
17. Ibid., p. 102.
18. A. von Speyr, *Handmaid of the Lord* (Et: New York, N.Y., 1955).
19. H. U. von Balthasar, *First Glance at Adrienne von Speyr* (Et: San Francisco, Calif., 1981), pp. 51–4.
20. B. Albrecht, *Eine Theologie des Katholischen. Einführung in das Werk Adrienne von Speyrs. I Durchblick in Texten* (Einsiedeln 1972), pp. 99–100.
21. Ibid., pp. 100–2.
22. Ibid., p. 109.
23. Ibid., pp. 122–3.
24. Ibid., p. 126.
25. H. U. von Balthasar, *Mysterium Paschale* (Et: Edinburgh

1990); cf. *idem.*, *First Glance at Adrienne von Speyr* (Et: San Francisco, Calif., 1981), p. 13.

26. See 'La théologie de la Descente aux enfers', in H. U. von Balthasar, G. Chantraine, S. Scola (eds), *La Mission ecclésiale d'Adrienne von Speyr* (Paris 1986), pp. 151–60.

27. See, for example, A. Nichols, *From Newman to Congar. The Idea of Doctrinal Development from the Victorians to the Second Vatican Council* (Edinburgh 1990), pp. 190–3.

Chapter XIII: *Walter Kasper and his Theological Programme*

1. W. Kasper, *The God of Jesus Christ* (Et: London 1984. Originally published Mainz 1982).

2. W. Kasper, *Jesus the Christ* (Et: London 1976. Originally published Mainz 1974).

3. 'Ratzinger on the Faith: a Response', *New Blackfriars* LXVI, 780 (June 1985), *passim*. For an alternative view: see A. Nichols, 'The Pope and his Critics', *The Tablet* (9 March 1985), p. 244; *idem*, 'In Support of Cardinal Ratzinger', *The Tablet* (20 July 1985), p. 749.

4. See E. Stolz *et al.*, 'Beitrage zur Geschichte der Universitat, besonders der katholisch-theologischen Fakultät in Tübingen', *Theologische Quartalschrift* 108 (1927), pp. 1–220.

5. Ibid., pp. 77–133.

6. See J. R. Geiselmann, *Die katholische Tübingen Schule: ihre theologische Eigenart* (Frieburg 1964). And cf. W. Kasper, *Jesus the Christ* (Et: London 1976), p. 9. Geiselmann writes: 'In contradistinction to many contemporary works on Jesus, they [the Tübingen theologians] had no doubt that that origin [the origin of Christianity in Jesus Christ] which is still normative for us, was accessible only through biblical and ecclesiastical tradition. They knew that we could dispense with that tradition only at the cost of a severe impoverishment of our resources. They differed from the neo-scholastic theology of their time in their parallel conviction that tradition had to be handed on as something living; that is, in conjunction and confrontation with the comments and questions of a particular time.'

7. P. Hünermann, 'Der Reflex des deutschen Idealismus in der Theologie der katholischen Tübingen Schule', *Philosophisches Jahrbuch der Görres-Gesellschaft* 72 (1964–65), pp. 161–79.

8. L. Lohmann, *Die Philosophie der Offenberung bei J. S. von Drey* (Frieburg 1953); P. Weindel, *Das Verhältnis von Glau-*

ben und Wissen in der Theologie F. A. Staudenmaiers (Dusseldorf 1940).

9. E. Klinger, 'Tübingen School', *Sacramentum Mundi* VI, pp. 318–20.
10. For Kasper's own critique of Neo-Scholasticism, see W. Kasper, *The Methods of Dogmatic Theology* (Et: Shannon 1969), chapter 2.
11. J. R. Geiselmann, *Lebendiger Glaube aus geheiligter Überlieferung. J. A. Möhler und die katholische Tübinger Schule* (Mainz 1972); H. Tristram, 'J. A. Moehler et J. H. Newman', *Revue des Sciences philosophiques et theologiques* XXVII (1938), pp. 184–204.
12. The Tübingen School did not suffer from *uncritical* openness: thus Staudenmaier attacked Hegel, Möhler disputed with L. Bautain and F. C. Baur, while J. E. Kuhn criticised D. F. Strauss.
13. W. Kasper, *Die Lehre von der Tradition in der römischen Schule* (Frieburg 1962).
14. See, for example, L. Scheffczyk, *Kursänderung des Glaubens? Theologische Gründe zur Entscheidung im Fall Küng* (Stein am Rhein 1980); Küng's critics seem borne out on this point by C. M. LaCugna's exhaustive investigation in her *The Theological Methodology of Hans Küng* (Chicago, Ill., 1982).
15. W. Kasper, *Die Lehre von der Tradition in der römischen Schule* (Frieburg 1962), pp. 420–2. And cf. J. R. Geiselmann, *Lebendiger Glaube aus geheiligter Überlieferung. J. A. Möhler und die katholische Tübinger Schule* (Mainz 1972), p. viii.
16. G. Perrone, *Il Protestantesimo e la regola di fede* (Rome 1853), II. c. I, a.2, p. 41.
17. W. Kasper, *Das Absolute in der Geschichte. Philosophie und Theologie der Geschichte in der Spätphilosophie Schellings* (Mainz 1965).
18. But see R. Gray-Smith, *God in the Philosophy of Schelling* (London 1933). The most painless way for an English reader to approach Schelling is, perhaps, by way of Coleridge: see, for example, A. C. Dunstan, 'The German influence on Coleridge', *Modern Language Review* 19 (1923), pp. 183–200.
19. X. de Tilliette, *Schelling. Une Philosophie en devenir* (Paris 1970), I, pp. 24–7.
20. J. W. Rathburn and F. Burwick, 'Paul Tillich and the philosophy of Schelling', *International Philosophical Quarterly* 4 (1964), pp. 373–93.

21. J. Habermas, *Das Absolute und die Geschichte: von der Zweispältigkeit in Schellings Denken* (Bonn 1954).
22. This interpretation of Schelling was first clearly stated by H. Fuhrmans in *Schellings letzte Philosophie. Die negative und positive Philosophie im Einsatz des Spätidealismus* (Bonn 1940).
23. Cf. W. Schultz, *Die Vollendung des Deutschen Idealismus in der Spätphilosophie Schellings* (Stuttgart 1955), pp. 86–7; 300–7.
24. X. de Tilliette, *Schelling. Une Philosophie en devenir* (Paris 1970), I, p. 50.
25. W. Kasper, *Das Absolute in der Geschichte, Philosophie und Theologie der Geschichte in der Spätphilosophie Schellings* (Mainz 1965).
26. W. Kasper, *The Methods of Dogmatic Theology* (Et: Shannon 1969. Originally published Munich 1967).
27. Ibid., pp. 42–3.
28. W. Kasper, *The God of Jesus Christ* (Et: London 1984. Originally published Mainz 1982), p. ix.
29. W. Kasper, *The Methods of Dogmatic Theology* (Et: Shannon 1969. Originally published Munich 1967), pp. 3–4.
30. W. Kasper, *The God of Jesus Christ* (Et: London 1984. Originally published Mainz 1982), p. 15.
31. Ibid.
32. Ibid., p. 316.
33. I. Berlin, *Two Concepts of Liberty* (Oxford 1958).
34. W. Kasper, *The God of Jesus Christ* (Et: London 1984. Originally published Mainz 1982), p. 15.
35. J. Ratzinger, 'Loi de l'Eglise et liberté du chrétien', Service culturel de l'Ambassade de France près la Saint-Siège, (Centre d'Etudes Saint-Louis de France, Rome, 24 November 1983). Ratzinger's account is indebted for its exegetical and theological foundations to D. Nestle, *Eleutheria. Studien zum Wesen der Freiheit bei den Griechen und im Neuen Testament* (Tübingen 1967), and to E. Coreth, 'Zur Problemgeschichte menschlicher Freiheit', *Zeitschrift für katholische Theologie* 94 (1972), pp. 258–89.
36. Ibid.

Chapter XIV: Lonergan's Method in Theology *and the Theory of Paradigms*

1. Commissione Teologico Internazionale, 'L'unità della fede e il pluralismo teologico', *Enchiridion Vaticanum* IV, sub die 11 October 1972.
2. B. Lonergan, *Method in Theology* (London 1972, 1973²).
3. Ibid., p. 3.
4. Ibid., p. 3.
5. Thomas Aquinas, *Summa Theologiae*, Ia, q.1, a.2.c.
6. B. Lonergan, *Insight: An Essay on Human Understanding* (London 1957).
7. The summary of *Insight's* transcendental method is given in *Method in Theology*.
8. See Roger Scruton's interpretation of the 'Critique of Judgment' in *Kant* (Oxford 1982), p. 87.
9. See B. Reardon, 'Maurice Blondel and the philosophy of action' in B. Reardon, *Liberalism and Tradition: Aspects of Catholic Thought in Nineteenth Century France* (Cambridge 1975). Thus in Blondel's terminology action is man's spiritual existence as manifested in every phase of his being. Investigation of it, however, must reach back beyond all specific articulations of the understanding and the will to the point indeed where they both have a common origin in the primal *élan* of spirit itself, since it is there that all human activity has its source and from which it derives its strength.
10. B. Lonergan, *Method in Theology* (London 1972, 1973²).
11. Post-Newmanian attempts to identify the dynamic structure of doctrinal development are discussed in J. H. Walgrave, *Unfolding Revelation* (London 1972), pp. 332–47.
12. Thomas Aquinas, *Summa Theologiae*. Ia, q.1, a.1, ad ii.
13. B. Lonergan, *Method in Theology* (London 1972, 1973²).
14. Ibid., p. 39.
15. Ibid., p. 105.
16. Ibid., p. 12. But the metaphor may not do justice to Lonergan's meaning: the 'outer word' is at once extrinsic to the essential God-man relationship and yet at the same time plays a 'rôle' in constituting it. Yet the frequently 'Buddhist' sounding language used in *Method* exemplifies von Balthasar's basic point that where the concept of revelation is not adequately controlled by the 'objective form' of revelation in Christ, the sense of revelation may drift off into a diffuse mysticism which

is not properly Christian at all. See H. U. von Balthasar, *Love Alone: The Way of Revelation* (London 1968), pp. 43–50.

17. On the rise of theological specialisation, see Y. Congar, *A History of Theology* (Et: New York 1968), pp. 165–76; and on the dislocation caused by the prizing apart of historical and dogmatic theology, M. Schoof, *A Survey of Catholic Theology 1800–1970* (New York, N.Y., 1970), pp. 35–7.

18. B. Lonergan, *Method in Theology* (London 1972, 1973²), p. 126.

19. Ibid., p. 271.

20. B. Lonergan, *Insight: An Essay on Human Understanding* (London 1957), p. 299.

21. Ibid., p. 311.

22. Ibid., pp. 326–33.

23. B. Lonergan, *Method in Theology* (London 1972, 1973²), p. 126.

24. Commissione Teologico Internazionale, 'L'unità della fede e il pluralismo teologico' *Enchiridion Vaticanum* I, sub die 11 October 1972.

25. Not that these formal authorities have always been spoken of in the same way (e.g. 'magisterium') or even explicitly at all (e.g. 'Christian experience') in the history of theology.

26. B. Lonergan, *Methods in Theology* (London 1972, 1973²), virtually *passim*; but see especially, pp. 271–80 and 326–9.

27. One thinks here of R. G. Collingwood's remarks on the major effects of putting one question rather than another to one's materials.

28. See F. Ferré, 'Mapping the Logic of Models in Science and Theology', *The Christian Scholar* 46 (1963).

29. On the crucial rôle of metaphor see P. Wheelwright, *Metaphor and Reality* (Bloomington, Ind., 1962), and for an application to theology, A. Farrer, *The Glass of Vision* (London 1948).

30. I am indebted here to T. S. Kuhn, *The Structure of Scientific Revolutions* (Chicago, Ill., 1962; 1970²). The second edition of this book is a good deal more realist than the first; to maintain a sense of objectivity in the exploration of revelation (theology as *scientia*), it is necessary to avoid an idealist understanding of both Kuhn on paradigm and Collingwood on question. For a discussion of these important nuances, see, especially for T. S. Kuhn, I. G. Barbour, *Myths, Models and Paradigms: The Nature of Scientific and Religious Language* (London 1974); and for the 'logic of question and answer', M. Krausz (ed.)

Critical Essays on the Philosophy of R. G. Collingwood (Oxford 1973), pp. 222–40.
31. E. Schillebeeckx, *Revelation and Theology* (London 1967), pp. 155–6.

Chapter XVI: Chesterton and Modernism

1. G. K. Chesterton, *The Victorian Age of Literature* (London 1913), p. 11.
2. George Tyrrell, cited in M. D. Petre, *Autobiography and Life of George Tyrrell* (London 1912), II, p. 350.
3. Cited in E. Poulat, *Intégrisme et catholicisme intégral* (Paris 1969), pp. 119–21. See translation in L. R. Kurtz, *The Politics of Heresy: The Modernist Crisis in Roman Catholicism* (Berkeley, Calif., 1986), p. 162.
4. See Alzina Dale, *The Outline of Sanity: A Biography of G. K. Chesterton* (Grand Rapids, Mich., 1982), p. 103.
5. Jacques Maritain, *Anti-moderne* (Paris 1922).
6. Jacques Maritain, *Trois Réformateurs: Luther, Descartes, Rousseau* (Paris 1925).
7. G. K. Chesterton, *The Well and the Shallows* (London 1935), p. 40.
8. Ibid., p. 119.
9. G. K. Chesterton, *The Daily News*, 2 January 1902, as cited by Lynette Hunter, *G. K. Chesterton: Explorations in Allegory* (London 1979), p. 10.
10. G. K. Chesterton, 'The Staleness of Modernism', *Church Socialist Quarterly* 8 (1909), pp. 199–200.
11. Ibid., p. 201.
12. Ibid., p. 202.
13. G. K. Chesterton, *The Defendant* (London 1901), p. 7.
14. G. K. Chesterton, *The Well and the Shallows* (London 1935), p. 246.
15. Pope John Paul II, *Sollicitudo rei socialis*, 15.
16. N. Boyle, 'Understanding Thatcherism', *New Blackfriars* 69, 318 (July-August 1988), pp. 307–24.
17. Cited in Robert Speaight, *George Bernanos: A Study of the Man and the Writer* (London 1973), pp. 178–9. See also Jacques Maritain, *Une opinion sur Charles Maurras et le devoir des Catholiques* (Paris 1926), and *La Primauté du spirituel* (Paris 1927).
18. John Coates, *Chesterton and the Edwardian Cultural Crisis* (Hull 1984).

19. G. K. Chesterton, *What's Wrong with the World* (London 1910), p. 24.

20. G. K. Chesterton, *The Thing* (London 1929), p. 93.

21. George Tyrrell, *Mediaevalism* (London 1908, 1920), p. 119.

22. Michael Mason, *The Centre of Hilarity* (London 1959), p. 124. See also Alzina Dale, *The Outline of Sanity: A Biography of G. K. Chesterton* (Grand Rapids, Mich), p. 286.

23. *The Times*, 26 August 1988.

24. *The Times*, 27 August 1988.

25. G. K. Chesterton, *The Well and the Shallows* (London 1935), p. 15.

26. H. Hensley Henson, Bishop of Durham, as cited in J. Barnes, *Ahead of his Age. Bishop Barnes of Birmingham* (London 1979), p. 196.

27. F. Woodlock, *Modernism and the Christian Church* (London 1925), p. 28. I must thank Mr Aidan Mackey for drawing my attention to this work, and for loaning me his copy.

28. J. A. T. Robinson, *The Priority of John* (London 1985).

29. François Dreyfus, *Jésus, savait-il qu'il était Dieu?* (Paris 1987).

30. John Henry Newman, *Essays on Miracles* (London 1870, 1890), pp. 4–5.

31. G. K. Chesterton, 'Preface' in F. Woodlock, *Modernism and the Christian Church* (London 1925), p. vi.

32. George Tyrrell, 'Ecclesiastical Development', *The Month* 90 (1897), p. 388.

33. G. K. Chesterton, *St Thomas Aquinas* (London 1933), p. 24.

34. G. K. Chesterton, Letter to *The Nation*, 21 December 1907. I am most grateful to Father Ian Boyd for procuring for me a copy of these 'Letters to *The Nation*' on the issue of 'the decline of the Oxford Movement.'

35. Cecil Chesterton, *G. K. Chesterton: A Criticism* (London 1908), pp. xiv–xv.

36. P. N. Furbank, 'Chesterton the Edwardian' in John Sullivan (ed.), *G. K. Chesterton: A Centenary Appraisal* (London 1974), p. 18.

37. Dorothy L. Sayers, 'Preface' in G. K. Chesterton, *The Surprise* (London 1952 reprint), p. 5.

Chapter XVII: The Rise and Fall of Liberation Theology?

1. For documentation, see B. Chenu and B. Lauret (eds), *Théologies de la libération. Documentation et débats* (Paris 1955). This collection includes a French translation of M. Alcalá's

account of the history of liberation theology up to the early 1980s, which originally appeared in Spanish in *Razón y Fe* for June 1984, and to which the early sections of this chapter are indebted. See also A. T. Hennelly (ed.), *Liberation Theology. A Documentary History* (Maryknoll, NY., 1990).

2. The original inspiration of 'historic theology' is best reflected in the work of the Argentinian E. Dussel, who combines liberation theology with Church history, as in his *History and the Theology of Liberation* (Et: New York, NY., 1976); *A History of the Church in Latin America* (Et: Grand Rapids, Mich., 1981).

3. The background was the Bandung Conference of 1955 with its deepened awareness of Third World countries. Also of this phase was the creation in 1968 by the Pontifical Commission on Justice and Peace together with the World Council of Churches of the joint venture, the Committee on Society, Development and Peace (SODEPAX). See, for example, for the theology of development and its ethics: G. H. Dunne, *The Right to Development* (New York, NY., 1974); D. Goulet, *The Cruel Choice: A New Concept on the Theory of Development* (New York, NY., 1971); and some remarks in J. Moltmann, *The Crucified God: the Cross of Christ as the Foundation and Criticism of Christian Theology* (Et: New York, NY., 1974), pp. 317–40.

4. For the text, see 'The Medellín statement by the Bishops of Latin America', *New Blackfriars* 50. 582 (November 1968), pp. 72–8.

5. G. Gutiérrez, *A Theology of Liberation* (Et: New York, NY., 1973; London, 1974); L. Boff, *Jesus Christ Liberator* (Et: London 1980).

6. G. Gutiérrez, *We Drink from Our Own Wells* (Et: New York, NY., 1984); a parallel attempt to provide a spirituality for liberation theology would be L. Boff and C. Boff, *Salvation and Liberation: In Search of a Balance between Faith and Politics* (Et: New York, NY., 1984).

7. J. L. Segundo's five volume *Teologia abierta para el laico adulto* is perhaps the fullest attempt to provide for Church workers a theology so understood. See also his manifesto *The Liberation of Theology* (Maryknoll, NY., 1982), p. xvi. Here Segundo proposes a ministerial training composed partly of the study of social pathology, and partly of the critical use of Scripture and Church dogma, 'suspecting that the whole

present way of training clergy or pastoral agents is merely a
way for society to protect itself right from the start from theologians by replacing their ability to analyse and criticise with
endless erudite bibliographies'.

8. See for example B. Kloppenburg, *Temptations for the Theo-
logy of Liberation* (Et: Chicago, Ill., 1974); C. P. Wagner,
Latin American Theology: Radical or Evangelical? (Grand
Rapids, Mich., 1970).

9. A. Barreiro, *Basic Ecclesial Communities. The Evangelisation
of the Poor* (New York, NY., 1982).

10. D. A. López Trujillo, 'Les problèmes de l'Amérique latine',
Documentation Catholique No. 1816 (18 October 1981).

11. Commission Théologique Internationale, Promotion humaine
et salut chrétien', *Textes et documents*, 1969–85 (Paris 1988),
pp. 167–8.

12. D. W. Fern, *Third World Liberation Theologies. An Introductory Survey* (New York, NY., 1986).

13. G. Gutiérrez, *The Power of the Poor in History* (Et: New York,
NY., 1983); J. Sobrino, *Christology at the Crossroads* (Et:
New York, NY., 1978). For Boff, see the bibliography in H.
Cox, *The Silencing of Leonardo Boff: The Vatican and the
Future of World Christianity* (London 1989).

14. *Documentation Catholique* No. 1758 (18 February 1979).

15. P. Arrupe, 'L'analyse marxiste. Lettre aux provinciaux jésuites'
d' Amérique latine', *Documentation Catholique* No. 1808 (17
May 1981), para. 13.

16. Congrégation pour la Doctrine de la Foi, 'Dix Observations sur
la théologie de Gustavo Gutiérrez', *Dialogue* No. 925 (22
March 1984).

17. *Trenta Giorni*, 3 March 1984.

18. My analysis appeared in Bishops' Conference of England and
Wales, *Briefing* 84, Vol. 14, No. 20, 17 September 1984.

19. Congregazione per la dottrina della Fede, 'Notificazione sul
volume Chiesa: *Carisma e Potere. Saggio di ecclesiologia mili-
tante* del padre Leonardo Boff, *Osservatore Romano*, 20–21
March 1985.

20. J. L. Segundo, *Theology and the Church. A Response to
Cardinal Ratzinger and a Warning to the Whole Church* (Et:
Minneapolis–Chicago–New York–London 1985).

21. Congregation for the Doctrine of the Faith, *Instruction on
Christian Freedom and Liberation*, Vol. 71.

22. L. Boff, *E a Igreja se fez povo* (Petrópolis 1986).

23. H. Cox, *The Silencing of Leonardo Boff: The Vatican and the Future of World Christianity* (London 1989), pp. 146–88.
24. It should be noted, however, that as early as 1986 liberation theologians in Latin America were already stressing the importance of political democracy as providing a space where the poor could gain a voice. See A. McGovern, 'Liberation Theology is Alive and Well', *Tablet*, 15 September 1990, pp. 1156–7, and more widely his *Liberation Theology and its Critics* (Maryknoll, N.Y., 1989).
25. Frei Betto, *Fidel and Religion. Castro Talks on Revolution and Religion with Frei Betto* (Et: New York, N.Y., 1987).
26. See P. Higgonet, 'When Man eats Man', a review of three studies of revolutionary France, in *The Times Literary Supplement*, No. 4565, 28 September–4 October 1990, pp. 1028–9.
27. G. MacEoin, 'Latin America turns its back on the faith of its past', *Catholic Herald* for 5 October 1990.

Chapter XVIII: The Story of Praxis: *Liberation Theology's Philosophical Handmaid*

1. *Politicus*, 294, D-E; *Nicomachean Ethics* 1.3, 1094 b 20. Cf. E. Kapp, 'Theorie und Praxis bei Aristoteles und Platon', *Mnesmosyne* Vol. 5 (1937), pp. 179–94.
2. N. Lobkowicz, *Theory and Practice. History of a Concept from Aristotle to Marx* (Notre Dame, Ind., and London 1976), pp. 17–33.
3. Ibid., p. 51: 'the *theoria* of the Stoics was little more than the knowledge required for the *kata phusin zên* (the life according to nature)'.
4. R. Arnou, *Theoria et Praxis. Une étude de détail sur le vocabulaire et la pensée des Ennéades de Plotin* (Paris 1921).
5. Lk 10: 38–42.
6. Jn 1:16, with reference to Prov 16:5.
7. N. Lobkowicz, *Theory and Practice. History of a Concept from Aristotle to Marx* (Notre Dame, Ind., and London 1976), p. 66.
8. Cf. J. Mausbach, *Die Ethik des heiligen Augustinus* (Freiburg 1909), Vol. I, pp. 264–98, 414–27.
9. *Summa Theologiae* IIa, IIae, q. 179, a. 2.
10. John Duns Scotus, Ordinatio, prologus, pars V, q. 2, n. 1.
11. N. Lobkowicz, *Theory and Practice. History of a Concept*

from Aristotle to Marx (Notre Dame, Ind., and London 1976), pp. 78–9.

12. L. White, *Mediaeval Technology and Social Change* (Oxford 1962).

13. N. Lobkowicz, *Theory and Practice. History of a Concept from Aristotle to Marx* (Notre Dame, Ind., and London 1976), p. 87.

14. E. Zilsel, 'The Genesis of the Concept of Scientific Progress', *Journal of the History of Ideas* 6 (1945), pp. 325–49.

15. F. Anderson, *The Philosophy of Francis Bacon* (Chicago, Ill., 1948), p. 183.

16. Ch. Adams and P. Tannery (ed.), *Oeuvres de Descartes* (Paris 1897), VI, p. 22.

17. N. Lobkowicz, *Theory and Practice. History of a Concept from Aristotle to Marx* (Notre Dame, Ind., and London 1976), pp. 119–20.

18. E. Cassirer (ed.) *Werks* (Berlin 1922), V, p. 239ff.

19. The *Philosophy of History* and the *Phenomenology of Mind* consider this from different perspectives.

20. See E. Benz, 'Die Mystik in der Philosophie des deutschen Idealismus', *Euphorion* 46 (1952), pp. 280–300; *idem.*, 'Johann Albrecht Bengel und die Philosophie des deutschen idealismus', *Deutsche Vierteljahrschrift für Literatur-wissenschaft und Geistesgeschichte* 27 (1953), pp. 528–54.

21. G. Cottier, *Du romantisme au Marxisme* (Paris 1961).

22. H. Glockner (ed.) *Sämtliche Werke* (Stuttgart 1932), VII, p. 456ff.

23. N. Lobkowicz, *Theory and Practice. History of a Concept from Aristotle to Marx* (Notre Dame, Ind., and London 1976), p. 185.

24. Ibid., pp. 193–206 for a presentation of the man and his work. See also August Cieszkowski, *Prolegomena zur Historiosophie* (Berlin 1838).

25. J. Gerhardt, 'Karl Marx und Bruno Bauer', in *Politische Ordnung und menschliche Existenz. Festschrift E. Voegelin* (Munich 1952), pp. 202–42.

26. W. Neher, *Arnold Ruge also Politiker und politischer Schriftsteller* (Heidelberg 1933). The brief citation is from Arnold Ruge, *Aus früherer Zeit* (Berlin 1863), IV, p. 569ff.

27. N. Lobkowicz, *Theory and Practice. History of a Concept from Aristotle to Marx* (Notre Dame, Ind., and London 1976), pp. 231–5.

28. Ibid., p. 276: cf. K. Marx, *Early Writings*, T. B. Bottomore (tr.) (London 1963), p. 58; Karl Marx-Friedrich Engels, *Historisch-kritisch Gesamtsausgabe*, D. Rjazanov and V. Adoratskij (eds) (Frankfurt 1927), Vol. I, p. 614.
29. N. Lobkowicz, *Theory and Practice. History of a Concept from Aristotle to Marx* (Notre Dame, Ind., and London 1976), pp. 278–82.
30. L. von Stein, *Der Socialismus und Communismus des heutigen Frankreich* (Leipzig 1842), pp. 8–12.
31. A. Sánchez Vásquez, *The Philosophy of Praxis* (London 1977), p. xi.
32. Ibid., p. 2.
33. Ibid., p. 4.
34. Ibid., p. 25.
35. Ibid., p. 32.
36. Ibid., p. 165.
37. C. Boff, *Theology and Praxis, Epistemological Foundations* (Et: Maryknoll, NY., 1987), p. 159.
38. Ibid., p. 167.
39. Ibid., p. 198.
40. For the continuing importance of the idea of totality in even radically revisionist Marxism, see M. Jay, *Marxism and Totality. The Adventures of a Concept from Lukács to Habermas* (Cambridge 1984).
41. This prescription is based on the accounts of biblical exegesis and dogmatic theology offered by the Second Vatican Council, and notably in the documents *Dei Verbum* and *Optatam totius*.
42. C. Boff, *Theology and Praxis, Epistemological Foundations* (Et: Maryknoll, NY., 1987), pp. 204–5.

Chapter XIX: Rex gentium*: History, Nationalism, Christ*

1. O *Rex Gentium*: antiphon at the Magnificat for 22 December in the Liturgy of the Hours of the Roman rite.
2. A. J. Toynbee, *A Study of History* (London 1934–54). I ought also to mention here the work of a contemporary of Toynbee's at Winchester School, Christopher Dawson. See C. Scott, *A Historian and his World: A Life of Christopher Dawson 1889–1970* (London 1984), with full bibliography.
3. See W. B. Gallie, *Philosophy and the Historical Understanding* (London 1964), p. 11.

4. With some exceptions listed conveniently in the bibliography of O. Lowry, *The Theology of History* (Cork 1969).
5. J. Daniélou, *The Lord of History* (Et: London 1960).
6. H. U. von Balthasar, *A Theology of History* (Et: London 1964); also cited in H. U. von Balthasar, *Man in History: A Theological Study* (Et: London 1968).
7. On this patristic background, see R. L. P. Milburn, *Early Christian Interpretations of History* (London 1954); L. G. Patterson, *God and History in Early Christian Thought* (London 1967).
8. See R. Gibellini, 'Una teologia dal rovescio della storia' in R. Gibellini, *Il dibattito sulla teologia della liberazione* (Brescia 1986), pp. 9–20.
9. On the Aldenham library, now at Cambridge, see D. Mathew, *Acton: the Formative Years* (London 1946), pp. 159–64.
10. What we have of the 'History of Freedom' is the fragment published by J. N. Figgis and R. V. Laurence in *The History of Freedom and Other Essays* (London 1907).
11. E. Gellner, *Plough, Sword and Book: the Structure of Human History* (London 1988).
12. Ibid., pp. 11–12.
13. Ibid., p. 13.
14. H. U. von Balthasar, *A Theology of History* (Et: London 1964), p. 98.
15. Ibid., p. 59.
16. Ibid., p. 99.
17. Ibid.
18. Ibid., pp. 67–8.
19. Mk 7: 24–30; Mt 15: 21–8.
20. Jn 4: 4–42.
21. Mt 8: 5–13; Lk 7: 1–10.
22. Jn 12: 20–1.
23. See J. Jeremias, *Jesus' Promise to the Nations* (Et: London 1958); and F. Hahn, *Mission in the New Testament* (Et: London 1965) for full discussion of the significance of these references.
24. Mt 27: 54b.
25. Eph 2:14.
26. For an illuminating account of the Church as communion, by an Orthodox open to the notion of a (Roman) universal *centre d'accord*, see O. Clément, 'L'Ecclésiologie orthodoxe comme ecclésiologie de communion', *Contacts* 61 (1968), pp. 10–36.

27. H. U. von Balthasar, *A Theology of History* (Et: London 1964), p. 137.
28. E. Gellner, *Plough, Sword and Book: the Structure of Human History* (London 1988), pp. 213–33.
29. E. Gellner, *Nations and Nationalism* (Oxford 1983).
30. E. Kedourie, *Nationalism* (London 1985), p. 9.
31. C. Moorhead, 'Pursuit of an Elusive Ideal', *The Independent* 8 December 1988, p. 29.
32. E. Kedourie, *Nationalism* (London 1985), pp. 138–9. See also his *Nationalism in Asia and Africa* (London 1970), pp. 1–152.
33. E. Kedourie, *Nationalism* (London 1985), p. 140.
34. Published as 'Europe Tomorrow', in *Briefing* 18:22 (11 November 1988), pp. 471–3.
35. Ibid., p. 473.
36. It might be opportune to re-publish Christopher Dawson's *The Making of Europe. An Introduction to the History of European Unity* (London 1932; New York, NY., 1958), and *The Modern Dilemma: The Problem of European Unity* (New York, NY., 1932). Also highly relevant are the closing chapter of his *The Judgment of the Nations* (London 1942), and the whole of *Understanding Europe* (London 1952; New York, NY., 1960).
37. R. A. Kann, *The Multinational Empire. Nationalism and National Reform in the Habsburg Monarchy, 1848–1918* (2 vols., Washington, DC., 1950). For a balanced assessment of the contributions of internal, centrifugal forces and the First World War in the monarchy's downfall, see J. W. Mason, *The Dissolution of the Austro-Hungarian Empire, 1867–1918* (London and New York, NY., 1985), pp. 80–4.
38. For a recrudescence of such anxieties, as registered or observed by otherwise relatively sympathetic Anglican critics, see, for instance, the remarks of the Bishop of London in *The Universe*, 27 November 1988, p. 11. Also, on the Roman Church's 'foreignness', Frank Field, M.P., in the *Catholic Herald*, 9 December 1988, p. 4. Of course, if these references are really covert allusions to the Irish, then it must be said that Irish nationalism (in its generally Roman Catholic dress) is no more acceptable, on the principles stated here, than is English nationalism (in its corresponding Anglican apparel).
39. Phil 3:20.
40. Rev 22:2.

244 Scribe of the Kingdom

Chapter XX: Dante's Way: Poetry and Grace

1. The late Kenelm Foster, of Blackfriars Cambridge, wrote: 'His response may most appropriately be called poetic if this term can denote a certain interplay of sense and intelligence issuing in a vivid imaginative apprehension of being in general', in his *The Two Dantes and Other Studies* (London 1977), p. 84. John Ruskin in *The Stones of Venice* had called Dante 'the central man of all the world', giving as his first reason Dante's holding in perfect balance 'the imaginative, moral and intellectual faculites at their highest', cited in W. Anderson, *Dante the Maker* (London 1983), p. 3.
2. K. Foster, 'Dante as a Christian Poet', in K. Foster, *God's Tree. Essays on Dante and Other Matters* (London 1957), pp. 5–6, with references.
3. Dante, *Paradiso* 33, 82–90.
4. A. Farrer, *The Glass of Vision* (London 1948) provides the case for Farrer's overall view of biblical revelation. He tested it in regard to one theological 'poem' within the canon in his *A Rebirth of Images. The Making of St John's Apocalypse* (London 1949).
5. See the lucid exposition of Karl Rahner's 'theology of the symbol' in J. H. P. Wong, *Logos-Symbol in the Christology of Karl Rahner* (Rome 1984), pp. 74–112. A more sober view of symbol would be to regard it as an efficacious manifestation – in diversely analogical ways – of *ens*, ontological reality: see F. D. Wilhelmsen, 'The Aesthetic Act and the Act of Being', *Modern Studies* (1952). In Dante's own period, a twofold appropriateness was sought in the symbol: a 'natural' fitness of some object to signify another reality, and its 'conventional' fitness so to do by virtue of tradition, or established usage. We should note, however, that this does not demand that something represented by the word had to exist outside the poem: the pelican of Thomas Aquinas's *Adoro te*, once its referential meaning is established, functions as a symbol providing insight into the eucharistic Lord – not independently of the referential meaning, though, but in dependence upon the meaning found through tradition and the nature of things.
6. L. Ouspensky, *La théologie de l'icône dans l'Eglie orthodoxe* (Paris 1960).
7. P. Mandonnet, *Dante le théologien* (Paris 1935).
8. K. Foster, 'St Thomas and Dante', in K. Foster, *The Two Dantes and Other Studies* (London 1977), pp. 56–65.

9. K. Smidt, *James Joyce and the Cultic Use of Fiction* (Oslo 1959), argues that while Joyce's telescoped words and neologisms constitute an incantatory attempt to grasp the indivisible Logos found in and through the *glossolalia* of speech, it is his Thomist conviction that all things are potentially beautiful, and that the laws governing perception of the beautiful are universal, which gives his art its all-embracing – and therfore 'cultic' – character. For that 'Thomism', see W. T. Noon, *Joyce and Aquinas* (New Haven, Conn., 1957).

10. J. Joyce, *Finnegan's Wake* (New York, NY., and London 1945), p. 611.

11. Ibid., p. 612.

12. Aristotle, *Metaphysics* A. 982b; cf. P. Boyde, *Dante Philomythes and Philosopher. Man in the Cosmos* (Cambridge 1981), p. vi.

13. Thomas Aquinas, *Libros Sententiarum* I, distinctio 34, 3, i.

14. Dante, *Paradiso*. As at 1, 73–5; 26, 10–12; 30, 49–51; cf. *Inferno* 1 118–22; 2, 10–42.

15. Dante, *Epistolae*, X. 15.

16. C. Ernst, *The Theology of Grace* (Cork–Dublin 1974), pp. 62–76.

17. Col 1; 15–20.

18. R. Pearce, 'The Eyes of Beatrice', *New Blackfriars* 54, 640 (1973), pp. 407–16.

19. Dante, *Paradiso* 18, 16–18.

20. Ibid., 19–21.

21. K. Foster, *The Two Dantes and Other Studies* (London 1977), pp. 126–7.

22. K. Foster, *God's Tree. Essays on Dante and Other Matters* (London 1957), pp. 43–4.

23. C. Williams, *The Figure of Beatrice. A Study in Dante* (London 1943). But note that, commenting on his own suggestion that in her formal doctrine the Church sees the *via negativa* as the key to the understanding of the *via positiva*, and vice versa, Williams explained in a letter of March 1945: 'The essentials of the one way are the accidents of the other ... There must be, sooner or later, even in the Way of Affirmation, some sort of seclusion of the soul to the Omnipotence. It must, in some sense, be divided from all else – for ever or for a time. I think, for a time; but it will not at the moment feel this. The Rejection aims at this as a continual method; the Affirmation endures it, when it comes. As the Rejection has always to allow its debt

to its parents, its teachers, its food and shelter, perhaps its loves. These are accidents of its calling, so the separation is an accident – necessary somehow and somewhere – of the Affirmation.' Cited by A. Ridler (ed.), *Charles Williams, The Image of the City, and Other Essays* (London 1958), p. xl.

24. A. C. Charity, *Events and their After-Life. The Dialectics of Christian Typology in the Bible and Dante* (Cambridge 1966), pp. 227–56.

25. Dante, *Paradiso* 20, 57.

26. C. T. Davis, *Dante and the Idea of Rome* (Oxford 1957).

27. Dante, *Purgatorio* 32.

28. Dante, *Paradiso* 27; see also K. Foster, 'The Canto of the Damned Popes: Inferno XIX', in K. Foster, *The Two Dantes and Other Studies* (London 1967), pp. 86–106.

29. Dante, *Purgatorio* 32, 102.

30. B. J. F. Lonergan, *Grace and Freedom. Operative Grace in the Thought of St Thomas Aquinas* (London 1971), p. 143, speaks of how, in Aquinas's theology, 'metaphysics and psychology, divine providence and human instrumentality, grace and nature, at last have meshed their intricacies in synthesis'.

Chapter XXI: Imaginative Eschatology: Benson's The Lord of the World

1. For Benson's life, see C. C. Martindale, *The Life of Monsignor Robert Hugh Benson* (London 1916, two volumes).

2. R. H. Benson, *Confessions of a Convert* (London 1920), p. 107.

3. C. C. Martindale, *The Life of Monsignor Robert Hugh Benson* (London 1916), Vol. I, p. 434.

4. Ibid., p. 78.

5. On his debt to Julian, see *Spiritual Letters of Monsignor Robert Hugh Benson* (London 1915), p. 6; Richard Rolle was the historical model for the fictional 'Raynal' in Benson's *Richard Raynal, Solitary* (London 1906). Note also his collection of pre-Reformation devotions, *A Book of the Love of Jesus* (London 1905) which he feared English Catholics, used to more Baroque fare, would find insufficiently warm – 'too Saxon' – but whose ethos he described as 'an extraordinary mixture of passion and restraint, strength and delicacy', *Spiritual Letters*, p. 73. For his Christocentricism, see, above all, *The Friendship of Christ* (London 1912), but also *Christ in the Church* (London 1911).

6. Benson's work offers a theology of the *city* of Rome, as 'a sort of sacrament of the New Jerusalem. You meet the four marks of the Church, incarnate, in the streets and churches', *Spiritual Letters*, p. 49.

7. *The Queen's Tragedy* (London 1906); *By What Authority?* (London 1909); *Come Rack, Come Rope* (London 1912).

8. Benson did not scruple to speak of the importance of 'the materialisation of religion', which he defined as 'the supplying of acts and images on which religious emotion may concentrate itself. Extreme definiteness seems necessary, and that, not only in the bright and impressive adjuncts of worship, but in the modes in which individual approach to God is made', *Confessions of a Convert*, pp. 37–8.

9. E. Gellner, *Plough, Sword and Book: the Structure of Human History* (London 1988).

10. Francis Fukiyma, 'The End of History', *The Independent*, 20–21 September 1989; for a Catholic response, Eamon Duffy, 'A Pot of Hubris at the Rainbow's End', *The Independent*, 3 October 1989.

11. Heb 11: 37–8. Benson also created, at his readers' instigation and with less enthusiasm, an alternative account of the End to this 'remnant' version: *The Dawn of All* (London 1911). But the author's heart is not in it; his conviction that salvation moves over through Cross to resurrection could not be married with such a non-dialectical view of the Church's triumph.

Chapter XXII: On Baptising the Visual Arts: A Friar's Meditation on Art

1. W. Wilson, *Christian Art since the Romantic Movement* (London 1965), p. 13. On Wackenroder's work, see B. Tecchi, *Introduzione agli scritti di poesia e di estetica di W. H. Wackenroder* (Florence 1934).

2. *Lumen Gentium* 67.

3. *Sacrosanctum Concilium* 122. For an overview of the Council's references to images, and allusions in other contemporary documents of the Church of Rome, see G. Rapisarda, 'Le immagini sacre nelle indicazione del Vaticano II e della riforma liturgica', in [Auctores varii] *Culto delle immagini e crisi iconoclasta* (Palermo 1986), pp. 153–73.

4. *Summa Theologiae*, IIa. IIe., q. 81, a. 7.

5. E. Masure, *Le Signe. Le passage du visible à l'invisible* (Paris 1954), p. 42.

6. E. Lanne, 'Rome et les images saintes', *Irénikon* (1986), pp. 163–88.
7. See A. Nichols, *The Art of God Incarnate. Theology and Image in Christian Tradition* (London 1980), pp. 11–12.
8. See R. Rosenblum, *Modern Painting and the Northern Romantic Tradition. Friedrich to Rothko* (London 1975).
9. See M. Betz, 'The Icon and Russian Modernism', *Artforum* (Summer 1977), pp. 38–45; and J. Masheck, 'Iconicity', in J. Masheck, *Historical Present. Essays of the 1970's* (Ann Arbor, Mich., 1984), pp. 209–28.
10. S. Gablik, *Has Modernism Failed?* (London 1985), p. 13.
11. I take the concept of 'secular fundamentalism' here from G. D'Costa, 'Secular Discourses and the Clash of Faith: *The Satanic Verses* in British Society', *New Blackfriars* 71, 842 (October 1990).
12. P. Fuller, *Beyond the Crisis in Art* (London 1980); *Art and Psycho-analysis* (London 1980); *The Naked Artist* (London 1983).
13. S. Gablik, *Has Modernism Failed?* (London 1985), p. 77; cf. Fuller's reprint, with a new prefatory essay in 1990, of his *Images of God. The Consolations of Lost Illusions* (originally published in London, 1982).
14. S. Gablik, *Has Modernism Failed?* (London 1985), p. 80.
15. *Nostra aetate* (The Declaration of the Second Vatican Council on Non-Christian Religions), 1.
16. C. Walter, 'The Icon and the Image of Christ: the Second Council of Nicaea and Byzantine Tradition', *Sobornost* N. S. 10, 1 (1988), pp. 23ff.
17. Cf. E. Fortino, 'The Role and Importance of Icons: a Roman Catholic Perspective', in G. Limouris, *Icons. Windows on Eternity* (Geneva 1990, Faith and Order Paper 147), pp. 124–31.
18. W. Wilson, *Christian Art since the Romantic Movement* (London 1965), p. 59.
19. W. Bulst and H. Pfeiffer, *Das Turiner Grabtuch und das Christusbild* I (Frankfurt 1987), pp. 95–136.
20. I draw this term from G. Goethals, 'The Church and the Mass Media: Competing Architects of our Dominant Symbols, Rituals and Myths', in J. McDonnell and F. Trampiets (eds), *Communicating Faith in a Technological Age* (Slough 1989), p. 77.

Chapter XXIV: Ekaterina Sienskaya Abrikosova: A Dominican Uniate Foundress in the Old Russia

1. Most of the biographical information about the Abrikosovs found in this chapter derives from A. K. Eszer, 'Ekaterina Sienskaja (Anna I.) Abrikosova und die Gemeinschaft der Schwestern des III. Ordens vom heiligen Dominikus zu Moskau', *Archivum Fratrum Praedicatorum* XL (1970), pp. 277–373. Fr Eszer, an official of the Congregation for the Causes of Saints, and Professor of Church History at the Pontifical University of St Thomas, Rome, based his work on a large number of letters in private possession.

2. She was placed, in 1903, in the first class of the History Tripos, part 1. (Information furnished by the archives of Girton College, via Ian Gorman, Esq.)

3. N. Zernov, *The Russian Religious Renaissance of the Twentieth Century* (London 1963).

4. K. Foster and M. J. Ronayne (eds), *I, Catherine. Selected Writings of St Catherine of Siena* (London 1980), p. 281.

5. A. K. Eszer, 'Ekaterina Sienskaja (Anna I.) Abrikosova und die Gemeinschaft der Schwestern des III. Ordens vom heiligen Dominikus zu Moskau', *Archivum Fratrum Praedicatorum* XL (1970), p. 285.

6. For Fe'dorov, see P. Mailleux, *Entre Rome et Moscou: L'Exarque Léonide Féodoroff* (Brussels 1966); Diakon Vasilii, *Leonid Federov. Žizn i deyatelnost* (Rome 1966). A brief sketch in the context of *fin-de-siècle* Russian attitudes to Catholicism is offered by I. Posnoff, 'Russian Catholics and Ecumenism', in A. H. Armstrong and J. B. Fry (eds), *Re-Discovering Eastern Christendom* (London 1963), pp. 135–53.

7. On Solov'ev, see E. Munzer, *Solovyev. Prophet of Russian and Western Unity* (London 1956); a précis of his thought is found in A. Nichols, *Theology in the Russian Diaspora* (Cambridge 1989), pp. 27–9.

8. For Szepticky's life up to 1920, see C. Korolevsky, *Le métropolite André Szeptickyj* (Grottaferrata 1921). A perceptive overview is D. Attwater, 'Andrew Szepticky, Father Metropolitan', *Blackfriars* (February 1948), pp. 53–9.

9. J. S. Curtiss, *Church and State in Russia: the Last Years of the Empire, 1900–1917* (New York, NY., 1940).

10. P. Mailleux, *Entre Rome et Moscow: l'Exarque Léonide Féodoroff* (Brussels 1966), p. 49.

11. Ibid., p. 84.

12. T. G. Stavrou and R. L. Nichols (eds), *Russian Orthodoxy under the Old Régime* (Minneapolis, Minn., 1978); and more specifically on the attempts at reform, A. A. Bogolepov, 'Church Reform in Russia 1905–1918', *Saint Vladimir's Seminary Quarterly* 10 (1966), pp. 12–66; J. W. Cunningham, *A Vanquished Hope. The Movement for Church Renewal in Russia 1905–1906* (Crestwood, NY., 1981).

13. For the complete text see *Eastern Churches Review* VII, 1 (1975), pp. 40–65.

14. A. K. Eszer, 'Ekaterina Sienskaja (Anna I.) Abrikosova und die Gemeinschaft der Schwestern des III. Ordens vom heiligen Dominikus zu Moskau', *Archivum Fratrum Praedicatorum* XL (1970), pp. 300–4.

15. Ibid., p. 310.

16. On this see H. J. Stehle, *Die Ostpolitik des Vatikans 1917–1975* (Munich 1975), ch. 1.

17. A. K. Eszer, 'Ekaterina Sienskaja (Anna I.) Abrikosova und die Gemeinschaft der Schwestern des III. Ordens vom heiligen Dominikus zu Moskau', *Archivum Fratrum Praedicatorum* XL (1970), p. 313.

18. Ibid., pp. 336–8. This gives a fuller account of the couple's ecumenical activities, on the Catholic side definitely pioneering for their period.

19. Ibid., p. 318.

20. Cited P. Mailleux, *Entre Rome et Moscow: l'Exarque Léonide Féodoroff* (Brussels 1966), pp. 101–2.

21. For the wider process, see J. Zatko, *Descent into Darkness. The Destruction of the Roman Catholic Church in Russia, 1917–1922* (Notre Dame, Ind., 1965).

22. A. K. Eszer, 'Ekaterina Sienskaja (Anna I.) Abrikosova und die Gemeinschaft der Schwestern des III. Ordens vom heiligen Dominikus zu Moskau', *Archivum Fratrum Praedicatorum* XL (1970), p. 359.

23. I. Smolitsch, *Russisches Mönchtum. Entstehung, Entwicklung und Wesen* (Würzburg 1953), pp. 433–41.

24. A. K. Eszer, 'Ekaterina Sienskaja (Anna I.) Abrikosova und die Gemeinschaft der Schwestern des III. Ordens vom heiligen Dominikus zu Moskau', *Archivum Fratrum Praedicatorum* XL (1970), pp. 371–3.

Index of Names

Abelard, P. 72
Abrikosov, V. V. 207, 210, 213, 215, 219, 220
Abrikosova, E. S. (A. I.) 207–24
Acton, J. E. E. D. 143
Adam 174, 190
Albert of Cologne 204
Albrecht, B. 36
Allende, S. 109
Allwohn, A. 49
Andronikof, C. 16–18
Angelico, Fra: see John of Fiesole
Anselm 74
Aquinas: see Thomas Aquinas
Aristotle 124, 125, 127, 168, 169
Arnold, T. 95
Arns, E. 110, 117
Arrupe, P. 103, 114, 115
Asquith, H. 85
Athanasius 4
Augustine 4, 55, 99, 105, 126, 144, 199
Avicenna 127

Bacon, F. 128
Balthasar, H. U. von 20–8, 29, 31, 32–4, 42, 43, 70, 71, 142, 147, 148, 151, 158
Barnes, E. W. 95
Barth, K. 24
Bauer, B. 133
Beatrice 166, 167, 169, 172, 173

Belavin, T. 5, 219
Belloc, H. 86
Benedict XV 46, 84, 85
Benigni, U. 84, 99
Benjamin, metropolitan 219
Benson, E. W. 177
Benson, R. H. 176–82
Bentham, J. 191
Berdyaev, N. A. 220
Bergson, H. 94
Berlin, I. 52
Bernanos, G. 23, 33
Bernard 72, 74, 106, 158
Betto, F. 122
Bismarck, O. 154
Bloch, E. 21
Blondel, M. 58
Boff, C. 138, 139, 140
Boff, L. 104, 106, 107, 112, 115, 117, 119, 120, 122, 138
Bonhoeffer, D. 108
Boniface VIII 211
Bouyer, L. 4
Buffet, B. 192
Bulgakov, S. N. 1–19, 220
Bunyan, J. 73
Burckhardt, J. 31

Calderón de la Barca, P. 23
Campbell-Bannerman, Sir H. 85
Câmara, H. 101, 103
Capreolus 127
Casaldáliga, P. 103, 104
Casas, B. de las 105